# THE CLAY SANSKRIT LIBRARY

FOUNDED BY JOHN & JENNIFER CLAY

GENERAL EDITOR

SHELDON POLLOCK

EDITED BY

ISABELLE ONIANS

WWW.CLAYSANSKRITLIBRARY.ORG
WWW.NYUPRESS.ORG

*Artwork by Robert Beer.*
*Typeset in Adobe Garamond Pro at 10.25 : 12.3+pt.*
*Editorial input from Dániel Balogh, Ridi Faruque,*
*Chris Gibbons, Tomoyuki Kono & Eszter Somogyi.*
*Printed and Bound in Great Britain by*
*TJ Books, Cornwall on acid free paper*

# THE RISE OF WISDOM MOON

by KṚṢṆAMIŚRA

EDITED AND TRANSLATED BY

Matthew T. Kapstein

WITH A FOREWORD BY J. N. MOHANTY

NEW YORK UNIVERSITY PRESS

JJC FOUNDATION

2009

First Edition 2009

The Clay Sanskrit Library is co-published by
New York University Press
and the JJC Foundation.

Further information about this volume
and the rest of the Clay Sanskrit Library
is available on the following websites:
**www.claysanskritlibrary.org**
**www.nyupress.org**

ISBN 978-08147-4838-1

**Library of Congress Cataloging-in-Publication Data**
Kṛṣṇamiśra
[Prabodhacandrodaya. English & Sanskrit]
The rise of wisdom moon / by Kṛṣṇamiśra ;
translated by Matthew T. Kapstein ;
with a foreword by J. N. Mohanty. -- 1st ed.
p. cm. -- (The Clay Sanskrit Library)
In English and Sanskrit (romanized) on facing pages.
Includes bibliographical references.
ISBN 978-0-8147-4838-1
1. Hinduism--Drama. 2. Sanskrit drama--Translations in English.
I. Kapstein, Matthew. II. Title.
PK3798.K65P713 2009
891'.21 dc--22
2009021929

# CONTENTS

# CSL CONVENTIONS

## Sanskrit Alphabetical Order

| | |
|---|---|
| Vowels: | *a ā i ī u ū ṛ ṝ ḷ ḹ e ai o au ṃ ḥ* |
| Gutturals: | *k kh g gh ṅ* |
| Palatals: | *c ch j jh ñ* |
| Retroflex: | *ṭ ṭh ḍ ḍh ṇ* |
| Dentals: | *t th d dh n* |
| Labials: | *p ph b bh m* |
| Semivowels: | *y r l v* |
| Spirants: | *ś ṣ s h* |

## Guide to Sanskrit Pronunciation

| | |
|---|---|
| *a* | b*u*t |
| *ā, â* | f*a*ther |
| *i* | s*i*t |
| *ī, î* | f*ee* |
| *u* | p*u*t |
| *ū,û* | b*oo* |
| *ṛ* | vocalic *r*, American p*ur*dy or English p*re*tty |
| *ṝ* | lengthened *ṛ* |
| *ḷ* | vocalic *l*, ab*le* |
| *e, ê, ē* | m*a*de, esp. in Welsh pronunciation |
| *ai* | b*i*te |
| *o, ô, ō* | r*o*pe, esp. Welsh pronunciation; Italian s*o*lo |
| *au* | s*ou*nd |
| *ṃ* | *anusvāra* nasalizes the preceding vowel |
| *ḥ* | *visarga*, a voiceless aspiration (resembling the English *h*), or like Scottish lo*ch*, or an aspiration with a faint echoing of the last element of the preceding vowel so that *taiḥ* is pronounced $\textit{taih}^{i}$ |
| *k* | lu*ck* |
| *kh* | blo*ckh*ead |
| *g* | *g*o |
| *gh* | bi*gh*ead |
| *ṅ* | a*n*ger |
| *c* | *ch*ill |
| *ch* | mat*chh*ead |
| *j* | *j*og |
| *jh* | aspirated *j*, he*dgeh*og |
| *ñ* | ca*ny*on |
| *ṭ* | retroflex *t*, *t*ry (with the tip of tongue turned up to touch the hard palate) |
| *ṭh* | same as the preceding but aspirated |
| *ḍ* | retroflex *d* (with the tip |

| | |
|---|---|
| | of tongue turned up to touch the hard palate) |
| *ḍh* | same as the preceding but aspirated |
| *ṇ* | retroflex *n* (with the tip of tongue turned up to touch the hard palate) |
| *t* | French *t*out |
| *th* | ten*t h*ook |
| *d* | *d*inner |
| *dh* | guil*dh*all |
| *n* | *n*ow |
| *p* | *p*ill |
| *ph* | u*ph*eaval |
| *b* | *b*efore |
| *bh* | a*bh*orrent |
| *m* | *m*ind |
| *y* | *y*es |
| *r* | trilled, resembling the Italian pronunciation of *r* |
| *l* | *l*inger |
| *v* | *w*ord |
| *ś* | *sh*ore |
| *ṣ* | retroflex *sh* (with the tip of the tongue turned up to touch the hard palate) |
| *s* | hi*ss* |
| *h* | *h*ood |

## CSL Punctuation of English

The acute accent on Sanskrit words when they occur outside of the Sanskrit text itself, marks stress, e.g., Ramáyana. It is not part of traditional Sanskrit orthography, transliteration, or transcription, but we supply it here to guide readers in the pronunciation of these unfamiliar words. Since no Sanskrit word is accented on the last syllable it is not necessary to accent disyllables, e.g., Rama.

The second CSL innovation designed to assist the reader in the pronunciation of lengthy unfamiliar words is to insert an unobtrusive middle dot between semantic word breaks in compound names (provided the word break does not fall on a vowel resulting from the fusion of two vowels), e.g., Maha·bhárata, but Ramáyana (not Rama·áyana). Our dot echoes the punctuating middle dot (·) found in the oldest surviving samples of written Indic, the Ashokan inscriptions of the third century BCE.

The deep layering of Sanskrit narrative has also dictated that we use quotation marks only to announce the beginning and end of every direct speech, and not at the beginning of every paragraph.

## CSL Punctuation of Sanskrit

The Sanskrit text is also punctuated, in accordance with the punctuation of the English translation. In mid-verse, the punctuation will not alter the sandhi or the scansion. Proper names are capitalized. Most Sanskrit meters have four "feet" (*pāda*); where possible we print the common *śloka* meter on two lines. In the Sanskrit text, we use French *Guillemets* (e.g., *«kva saṃcicīrṣuḥ?»*) instead of English quotation marks (e.g., "Where are you off to?") to avoid confusion with the apostrophes used for vowel elision in sandhi.

### SANDHI

Sanskrit presents the learner with a challenge: *sandhi* (euphonic combination). Sandhi means that when two words are joined in connected speech or writing (which in Sanskrit reflects speech), the last letter (or even letters) of the first word often changes; compare the way we pronounce "the" in "the beginning" and "the end."

In Sanskrit the first letter of the second word may also change; and if both the last letter of the first word and the first letter of the second are vowels, they may fuse. This has a parallel in English: a nasal consonant is inserted between two vowels that would otherwise coalesce: "a pear" and "an apple." Sanskrit vowel fusion may produce ambiguity.

The charts on the following pages give the full sandhi system.

Fortunately it is not necessary to know these changes in order to start reading Sanskrit. All that is important to know is the form of the second word without sandhi (pre-sandhi), so that it can be recognized or looked up in a dictionary. Therefore we are printing Sanskrit with a system of punctuation that will indicate, unambiguously, the original form of the second word, i.e., the form without sandhi. Such sandhi mostly concerns the fusion of two vowels.

In Sanskrit, vowels may be short or long and are written differently accordingly. We follow the general convention that a vowel with no mark above it is short. Other books mark a long vowel either with a bar called a macron (*ā*) or with a circumflex (*â*). Our system uses the

## VOWEL SANDHI

*Final vowels:*

| a | ā | i | ī | u | ū | ṛ | e | ai | o | au | *Initial vowels:* |
|---|---|---|---|---|---|---|---|---|---|---|---|
| ' â | " â | y a | y a | v a | v a | r a | e ' | ā a | o ' | āv a | a |
| ' ā | " ā | y ā | y ā | v ā | v ā | r ā | a ā | ā ā | a ā | āv ā | ā |
| ' ê | " ê | ' î | " î | v i | v i | r i | a i | ā i | a i | āv i | i |
| ' ē | " ē | ' ī | " ī | v ī | v ī | r ī | a ī | ā ī | a ī | āv ī | ī |
| ' ô | " ô | y u | y u | ' û | " û | r u | a u | ā u | a u | āv u | u |
| ' ō | " ō | y ū | y ū | ' ū | " ū | r ū | a ū | ā ū | a ū | āv ū | ū |
| a' r | a" r | y ṛ | y ṛ | v ṛ | v ṛ | ' ṛ̂ | a ṛ | ā ṛ | a ṛ | āv ṛ | ṛ |
| ' âi | " âi | y e | y e | v e | v e | r e | a e | ā e | a e | āv e | e |
| ' āi | " āi | y ai | y ai | v ai | v ai | r ai | a ai | ā ai | a ai | āv ai | ai |
| ' âu | " âu | y o | y o | v o | v o | r o | a o | ā o | a o | āv o | o |
| ' āu | " āu | y au | y au | v au | v au | r au | a au | ā au | a au | āv au | au |

## CONSONANT SANDHI

| *Permitted finals:* k | ṭ | t | p | ṅ | n | m | *(Except āḥ/aḥ)* ḥ/r | āḥ | aḥ | *Initial letters:* |
|---|---|---|---|---|---|---|---|---|---|---|
| k | ṭ | t | p | ṅ | n | ṃ | ḥ | āḥ | aḥ | k/kh |
| g | ḍ | d | b | ṅ | n | ṃ | r | ā | o | g/gh |
| k | ṭ | c | p | ṅ | ṃś | ṃ | ś | āś | aś | c/ch |
| g | ḍ | j | b | ṅ | ñ | ṃ | r | ā | o | j/jh |
| k | ṭ | ṭ | p | ṅ | ṃṣ | ṃ | ṣ | āṣ | aṣ | ṭ/ṭh |
| g | ḍ | ḍ | b | ṅ | ṇ | ṃ | r | ā | o | ḍ/ḍh |
| k | ṭ | t | p | ṅ | ṃs | ṃ | s | ās | as | t/th |
| g | ḍ | d | b | ṅ | n | ṃ | r | ā | o | d/dh |
| k | ṭ | t | p | ṅ | n | ṃ | ḥ | āḥ | aḥ | p/ph |
| g | ḍ | d | b | ṅ | n | ṃ | r | ā | o | b/bh |
| ṅ | ṇ | n | m | ṅ | n | ṃ | r | ā | o | *nasals* (n/m) |
| g | ḍ | d | b | ṅ | n | ṃ | r | ā | o | y/v |
| g | ḍ | d | b | ṅ | n | ṃ | *zero*[1] | ā | o | r |
| g | ḍ | l | b | ṅ | l̃[2] | ṃ | r | ā | o | l |
| k | ṭ | c ch | p | ṅ | ñ ś/ch | ṃ | ḥ | āḥ | aḥ | ś |
| k | ṭ | t | p | ṅ | n | ṃ | ḥ | āḥ | aḥ | ṣ/s |
| gg h | ḍḍ h | dd h | bb h | ṅ | n | ṃ | r | ā | o | h |
| g | ḍ | d | b | ṅ/ṅṅ[3] | n/nn[3] | m | r | ā | a[4] | *vowels* |
| k | ṭ | t | p | ṅ | n | m | ḥ | āḥ | aḥ | *zero* |

[1]ḥ or r disappears, and if a/i/u precedes, this lengthens to ā/ī/ū. [2]e.g. tān+lokān=tāl̃ lokān.
[3]The doubling occurs if the preceding vowel is short. [4]Except: aḥ+a=o '.

macron, except that for initial vowels in sandhi we use a circumflex to indicate that originally the vowel was short, or the shorter of two possibilities (*e* rather than *ai*, *o* rather than *au*).

| When we print initial | before sandhi that vowel was |
|---|---|
| *â*, | *a* |
| *î* or *ê*, | *i* |
| *û* or *ô*, | *u* |
| *âi*, | *e* |
| *âu*, | *o* |
| *ā*, | *ā* |
| *ī*, | *ī* |
| *ū*, | *ū* |
| *ē*, | *ī* |
| *ō*, | *ū* |
| *ai*, | *ai* |
| *āu*, | *au* |
| ’, before sandhi there was a vowel *a* | |

When a final short vowel (*a*, *i*, or *u*) has merged into a following vowel, we print ’ at the end of the word, and when a final long vowel (*ā*, *ī*, or *ū*) has merged into a following vowel we print ” at the end of the word. The vast majority of these cases will concern a final *a* or *ā*. See, for instance, the following examples:

| What before sandhi was | is represented as |
|---|---|
| *atra asti* | *atr’ âsti* |
| *atra āste* | *atr’ āste* |
| *kanyā asti* | *kany” âsti* |
| *kanyā āste* | *kany” āste* |
| *atra iti* | *atr’ êti* |
| *kanyā iti* | *kany” êti* |
| *kanyā īpsitā* | *kany” ēpsitā* |

Finally, three other points concerning the initial letter of the second word:

(1) A word that before sandhi begins with *ṛ* (vowel), after sandhi begins with *r* followed by a consonant: *yatha” rtu* represents pre-sandhi *yathā ṛtu*.

(2) When before sandhi the previous word ends in *t* and the following word begins with *ś*, after sandhi the last letter of the previous word is *c*

and the following word begins with *ch*: *syāc chāstravit* represents pre-sandhi *syāt śāstravit*.

(3) Where a word begins with *h* and the previous word ends with a double consonant, this is our simplified spelling to show the pre-sandhi form: *tad hasati* is commonly written as *tad dhasati*, but we write *tadd hasati* so that the original initial letter is obvious.

### COMPOUNDS

We also punctuate the division of compounds (*samāsa*), simply by inserting a thin vertical line between words. There are words where the decision whether to regard them as compounds is arbitrary. Our principle has been to try to guide readers to the correct dictionary entries.

## Exemplar of CSL Style

Where the Devanagari script reads:

कुम्भस्थली रक्षतु वो विकीर्णसिन्धूररेणुर्द्विरदाननस्य ।
प्रशान्तये विघ्नतमश्छटानां निष्ठ्यूतबालातपपल्लवेव ॥

Others would print:

kumbhasthalī rakṣatu vo vikīrṇasindūrareṇur dviradānanasya /
praśāntaye vighnatamaśchaṭānāṃ niṣṭhyūtabālātapapallaveva //

We print:

kumbha|sthalī rakṣatu vo vikīrṇa|sindūra|reṇur dvirad'|ānanasya
praśāntaye vighna|tamaś|chaṭānāṃ niṣṭhyūta|bāl'|ātapa|pallav" êva.

And in English:

May Ganésha's domed forehead protect you! Streaked with vermilion dust, it seems to be emitting the spreading rays of the rising sun to pacify the teeming darkness of obstructions.

("Nava·sáhasanka and the Serpent Princess" I.3)

### Drama

Classical Sanskrit literature is in fact itself bilingual, notably in drama. There women and characters of low rank speak one of several Prakrit dialects, an "unrefined" *(prākṛta)* vernacular as opposed to the "refined" *(saṃskṛta)* language. Editors commonly provide such speeches with a Sanskrit paraphrase, their "shadow" *(chāyā)*. We mark Prakrit speeches with ⌜opening and closing⌟ corner brackets, and supply the Sanskrit *chāyā* in endnotes. Some stage directions are original to the author but we follow the custom that sometimes editors supplement these; we print them in italics (and within brackets, in mid-text)

# FOREWORD

THIS NEW TRANSLATION of Krishna·mishra's "The Rise of Wisdom Moon" will be, I believe, welcomed by all lovers of Sanskrit literature and especially by admirers of this marvelous drama. MATTHEW KAPSTEIN brings out the work's literary qualities in a manner the earlier translators could not, all the more for the modern literary sensibility. Some of his renderings of Sanskrit proper names are particularly ingenious.

"The Rise of Wisdom Moon" belongs to a literary genre that requires from readers both philosophical knowledge and literary sensibility in order to be able to appreciate it. The work cannot be reduced to a merely philosophical treatise, so compelling is its literary and dramatic effect. The cast of characters, each representing a power of sensible, erotic, intellectual and spiritual life, is at first confounding, but soon, as one identifies each power's characteristic, familiar role, the entire story of conflict, struggle, and eventual resolution coheres in its depiction of man's inner life, and is comparable in this respect to HEGEL's "Phenomenology of Spirit." For while HEGEL's is a philosophical treatise cast, rather severely, as a dramatization, Krishna·mishra's is ostensibly a drama meant to be staged, but is also explicitly philosophical.

MATTHEW KAPSTEIN highlights, as contrasted with earlier translators and writers on the text, its literary quality and wishes to underplay its philosophical nature. The irony lies precisely here, in the work's literary style. This irony of style, I would suggest, is particularly suited to conveying the philosophy it does convey in this case, that is, Adváita Vedánta. This is so because, looked at closely, Adváita Vedánta contains a deep irony: knowledge, or pure consciousness, is itself the locus of ignorance, and yet ignorance seeks to conceal just that which harbors and manifests it. Pure knowledge does not destroy, but rather manifests ignorance. Hence, in Krishna·mishra's play, ignorance and knowledge are cousins, as are the Káuravas and the Pándavas of the great epic. The infinite pure Self *chooses* to be ensnared by illusion, and then does not strive to free itself. Those who act to free the Self are characters who are themselves the kin of illusion. In fine, they are all bound together, and our initial dichotomous, opposition thinking fails.

What a wonderful portrayal of the inner history of the spirit.

J.N. Mohanty
Philadelphia
12 September, 2008

# INTRODUCTION

Throughout the long history of the Sanskrit literary tradition, few texts have enjoyed a success comparable to that of "The Rise of Wisdom Moon" (*Prabodhacandrodaya*), the sole extant work of the otherwise unknown playwright Krishna·mishra·yati, or Krishna·mishra "the ascetic" (*yati*). Composed during the mid eleventh century in north-central India, it came to be translated numerous times over the centuries into both Indian and foreign languages, and was the subject of as many as a dozen Sanskrit commentaries. What is more, "The Rise of Wisdom Moon" is generally credited with having given birth to a distinctive genre of Sanskrit drama, that of the allegorical play. If imitation is the sincerest form of flattery, Krishna·mishra's creation has earned high praise indeed.

"The Rise of Wisdom Moon" entered the Western canon of Sanskrit studies early in the nineteenth century: an English translation by J. Taylor appeared in Bombay in 1812 and has been intermittently reprinted ever since; and in 1845 an edition of the Sanskrit text, prepared by Hermann Brockhaus, was published in Leipzig, Germany. By the end of that century, Krishna·mishra's work was available in German (1820, 1842, 1846), Russian (1847), Dutch (1869) and French (1899) versions in addition to Taylor's pioneering effort.[1] We will examine aspects of the historical background for the early success of "The Rise of Wisdom Moon" in the West later in this introduction. At the outset, however, it will be useful to be familiar with the story told in the play itself.

## Plot Summary

As the scene opens, following the required benedictions, the Stage-manager relates that he has received an order from Gopála, a lord allied with king Kirti·varman. Gopála, thanks to his valiant conduct in battle, has succeeded in restoring Kirti·varman to the throne after the latter had suffered defeat at the hands of his rival Karna, the ruler of the kingdom of Chedi. Following a period of boisterous celebration, Gopála feels that the time has come to extol the virtue of spiritual peace, and so commands that "The Rise of Wisdom Moon," a work composed by his own guru Krishna·mishra, be performed before the king. The Stage-manager, speaking to his actress wife of Gopála's heroism, recites a verse comparing the downfall of Karna and reinstallation of Kirti·varman to spiritual intuition's overcoming of ignorance, and the birth of wisdom that thereby ensues. The frame of the allegory is thus introduced, together with its protagonists Intuition, Magnus Nescience, and Wisdom Moon.

At the recitation of this verse a commotion is heard backstage: Kama, or Lord Lust in our translation, is indignant that his master Magnus Nescience should be disparaged by a mere actor, and he airs his complaint to his wife, Lady Passion. She, however, senses that Intuition and his party may be more formidable than her husband believes and raises a delicate question: is it true, as she has heard, that Lust—and by implication Magnus Nescience with his entire faction—in fact share common origins with their hated enemies, Intuition and his allies? Lust confirms her suspicions in revealing that Nescience and Intuition are paternal half-siblings, having been born to one or another of the two wives of Thought, and that the latter, in turn, was the unique son of the Supreme Lord's marriage with Maya, the cosmic illusion underlying all creation. Intuition and Magnus Nescience, therefore, are now the chiefs of two rival, but consanguine, clans.

Lust also reveals to Passion a terrifying secret: he has heard a prophecy that a spell-wielding demoness, Scientia, will arise to put an end to both branches of the family at once. Her birth, like that of her brother Wisdom Moon, will follow from Intuition's marriage to Lady Úpanishad. As Lust loudly condemns those who would thus seek to destroy their own clan, a new commotion is heard. But this time it is Intuition reacting in his turn to Lust's deprecations of him.

Intuition now discusses the family's fate with his wife, Lady Intelligence, seeking to explain just how it is that the Supreme Lord—the highest principle that is the true and eternal Self, or Brahman—came to be entangled in the snares of Illusion, who has lulled the Lord into a profound, fitful sleep. When Intelligence inquires as to what might be done to rouse him so that he may be awakened once again, Intuition is embarrassed. Fearing his wife's reaction, he hesitates to reveal that she will have to accept Úpanishad as her co-wife. Intelligence, however, assures him that she is not one given to jealousy. As the first act concludes, they plot together to bring about Intuition's union with Úpanishad so that Wisdom Moon may be born.

The setting shifts to Varánasi, where the second act begins. The holy city, a place promising liberation on this earth, is now in the clutches of one of Magnus Nescience's main henchmen, Hypocrite, who has adopted the guise of a pious brahmin. A boastful stranger arrives, seeking to find lodging in Hypocrite's household, but the two merely annoy one another before realizing that they are in fact close relations; for the stranger is Egoismo, the "I-maker," who is the source of our conviction that we are discrete selves, separate from both the true and absolute self, as well as from one another. Hypocrite is none other than his grandson, the child of Lady Craving and Lord Greed. Their entire branch of the family, it emerges, has been ordered to Varánasi by Magnus Nescience, who soon arrives on stage with much fanfare. It is not long before he is joined by Hedonist, the representative of worldliness and materialism, and here embodying the deepest folly into which philosophical thinking can fall.

Although Hedonist reports the victory of Nescience's forces in the world at large, he has also learned of a possible source of danger to their faction: there is a powerful female adept, Hail Vishnu, now active, who poses a threat that cannot be ignored. Nescience orders her elimination, but then discovers that he faces an additional problem. A messenger from Orissa, where the great temple of Jagan·natha is in the hands of Nescience's minions, brings the unwelcome news that the ladies Peace and Faith are serving as go-betweens to arrange Intuition's marriage with Úpanishad. Moreover, Lex, Dharma in Sanskrit, personifying the laws, duties and regulations of the world, was until recently allied with Lust, but now seems to have befriended Dispassion and is therefore changing camps. Nescience, furious at this defection, sends the order to Lust that Lex be brought under control. To ensure, too, that Peace, Faith and the other allies of Intuition are suitably neutralized, he sends for his leading partisans: Lord Anger and Sir Greed, Lady Craving and Mistress Harm. Despite their assurances, Nescience nonetheless remains concerned that Peace presents a graver risk than his followers can admit. As she is the daughter of Faith, and Faith, in turn, the constant companion of Úpanishad, he must devise a means to drive these last two apart. Peace, on learning of her mother's disappearance, will then be left off-guard and vulnerable. In the final scene of the act, he hatches his plan: the seductive and devious Miss Conception, the very incarnation of false ideas, is dispatched to work her wiles on hapless Faith.

As the third act unfolds, Peace is found weeping in distress at her mother's absence. She goes so far as to contemplate suicide, and is dissuaded only by the entreaties of her friend Mercy, who urges her not to abandon the search for her mother, even if it takes her among heretics and outcastes. The pair sets out, meeting in turn a Jain ascetic, a Buddhist monk, and a Skullman, who follows the transgressive path of tantric Shaivism. All three are found to be accompanied by their respective versions of Faith, but Mercy and Peace discern that none is true Faith, Peace's mother. They are not imbued with the principle of truth and purity (*sattva*), but are, rather, the daughters of the dark and dull element (*tamas*), or of energy and excitation (*rajas*). The Skullman, moreover, is an adept of the black arts and so sets about to deploy a potent spell called the "Great Terrorress" (*Mahābhairavī*) to capture true Faith, together with Lex.

Love meets Faith in the fourth act, after the latter has managed to escape from the Terrorress's clutches following the Skullman's conjurations. It was, indeed, the *yoginī* Hail Vishnu who succeeded in counteracting the spell, and she, too, has been busy organizing Intuition's forces in the struggle against Magnus Nescience. Intuition, for his part, weakened by the run-up to war, has retreated to Radha—the hometown of Egoismo—in Bengal, where, practicing austerities, he prepares himself for union with Úpanishad. He calls upon those among his forces who are most capable of defeating Nescience's greatest warriors: Analyst is to vie with Lust, Patience with Anger, and Contentment with Greed. Each is called upon in turn to explain the means for victory at their disposal. The troops assembled, they set out for battle. Intuition mounts his chariot and flies off for an aerial view of the rout of Nescience's armies in Varánasi. In the concluding portion of the act, he offers homage to Vishnu at the chief shrine in the holy city.

Although Intuition and his forces are now victorious, the war, like that of the "Maha·bhárata," has been waged among siblings. The joy of success, therefore, is dampened by grief at the fate of one's closest relations, much as it is in the hero Árjuna's laments in the first canto of the "Bhágavad·gita." Faith articulates this in the first lines of act five, and hastens to meet Hail Vishnu, to whom she is to report the events of the battle. She finds the goddess in conversation with her daughter, Peace. Joining them, she describes what has taken place.

After the armies had gathered, Intuition dispatched Reason as his messenger to Nescience, with the ultimatum that the latter and his party must quit Varánasi or face death in battle. Taking up the challenge, Nescience sends the heresies into action as the first wave of his attack. The goddess Sarásvati appears at the head of Intuition's army to rally his troops. She is soon joined by Lady Hermeneutics—the Mimánsaka philosophy—together with the other schools and traditions that affirm the authority of the Veda. Though they have often been discordant in the past, they are now united by a common purpose. As Faith explains it, all those that are founded in the Vedic revelation partake of the same inner light.

In the heat of the ensuing combat, the materialist system soon perishes, quickly abandoned by both sides. The surviving heretics are driven to the frontiers. Lust, Anger and the remaining close allies of Nescience are slain in individual combat, while Nescience himself has fled and gone into hiding no-one-knows-where. Thought, the father of both Intuition and Nescience, learning of the demise of so many of his progeny, now grows despondent and contemplates suicide. Once apprised of this, Hail Vishnu dispatches Sarásvati to console him.

The scene shifts: Thought is bemoaning his losses to Intention, when Sarásvati enters and, after instructing him on the means whereby he might regain his composure, encourages Thought to be reconciled with Dispassion, a son he had abandoned at birth long ago. Father and son joyfully reunite, and Sarásvati, recognizing that Thought cannot remain alone following the loss of his first wife, Eva Lucienne, or active engagement in the world, now confirms his marriage with Diva Lucienne, the process of disengagement.

Having set Thought's household in its new and proper order, the goddess commands the performance of memorial offerings for their deceased kin.

Faith and Peace are in dialogue, in the prologue to act six, revealing that, following Thought's reconciliation with Dispassion, the Inner Man, who is the Supreme Self, is now increasingly coming into his own. Owing to his newfound detachment even Lex has grown quiescent, as there is no longer reason to contemplate consequential actions, whether the goals be good or bad. Nevertheless, the old foe Magnus Nescience has been still able to stir up some trouble: he has managed to conjure up visions of the delectable state called the "Honeyed Realm," so that the Inner Man was for a while tempted to return to *saṃsāra*, until Reason entered the scene to snap him out of it. Faith and Peace conclude their discussion, hastening to arrange for Intuition's meeting at last with Úpanishad.

The Inner Man now sings the praises of Hail Vishnu, when Peace enters with Úpanishad. The latter is hesitant to approach, for she recalls that she had been rejected once before and thereafter fell into grave difficulty. Peace objects that the Inner Man was blameless and that it was Nescience whose nefarious schemes had caused Úpanishad to be separated from Intuition. She had taken refuge with her daughter Gita, that is, the "Bhágavad·gita," in order to escape from Reason, a state of affairs that Intuition finds puzzling. All gather before the Inner Man, who honors Úpanishad and inquires as to what she had suffered during her prolonged exile.

Úpanishad relates that she first dwelt among foolish persons, who understood nothing of what she had to say. She encountered the traditions of Vedic ritual and thought that she might stay with them, but was able to find only a temporary accommodation based on the mistaken assumption that the Self of which she spoke was the ritual agent. Eventually, these traditions, personified as Sacrificial Science, found her to be a bad influence and so asked her to leave. Meeting then Hermeneutics, the Mimánsaka school, her experience with Sacrificial Science was about to be repeated, when the famed Mimánsaka teacher Kumárila intervened to introduce the notion of the dual nature of the Self: the aspect of which Úpanishad spoke was, he thought, quite distinct from a second dimension, the agent invoked in the ritual traditions. Intuition interrupts her narrative at this point to praise Kumárila's good sense.

Úpanishad continues her story, recounting her experiences with the philosophical systems of Vaishéshika, Nyaya, and Sankhya, all of whom derided her teaching of the absolute Brahman in favor of cosmologies based on atoms or prime matter, and eventually condemned her as a nihilist. Fleeing, therefore, from philosophical arguments and speculations, she wandered until she found a safe haven in the ashram of her daughter Gita.

Her travails now exposed, the Inner Man engages both her and Intuition in dialogue to discover the true meaning of her teaching, whereby the great affirmations (*mahāvākya*) of the Úpanishads—such as the famous saying "thou art that"—are introduced. As their conversation advances, Contemplation joins them, carrying a message from Hail

Vishnu revealing that Úpanishad is already pregnant with Scientia and Wisdom Moon. Úpanishad then departs together with her husband Intuition. The Inner Man merges with Contemplation and, in his absorption, realizes that Scientia has taken birth and completed the conquest of Nescience. Wisdom Moon joins him on stage, they embrace joyfully, and the Inner Man praises Hail Vishnu for his good fortune. The goddess arrives, confirming that all that was to be done is now concluded. The play ends with final benedictions.

## A Bit of History

To appreciate "The Rise of Wisdom Moon" more fully, we must consider some salient points of its historical, literary, and religious-philosophical background. The first was largely forgotten in India itself prior to the reconstruction of India's pre-Islamic history as this emerged following the considerable archeological and epigraphical discoveries of the nineteenth century. Just how obscure the relevant history was prior to these developments may be gleaned from the dedication of TAYLOR's 1812 translation, where we read:

> Perhaps some conjecture may be formed concerning the age of the Play, from the mention which is made of the King Shri Kirti Varma, who is said to have attended its representation, along with his court. My Pandita, indeed, says, that he is a personification of the fame or glory of Gopala [the god Krishna]; but I am more inclined to think that he was a real personage, and that the poet, out of compliment or flattery, represents Gopala or Krishna as fighting his battles, and establishing him on the

> throne. If the Shri Kirti Varma was a real being, he probably reigned over Magadha or Behar, the sovereigns of which also extended their empire to the provinces which lie northward of the Ganges; for Varma, or warrior, was a family name assumed by the Magadha kings, and Shri was prefixed as a title, intimating success or prosperity. If the conjecture be correct, it would lead us to ascribe a considerable antiquity to the Play.[2]

He goes on to propose that it should be dated to the latter half of the first millennium CE, though without finding evidence for a more precise estimation.

That the pandit with whom TAYLOR worked was inclined to regard the occurrence of the name Gopála as strictly referring to god Krishna was perhaps a legacy of the popularity which the play came to enjoy in north Indian Váishnava circles from about the fifteenth century on, leading him to interpret away its historical references in the light of this understanding. TAYLOR, however, proved to be correct in his guess that Kirti·varman was a real individual, though his attempt to place him in the kingdom of Mágadha was in error. It was not, at any rate, until 1865, when ALEXANDER CUNNINGHAM discovered an inscription of the Chandélla dynasty at Mahoba, situated in modern Uttar Pradesh to the north of Khajuraho, that the evidence needed to decide the issue at last became available. Though CUNNINGHAM was aware of the significance of his find, the results were for the first time set out clearly by E. HULTZSCH, in a study of the Mahoba inscription published in 1888. For here, in the 26th verse, we read that Kirti·

varman "acquired fame by crushing with his strong arm the haughty Lakṣmīkarṇa, whose armies had destroyed many princes." (HULTZSCH 1888: 219–20). And in other sources the Chedi monarch Lakshmi·karna—Karna in our play—is mentioned as "death to the lord of Kālañjara,"[3] referring to his conquest of the Chandélla's chief fortress. Given the chronological knowledge derived from the broader study of medieval Indian epigraphy, "The Rise of Wisdom Moon" could now be understood to celebrate a Chandélla restoration that occurred sometime not long after 1060.[4]

The Chandélla dynasty had emerged from among feudatories of the Pratiháras who ruled in late first-millennium Western India, and they established themselves as the independent lords of much of what is today Madhya Pradesh by about the middle of the tenth century. Like many other royal families in India, their true beginnings, which were perhaps tribal, were disguised by a legend of divine origin, in this case stemming from the god of the moon, Chandra. This association was used to explain their name, Chandélla, and is mentioned early in the first act of our play, where we find a reference to Kirti·varman as belonging to the "lunar line" (1.16). The title of the play and the name of its character Wisdom Moon further celebrate this connection.

Kingship in India was always a rough and tumble business, and the Chandéllas, as was typical, were locked in shifting patterns of rivalries and alliances with their neighbors, including their former masters, the Pratiháras, as well as the Kala·churis who ruled in Chedi to the south, and the Palas and Senas to the east, in Bihar and Bengal, together with many less prominent players. The Chandéllas themselves were centered in the region that is today called Bundelkhand, in the northeast of Madhya Pradesh, where they commanded the fortress of Kalan·jara and had their cultural and religious capital at Khajuraho. Their territory at its greatest extent embraced much of present Madhya Pradesh, and to some degree reached beyond this as well. Chandélla dominance in this part of Central India endured for roughly three centuries. From the eleventh century on, they were among the north Indian dynasties that were regularly harassed by Muslim Turkic raiders first from Central Asia and later the Delhi Sultanate. The fortress of Kalan·jara was itself taken by the conqueror Qutb-ud-din Aibak in 1203, but appears to have been regained not more than two years later. The Chandéllas, though much weakened, continued to maintain a measure of sovereignty for another century, until they finally fade from the record with the reign of Hammíra·varman (c. 1288–1311), the last of their rulers to have left surviving inscriptions.

Among the Chandéllas, royal succession passed strictly from father to son, with only a small number of exceptions. One of these was the king with whom we are concerned, Kirti·varman, who inherited the throne from his elder brother Deva·varman (c. 1050–1060), apparently after the latter passed away leaving no heir. It is possible, though we do not have sufficient information to be sure, that this was due to the conquest of the Chandéllas by their Kala·churi foe Lakshmi·karna (c. 1040–1073), who had embarked upon a scheme of conquest so ambitious that he has sometimes been characterized as a "Napoléon" of medieval India (DIKSHIT 1977: 103). What both the Mahoba inscription and "The Rise of Wisdom Moon" make clear, however, is that Kirti·varman was installed (or reinstalled) following Karna's defeat by the resurgent Chandéllas. As we have seen above, this appears to have occurred during the 1060s, a period during which Karna's fortunes in general had begun to turn.

As the play affirms, but without a confirming record being found in the extant inscriptions, Kirti·varman's success was due to the heroic action of his "natural ally" (*sahajasuhṛt*) Gopála. Discounting TAYLOR's suggestion that this was but a reference to the divine aid of Krishna, we must assume that the testimony of the play is in essence true, for it is hardly possible that a literary work ascribing a royal restoration to a subsidiary lord could have circulated—and indeed present itself as a work to be performed before the king—if the court was not substantially in accord with the account given there. The description of Gopála as Kirti·varman's "natural ally" has sometimes been regarded as supplying a plausible explanation in this case, and, as some historians have noted, the term in fact had two precise significations in ancient Indian political theory, referring either to a king who was one's enemy's enemy, or to the lords and retainers belonging to one's maternal clan.[5] It seems therefore that Gopála must have been one of Kirti·varman's maternal uncles or cousins. I think that we can go beyond this, however, and suggest as an hypothesis that, given the unusual succession from elder to younger brother, and the likelihood in the light of what else may be known of Chandélla genealogy, that Kirti·varman must have been rather young, perhaps even a child, when he succeeded to the throne. For his was a notably long reign, spanning roughly four decades, until the closing years of the eleventh century. The Kala·churi Karna, therefore, may have invaded at a time when the Chandélla line was particularly vulnerable—when Deva·varman had not yet produced an heir—and it was because of his rescue of the dynasty under such circumstances that Gopála's deed could be publicly celebrated, not least at the court of the king he had succeeded in placing upon the throne.[6]

It is unfortunate that the spotty record of Chandélla history provides us with few indications concerning the events of Kirti·varman's rule following the defeat of Lakshmi·karna. The construction of three important reservoirs is attributed to him by local tradition, and two temples of Shiva, one at Mahoba and the other at Ajayagadh, in the immediate vicinity of Khajuraho, may have been built with his patronage. An inscription accompanying a Jain image found in a village near Mahoba confirms that he extended his protection to this religion and mentions two of his officers as Jain adherents. Other inscriptions laud his personal qualities, praising him as a righteous ruler whose good works purified the evil of the age of Kali (DIKSHIT 1977: 109).

An important historical problem that remains, of course, is the identity of the author of our play, Krishna·mishra. Besides the addition to his name of the title *yati*, or "ascetic," and the statement in the first act that he was Gopála's guru, nothing at all is known of him with certainty. Later tradition maintains that he was an ascetic of the *haṃsa* order, which, in the light of his clear affiliation with the philosophical tradition of Adváita Vedánta, is not an impossibility. However, because *yati* was sometimes adopted as a sobriquet by lay scholars, and because Krishna·mishra's roles as a poet and counselor of a lord seem most often to have been occupied by lay specialists and not renunciates, skepticism about this tradition seems warranted. And a tale found in the *Prakāśa* commentary relates that he wrote "The Rise of Wisdom Moon" on behalf of a disciple who was attached to poetry but disliked philosophy, and so needed to swallow the bitter dose of Vedánta mixed into the sugary syrup of the theater. This quaint story, however, must have come into circulation at some point after the real historical origins of the play were largely forgotten (KRISHNAMACHARIAR 1970 [1937]: 676).

Despite the extreme poverty of our knowledge of Krishna·mishra the man, his work permits us to make some judgments regarding his character. He was the confidant and teacher of a leading lord of his time, and his qualifications for this role included a broad philosophical and literary culture. His deep understanding of the spiritual tradition with which he was affiliated was leavened by an amused view of human weakness and folly. As we become more familiar with his work, we may imagine that we catch occasional glimpses within it of the workman as well.

## Literature or Philosophy?

Allegory was never recognized as a distinct genre by Sanskrit writers on literary criticism and poetics. It was not until recent times, after Western literary categories became known, that writers in the modern Indian languages coined the Sanskrit neologisms *pratīkanāṭaka* ("symbolic drama") and *rūpakanāṭaka* ("metaphorical drama") in order to describe "The Rise of Wisdom Moon" and works resembling it.[7] Nevertheless, allegory had in fact been used by Indian authors from the earliest times. The image of the two-headed bird, for instance, first found in the *Ṛgveda* (1.164.20), was taken over in the *Muṇḍaka Upaniṣad* as an allegory of the dimorphism of the soul. By citing this famous passage in act six (6.112 [20]), Krishna·mishra in effect plants the roots of his inspiration deep in the most ancient strata of Sanskrit literature.

Fragments of early Buddhist dramas, dating to the first centuries CE, also make use of allegory, and include characters with names like "Fame" and "Pride." Nevertheless, these plays, so far as we can now know them, do not appear to have been sustained allegories, that is, they were primarily stories of Buddhist saints, in which some episodes took allegorical form. And there is no evidence of knowledge of these works among later Indian writers, much less of their exerting any influence upon the way they wrote.[8]

At the same time, regarding several of the devices he employs in developing his allegory, Krishna·mishra's debts to earlier dramatic writing can sometimes be discerned. One example is to be found in his satire of the three heterodox schools—Jainism, Buddhism and Kapálika Shaivism—in the third act. In this case, the inspiration of the seventh-century farce *Mattavilāsa*, the "Madman's Play," of Mahéndra·varman seems unmistakeable.[9] And in Krishna·mishra's incorporation of elements of philosophical debate and dialogue into the drama at several points, he may well have the model of Jayánta·bhatta's *Āgamaḍambara*, "Much Ado

About Religion," in mind.[10] In sum, although Krishna·mishra's contribution to Indian literature was not the invention of allegory as such, he may nonetheless be credited with introducing its employment in order to structure an entire literary work from beginning to end. That the tradition itself recognized this to be an original contribution may be gathered from the fact that several of the later Sanskrit allegories, and more than a dozen are known, explicitly refer back to "The Rise of Wisdom Moon," often underscoring this fact by the use of clearly imitative titles (KRISHNAMACHARIAR 1970 [1937]: 675–85).

Allegory, however, is an unfortunate genre. It suffers from the constraint of its major premise, for it must tell a story that is in fact a second story, a double task restricting the author's free creation and often lending to allegorical works a rigid, contrived quality, as we know from European medieval mysteries like "Everyman," or from Bunyan's "Pilgrim's Progress." That Krishna·mishra succeeded in his task better than most is demonstrated by his work's enduring success. However, it is difficult in this case not to concur with the assessment of one of the path-breakers in the study of Sanskrit literary history, S.K. DE:

> With … abstract and essentially scholastic subject-matter, it is difficult to produce a drama of real interest. But it is astonishing that, apart from the handicaps inherent in the method and purpose, Kṛṣṇamiśra succeeds, to a remarkable degree, in giving us an ingenious picture of the spiritual struggle of the human mind in the dramatic form of a vivid conflict, in which the erotic, comic and

devotional interests are cleverly utilized. (Dasgupta & De 1962: 483)

As De rightly stressed, the demands of Krishna·mishra's subject-matter, the attainment of spiritual peace in the soul's liberation as understood within the tradition of the nondualist school of Vedánta (*advaita vedānta*), both pose a challenge to the author in relation to properly literary expression and at the same time inhibit the reader's properly literary reading of the text. An unfortunate result has been that modern readers have sometimes taken the work merely to be an elementary primer of Adváita philosophy, almost entirely ignoring its literary qualities. In the present translation, therefore, I have sought to lay stress on "The Rise of Wisdom Moon" as a clever and often quite funny play, quite apart from its message per se.

The message, however, is essential for any understanding of the work, and in seeking to address it in dramatic form, rather than in a formal theological treatise, Krishna·mishra was accepting a considerable risk. For above and beyond the difficulties inherent in dramatizing spiritual growth, he was taking a forthright stand in regard to one of the keenest disputes in classical Indian literary theory. In essence, the critics wished to establish whether, besides the aesthetic sentiments with which we are generally familiar—erotic love, humor, horror, and the like—is there additionally a distinct sentiment of peace?[11] Can the mystical realization of oneness and the void be the subject-matter of great literature, or does its awesome depths compel only a surpassing silence, from which no literary art can emerge? Krishna·mishra was among those who affirmed that a sentiment of peace can serve as an appropriate focus for literary creation, and he tells us this explicitly, affirming at the outset that he has written "a play conveying the sentiment of peace" (1.7).

But how to convey such a sentiment? To elicit horror, one can show frightening things, for humor things that are funny, and so on. The attempt to display peace directly—perhaps by depicting a group of persons in silent meditation—is guaranteed to be merely a bore. The only strategy that might work is to arrive at peace through contrast. Peace becomes dramatically interesting only in relation to its opposites: war, struggle, the erotic distractions, and so on. Krishna·mishra very well understood this and, using the contrastive categories underscored in Indian traditions, sought to realize the sentiment of peace as the conclusion of a journey through what peace is not.[12]

In order to achieve this end, Krishna·mishra's work depends on one of the fundamental dichotomies informing classical Indian thought, that between *pravṛtti* and *nivṛtti*.[13] The pair is often translated, misleadingly I think, as "activity" and "inactivity." It is important, however, to gain a more nuanced sense of their meaning, as this provides an essential key to understanding the play as whole.

To begin, we may cite a popular verse that states: "I know the *dharma*, but it is not what I engage in; I know non-*dharma*, too, but it is not what I desist from."[14] Here, I have translated *pravṛtti* as "what I engage in" and *nivṛtti* as "what I desist from." The relevant contrast is not one between activity and inactivity, but between the forward, outgoing channeling of energies into a particular pattern of action, and, oppositely, the withdrawal or turning away from that course. Though the verse nicely introduces the terms as they apply to our individual, active undertakings, we must recognize further that the distinction in question may be invoked in some rather different contexts. In Buddhist idealist philosophy, for instance, it pertains to perceptual processes, *pravṛtti* referring to the proliferations of consciousness which constructs the world as we perceive it, and *nivṛtti* to the inversion of that process in meditation, where our constructions are dissolved as tranquility and insight develop.[15] We should be aware, too, of the cosmological significance of these concepts in Brahmanical thought. In this case, *pravṛtti* indicates the emanation of the phenomenal world through the agency of *māyā*, creative illusion generating the world of appearance, while *nivṛtti* is the dissolution that occurs when *māyā*'s work is undone.

Several of these strands of meaning are beautifully woven together in the introduction to the commentary on the "Bhágavad·gita" attributed to the renowned Adváita Vedánta philosopher Shánkara (eighth century).[16] While it is not certain the Krishna·mishra had precisely this text in mind when he composed "The Rise of Wisdom Moon," he was no doubt thinking of closely similar materials. The philosopher's words, therefore, will help to clarify some essential elements in the structure of the play:

> The Lord, having created this world, desired to make it endure. Having first produced the lords of creatures—the sun and the others—he caused them to maintain the law (*dharma*) whose characteristic is engagement (*pravṛtti*),

> as taught in the Veda. Then, having given rise to others—Sánaka, Sanándana, etc.—he caused them to maintain the law whose characteristic is disengagement (*nivṛtti*) and whose characteristic is knowledge and dispassion. For twofold is the law taught in the Veda—that having the characteristic of engagement and that having the characteristic of disengagement—and this is the cause for the world's enduring. That which is the basis for the manifest well-being and beatitude of creatures, that law has been upheld for long ages by those who aspire for the good, brahmins and others, according to their caste (*varṇa*) and life-station (*āśrama*).[17]

As they are described here, *pravṛtti* and *nivṛtti* are complementary processes, that together are necessary so that the world is upheld overall. Krishna·mishra underscores this point at the very beginning of "The Rise of Wisdom Moon," in proclaiming the need to balance the festivities of the king's reinstallation with a work devoted to the "sentiment of peace," and, more pointedly still, in writing that:

> The divine light is by nature pacific, so that, if for whatever reason it suffers modification, it abides as it is in its essence. [Thus Gopála] undertook to shore up on this earth the rule of the princes of the lunar line, when they were uprooted by the Chedis' lord … [S]uch persons, ornaments of manliness, who are of a piece with Lord Naráyana [Vishnu], descend to earth for the sake of beings and when they have completed their tasks attain peace once again. (1.16–18)

The oscillation between active engagement in the maintenance of the world and withdrawal from it is thus characteristic both of the divinity and of kings.

For Krishna·mishra, in sum, the dichotomy of *pravṛtti* and *nivṛtti* functions on three basic levels: macrocosmically, it defines the order governing the universe as whole, and microcosmically, it describes individuals' patterned engagement in and disengagement from mundane activity. But it also operates mesocosmically, in relation to the order of the monarchal state, wherein the righteous king must achieve that delicate balance whereby martial force is neither oppressive nor overextended, and peace is not confounded with pusillanimity. The equilibrium that must be achieved here is further accentuated by Krishna·mishra in the general structure of his work. For the first three acts, in which Magnus Nescience and his gang enjoy the upper hand, concern engagement in mundane activity in the life of the individual who is bound to *saṃsāra*, while the final three acts are dedicated to *nivṛtti*, here the soteriologically valued withdrawal from worldliness through which enlightenment may be won.

Much has been made of the apparent synthesis of Adváita Vedánta philosophy with Váishnava devotionalism, or *bhakti*, that characterizes "The Rise of Wisdom Moon." My own belief is that this has been somewhat overblown, the result of reading the play through the lens of the later sectarian devotional movements that sometimes appropriated it. One author has even gone so far as to characterize Krishna·mishra's religious attitude as a "fanatic zeal for Vaisnavism" (Bose 1956: 161), but this is surely misleading. For several reasons, Krishna·mishra's sectarian inclinations appear to me to be weaker than is generally assumed, and the Vaishnavism of his work, while by no means to be denied, may be explained without reference to strong sectarian bias.

The Váishnava current in "The Rise of Wisdom Moon" is underscored principally by these features: the heroine of the drama is the character Vishnu·bhakti, Hail Vishnu in our translation; at the conclusion of act four, Intuition undertakes a pilgrimage to the shrine of Vishnu in Varánasi (4.123); in act five, Thought is instructed in meditation upon Vishnu as an alternative to absorption in the absolute Brahman (5.103 [27]); and references to a number of Vishnu's incarnations are found throughout the work. Taken together with arguments that have been most clearly presented by Paul Hacker, to the effect that early Adváita Vedánta, as represented above all by Shánkara, was mildly Váishnava in its leanings, it is undeniable that Krishna·mishra clearly expresses a similar partiality here, though "fanatic" is no doubt too strong a characterization of his leanings (Hacker 1965).

The Váishnava reading of the text is mitigated by a number of positive gestures to Shaivism, and indeed to other sectarian traditions, at various points in the play. This despite the wholesale rejection, in act three, of the transgressive Kapálika current of Shaivism as altogether heretical. Nevertheless, the second of the opening verses of benediction is dedicated to Shiva, with distinct allusions to systems of yoga that were often placed under that divinity's patronage. (The first of the benedictions concerns the nondual Brahman, and therefore has no distinct sectarian orientation, apart from its affirmation of Advánta Vedánta.) In act five (5.32), as Intuition's armies advance, the Shaiva traditions, on an equal footing with the Váishnava, are arrayed within the victorious ranks. And the ultimate equivalence of the three great Hindu divinities—Brahma, Vishnu, and Shiva—is unambiguously asserted some lines later:

The Light, at peace and limitless,
  without duality, unborn,
By the admixture of qualities varies,
  and is praised as "Brahma,"
  "Vishnu," or "Uma's Lord." (5.40 [9])

Moreover, the play's many references to Vishnu's incarnations—including boar, dwarf, man-lion, Axman Rama, and Rama—all follow well-established conventions whereby these avatars were analogized to the figure of the King. For Vishnu as the preserver of the world is the member of the trinity who provides the best template for righteous kingship, upholding the order of the cosmos and granting peace and security to its creatures.

These last observations allow us, I believe, to put Krishna·mishra's Vaishnavism into its proper perspective. The rulers of the Chandélla dynasty generally seem to have favored the worship of Shiva, but they were tolerant monarchs, who extended their patronage to the several major Brahmanical and Hindu traditions and to Jainism, and even countenanced a Buddhist presence within their domains as well.[18] Vaishnavism was, however, a strong current within Chandélla religion, and several of the monarchs appear to have regarded Vishnu as their personal tutelary divinity.

One of these was Kirti·varman (MITRA 1977 [1958]: 189). It becomes possible to imagine, therefore, that "The Rise of Wisdom Moon," in its leanings towards Vaishnavism, is primarily expressing an allegiance to the ruler in whose honor the play was written and produced.

We may press this point somewhat further. To mention our play and the famed temples of Khajuraho in a single breath may appear to be an incongruent pairing, for the great north Indian temple-complex, after all, is widely associated with the celebration of the erotic, while Krishna·mishra's drama represents orthodox Vedánta, a philosophy that values detachment from worldly delights in favor of the inner realization of an immutable, transcendent self. But Khajuraho's marvels and "The Rise of Wisdom Moon" both issued from the court of the Chandélla monarchs, and the period during which our play was composed was not far removed from the height of development at Khajuraho.[19] It is not difficult, in fact, to imagine that the play might have been performed among the temples and palaces there. While sexual frankness characterizes many of the scenes adorning the outer walls of Khajuraho's temples, in the interior they are almost all dedicated to the great gods of the Hindu pantheon, in forms that arouse not the slightest hint of tantric transgressions.[20] By the same token, "The Rise of Wisdom Moon," though surely ridiculizing our erotic proclivities, also sees a place for them in the order of things and can hardly be considered as prudish in its treatment of sexual desire:

She slithers hither:
slowed by the big burden of her booty,
and revealing by a little trick
of her flowing garland's pose,
pressed by playful arms,
breasts marked with lovers' scratches;
With glances as long as strings of blue lotuses
she drinks up your mind
while jingling her bangles
with the languid movements of her wrists. (2.162 [34])

To focus upon sex, however, is to miss the chief concerns of both the temples and the play. Just as the deity Vishnu, as honored by Intuition at the conclusion of act four, is clearly exempt from the fun and folly of the preceding acts, so too the great image of Vishnu as Vaikúntha, in Khajuraho's Lákshmana Temple, a temple with which Krishna·mishra may well have been familiar, transcends the swirling activity, erotic and otherwise, depicted on the shrine's outer walls.[21] The imperial order is silent at its center, but nonetheless this imperturbable calm forms the basis for both the love and the war whereby the kingdom thrives. Taken together, Khajuraho's temples and Krishna·mishra's play are perhaps best regarded as diverse iterations of the Chandélla royal religion, for which divinity and sovereignty, cosmos and realm, were never quite two. Our play's Vaishnavism, therefore, unmistakeable though it may be, was not yet distinguished from kingly cult and must not be assimilated to the devotional movements that would soon emerge as predominant throughout much of the North Indian religious scene.[22]

## Krishna·mishra's Legacy

The reception history of "The Rise of Wisdom Moon" in India has been studied in depth so far only with respect to one regional language, Hindi (including Braj).[23] It is clear, however, that, starting with its impact within Sanskrit literary culture itself, the play became established as a touchstone for the form of the allegorical drama, and more specifically a model for literary instruction in philosophical matters. The evidence available to us demonstrates both unusually broad diffusion and enduring popularity. The interest that its philosophical content generated is indicated by its widespread use as a source for knowledge of the "heretical" doctrine of the Charvákas (or Lokáyatas), the skeptical hedonists and materialists who had been among the bugbears of early Indian thought. Indeed, the fourteenth-century "Compendium of All Viewpoints" (*Sarvadarśanasaṃgraha*), among the best known of all Indian philosophical summations, bases its record of the Charvákas to a large extent upon their representation in "The Rise of Wisdom Moon."[24]

M. Krishnamachariar (1970 [1937]: 678), in his history of classical Sanskrit literature, mentions no fewer than ten commentaries on our play. This fact alone confirms the high regard with which it was held among Sanskrit scholars, and suggests, too, that it was frequently a subject of instruction. Not all learned readers of Sanskrit, however, followed Krishna·mishra in his adherence to Adváita Vedánta. This was surely one of the reasons for which imitations of his play proliferated, tailoring his model to the needs of differing philosophical or sectarian affiliations. These works often declare the source of their inspiration by the inclusion of the word *udaya*, "rise, ascent" in the title. More than a dozen such plays, some written as late as the nineteenth century, are known, of which several have enjoyed relative success. Among them, we may note in particular "The Sunrise of Comprehension" (*Saṅkalpasūryodaya*) by the famed teacher of the "qualified non-dualist" (*viśiṣṭādvaita*) Vedánta tradition, Vénkata·natha (fourteenth century, also known as Vedánta·déshika); the medical allegory entitled "The Rise of Ambrosia" (*Amṛtodaya*) of Gókula·natha (ca. early seventeenth century); and "The Rise of the Moon of Chaitánya" (*Caitanyacandrodaya*) of Karna·pura (early sixteenth century).[25] The latter is distinguished by its combining of allegory with historical elements drawn from the lives of Chaitánya (1486–1534), the renowned apostle of devotion to Krishna, and his contemporaries. A Jain play, "The Conquest of King Confusion" (*Moharājaparājaya*), composed by Yashah·pala in the thirteenth century similarly combines allegory with history in recounting the conversion to Jainism of King Kumára·pala of Gujarat.[26]

"The Rise of Wisdom Moon," written early in the second millennium, entered into circulation just as the regional languages of the subcontinent began gradually to supplant the dominance of Sanskrit in Indian literary cultures.[27] This process of vernacularization, however, offered new avenues for the diffusion of Krishna·mishra's play, and from the fifteenth century onward, we find it being translated or transfigured throughout a wide range of north and south Indian tongues, including Hindi, Braj, Bengali, Gujarati, Urdu, Tamil, Telegu, Malayalam, and no doubt others as well.[28] In Hindi and Braj, in particular, numerous versions are known. Most of these seem to have stemmed from the Váishnava *bhakti* movements that proliferated in late medieval North India, whose devotees were attracted to the play owing to its generalized Váishnava orientation, as we have discussed above. One such version, by Gulāb Siṅgh (1905), versifies the entire text in Braj, following prosodic conventions dear to the Braj *bhakti* poets.

Perhaps the most remarkable of the Indian translations of "The Rise of Wisdom Moon," however, was one that carried it beyond the Hindu fold. This was the Persian version that emerged from the circle of Prince Dara Shikoh (1613–59), the Emperor Akbar's ill-fated grandson, who, developing the implications of his forefather's syncretic imperial religion, sought a reconciliation between Hinduism and Islam. The translation was achieved by the prince's secretary and protégé Banwalidas Wali, also known as Baba Wali Ram, by origin a *kāyastha*—a member of the scribal and clerical caste—from Varánasi. Wali would become a renunciate in later life, closely associated with some of the leading Sufi masters of the age, and in the years before his death, in 1667/8, emerged as a revered mystic in his own right. Besides his Persian rendition of "The Rise of Wisdom Moon" as the *Gulzar-i-Hal* ("The Rose Garden of Absorption"), a number of other treatises and translations are attributed to him (Chand & Abidi ca. 1961). Although, unlike the Persian translation of the Upanishads that had been achieved by Dara Shikoh himself, "The Rise of Wisdom Moon" was not to reach the West in its Persian incarnation,[29] its preservation in a number of manuscripts suggests that it nevertheless enjoyed some favor in Mughal literary culture.

Given the exceptional diffusion of "The Rise of Wisdom Moon" within India, it should come as no surprise that European scholars became aware of it relatively early in the history of Sanskrit studies. The first to have referred to it appears to have been Henry Thomas Colebrooke (1765–1837), whose study "On Sanskrit and Prakrit Poetry" (1808) includes a brief notice of the play.[30] It is likely that John Taylor became aware of the work independently,[31] however, and his account of how he first took interest in it may be cited in order to explain the interest that it aroused in European Indological circles generally during the nineteenth century:

> For some months I was occupied in the perusal of books which treat [the Indian philosophical systems] in a dry didactic manner, and which, by announcing the doctrines dogmatically, instead of unfolding them in a connected series of reasoning and illustration, preserve, in many places, a degree of obscurity which it is almost impossible to remove. The experience of these difficulties naturally induced me to enquire if there was any book which explained the [Vedānta] system by a more easy method; and having heard from several Pandits that the Nâtak (Play), called the Prabôdha Chandrôdaya, or the Rise of the Moon of Intellect, was held in high estimation among them, and was written to establish the Vêdânta doctrines, I determined to read it, in hopes that the popular view it took of the subject would lead to a general

understanding of its doctrines, and of the principal technical terms. (TAYLOR 1893 [1812]: iii–iv)

Although TAYLOR's treatment of "The Rise of Wisdom Moon" as a primer of Vedánta philosophy had much to recommend it in 1812 when it was first published (it remains essential reading for serious students of early nineteenth-century Indology and still serves as an excellent example of Georgian Sanskrit translation), the play has perhaps suffered by having been consigned to this pigeon-hole in the Western study of Indian literatures. SYLVAIN LÉVI, in his *Le Théatre Indien*, clearly situated "The Rise of Wisdom Moon" in the context of dramatic and poetic art, but interest in the play has continued to be focused primarily upon its doctrinal content (LÉVI 1963 [1890]: 229–35). The more recent translation by Dr SITA K. NAMBIAR, based on her 1960 dissertation completed under the direction of the great Vedánta scholar PAUL HACKER, still exemplifies this, though it may be recommended for its overall accuracy and its close attention to the philosophical and theological aspects of the allegory.[32] Recent translations in French, Italian and especially Spanish have gone further in the way of exposing to the contemporary reader something of the text's pleasures as literature;[33] among them, the work of LOUIS RENOU's student ARMELLE PÉDRAGLIO should be noted in particular as the most thorough study of Krishna·mishra's play to date. Nevertheless, perhaps owing to the mustiness that now hangs over the allegorical form in general, "The Rise of Wisdom Moon" has not for some time seen the prominence among classical Indian works studied in the West that it enjoyed more than a century ago.

## The Play's Languages and the Present Translation

As is the norm in Sanskrit drama, "The Rise of Wisdom Moon" includes characters who speak not in fact Sanskrit, but dialects of Prakrit, the literary languages that were inspired by the colloquial tongues of North India during the last centuries BCE and for some time thereafter. The use of these languages in the theater was typically subject to strict codification: men of status spoke Sanskrit, while the women spoke the Shauraséni Prakrit that was associated with north-central India, but sung their verses in Maharáshtri, the language of the southwest that was renowned for poetic beauty. Lower class characters and some others, such as adherents of the Jain religion, however, used Mágadhi, derived from the speech of the northeastern regions around modern Bihar.[34]

"The Rise of Wisdom Moon" was clearly composed with these standards in mind, but it departs from them in a number of ways. As is the case in many other plays, the "Mágadhi" we find here is not really Mágadhi Prakrit at all, but rather Shauraséni modified by the introduction of a small number of Magadhisms. The *r*-s, for instance, are usually converted to *l*-s, in imitation of the Mágadhi accent. The effect is perhaps a bit like that made by the character of a Parisian waiter in an English sit-com, who speaks "French" by saying such things as, "Mais, Madame, zer eez no fly in zee soup!" And just as our use of stereotyped accents in this way is a device for suggesting foreign speech to audiences who may not be familiar with the actual languages the characters are supposed to employ, so the Sanskrit dramatist's "magadhized" Shauraséni doubtlessly reflects a situation in which the genuine Mágadhi Prakrit had become obscure. Poetic composition in the difficult Maharáshtri dialect, too, has been dropped by the author of "The Rise of Wisdom Moon." In fact, the entire play contains only two Prakrit verses recited by female characters (2.177 [39], 3.103 [17]) and these are in Shauraséni. In all, then, composition in Prakrit appears here to be restrained and simplified.

The play's most striking departure from the linguistic standards, however, is in its use of Sanskrit itself. For an unusual number of the female characters speak Sanskrit, and after the fourth act the use of Prakrit drops out entirely. Krishna·mishra's general principle seems to have been to use Sanskrit both where ordinary dramatic convention would require it, as well as for those characters who are most clearly aligned with the victory that brings about the birth of Wisdom Moon. Prakrit is thus coded here as a product of mundane confusion. That this is so is clearly suggested early in act four, where Love, who has so far been speaking in Prakrit, shifts to Sanskrit, with a specific stage-direction to this effect, when reciting a verse directly referring to Intuition's success (4.22–23 [5]).

I have made no effort to imitate the play's multilingualism in the translation. Although one can imagine using dialect variations of British and American English to indicate differences of social class and background, such distinctions within our culture are not gendered as they are in the Sanskrit theater. Best then to leave them to one side for the purpose of translation. In attempting here to create a new version of "The Rise of Wisdom Moon" for the contemporary anglophone reader, I have in general laid less emphasis upon philosophical purity than have previous translators and instead have sought to create a work that, like Krishna·mishra's original, is pleasant and amusing to read. How well or poorly I have succeeded in this I leave for my readers to judge. One of the major obstacles that I may note, however, stems from the allegorical form itself. Reading a work packed with characters with names like Ignorance, Discrimination, and Investigation-of-things can be a tedious exercise. How many of us recall reading Bunyan in school with much relish? I have therefore tried to mitigate somewhat the ponderousness of the form by finding, wherever possible, lighter ways to name the main characters, even at the expense of departing in some respects from literal precision. Thus, Big Ignorance is here Magnus Nescience and False Views (often misleadingly named as "Heresy") is Miss Conception. For similar reasons, I have added the occasional "lord" or "lady," even where there are no equivalents in Sanskrit: "Lady Craving" sounds like it might be a name, where "Craving" alone might not. Evidently, this approach could not be applied throughout without much contrivance, and so I have introduced it only occasionally, where it seems most useful in order to add some color to the translated text. The complete list of characters explains the usage that I have adopted in full.

I have also sought, so far as is possible, to translate whole thoughts and not just strings of words. Because we express our ideas in English quite differently than we do in Sanskrit, it will therefore be apparent to the reader who knows both languages that I have not always insisted upon the sort of philologically exact translation that is encouraged in university Sanskrit courses. To those who find my practice objectionable, I can only protest that my goal has been to produce a translation and not a crib.

Because Krishna·mishra's wit reflects much insight into human character, it is often possible to imagine transposing parts of his work into settings completely alien to it, to give it a thoroughly modern veneer. This, of course, would not be appropriate in a translation, even one that accepts as much freedom as sometimes I do here, but should anyone ever think to stage "The Rise of Wisdom Moon," or extracts from it, then I heartily recommend taking whatever liberties seem fit. Thus, act two, for instance, focusing on the dysfunctional family of Magnus Nescience, might be recast as an episode in the popular American mafia comedy, "The Sopranos," or transported to colonial India to be played out, as in the Hindi film *Lagaan*, among a suitably degenerate group of British cantonment residents. In act three, the Skullman can readily be imagined to be a member of the Hell's Angels motorcycle gang, with the racy Skullgirl as his biker babe. And, in the same context, the Jain ascetic might be replaced by a televangelist she seduces. It is perhaps more difficult to find the right template for the later acts—spiritual tranquility and enlightenment seem not to be the dominant tropes in popular culture just now—but we might go back just a few decades, to set the scene at the height of the Aquarian Age. For there, at the least, characters with names like Peace, Love, Mercy, Patience and Faith would surely find themselves right at home.

### The Sanskrit Text

"The Rise of Wisdom Moon" has never been adequately critically edited. The still useful editio princeps of Brockhaus (1845) was based primarily on six manuscripts that had become available in London early in the nineteenth century, thanks especially to the donations of Colebrooke and Taylor. (There is no evidence, so far as I am aware, to support Pédraglio's assertion that there may have existed an early xylographic edition which was used by Taylor.) The later nineteenth-century editions published in India appear mostly to be (semi-)diplomatic transcriptions—Bhaṭṭācārya's 1874 Kolkata edition is a case in point—though V. Paṇśīkar's 1898 Nirṇaya Sāgara Press edition, with its later reprintings, was based upon a selection of manuscripts. Since it was first published V. Paṇśīkar's has been widely adopted as the "standard" text, by both editors of subsequent editions and translators.

The 1936 Trivandrum text (Tr), edited by Sāmbaśiva Śāstrī, has been generally ignored but comes closest in some respects to laying the groundwork for a critical edition. It represents exclusively manuscripts from Kerala accompanied by the sixteenth-century *Nāṭakābharaṇa* commentary and thus, unlike any of the earlier editions, aspires to clarify a particular local recension. Although its readings seem, on semantic and aesthetic (that is to say, not necessarily text critical) grounds to be sometimes preferable to those found in the other available versions, this is by no means always so. Owing to its overall excellence, however, as well as to the fact that it has remained unknown to most modern readers of the play, I have adopted it as the basis for the text given here. Nevertheless, I have departed from it in certain particulars, of which those that seem to me to be the most important are mentioned in the accompanying notes. The key principles of which the reader should be aware are these:

- Where Tr and the other versions consulted differ, but the variants are closely synonymous, I have usually followed Tr with no comment.
- Where Tr and other versions differ, and the variants are not closely synonymous, I have preferred Tr unless it appears clearly inferior.
- In those cases in which Tr does not include verses or passages attested in the other versions consulted, I have nevertheless often included these in the text, but with their omission from Tr recorded here.
- Where Tr suspends normal external sandhi between words, as it does on some occasions, I have followed it where the word-break in question corresponds to a pause that may be indicated with appropriate punctuation. In other cases, I have followed the standard sandhi.
- Where a doubtful reading in Tr seems likely to be an uncorrected typographical error, this is corrected without further mention. Such apparent errors in Tr are quite rare, however.
- Small variations in the wording of stage directions are generally not commented upon here.

Unsurprisingly, Sanskrit verse passages are the most stable among the various editions consulted, followed by Sanskrit prose. Variations in these portions of the work are relatively few and seldom of great significance for our understanding of the text overall. More problematic is the Prakrit text, whose variations among the versions I have used are often considerable. It has gradually come to be recognized that the notable discrepancies found in the treatment of the dramatic Prakrits in general reflect in some measure differences among regional traditions, so that, in the present case, I have generally preferred to follow the Trivandrum text, much as I have in regard to the Sanskrit. However, some features of the Prakrit we find here seemed to warrant global emendation:

- Tr nowhere uses the semivowel *l* in Prakrit and instead has the intervocalic "flapped" *ḷ* (as found in Vedic, Pali, and Marathi, and not to be confused with the Sanskrit vowel *ḷ*, for instance in the root *kḷp*). I have replaced this with the semivowel *l* throughout.
- The aspirate nasals of Prakrit *ṇh*, *mh*, and the like, are given in Tr as *hṇ*, *hm*, etc. I have preferred the more typical forms.
- Tr on some occasions introduces *tatsama* forms—words given in Sanskrit instead of Prakrit—where they do not seem warranted. This most probably reflects the copying of the *chāyā* (the Sanskrit gloss of the Prakrit) into the Prakrit text itself. With one exception, the name of the "spell" *Mahābhairavī* in acts three and four, and the similar use of the hybrid form *Mahābhailava* at 3.116,

where I have retained the Sanskrit diphthong *ai*, I have restored the Prakrit in such cases.

On the other hand, I have not attempted to bring perfect consistency to the Prakrit text, and some irregularities, such as will be readily recognized by the intermediate or advanced student reading the Prakrit in comparison with the *chāyā*, have been allowed to stand.

## Acknowledgements

My first and foremost debt of gratitude is to John and Jennifer Clay, whose vision created and sustained the Clay Sanskrit Library. I thank, too, Richard Gombrich, who during his tenure as General Editor of the CSL commissioned me to undertake the present translation. Sheldon Pollock and Isabelle Onians, the present General Editor and Editor of this remarkable collection, have graciously shepherded my work through to its conclusion. In this, the CSL editorial team, including Chris Gibbons, Stuart Brown, Eszter Somogyi and Dániel Balogh, have done the yeoman's work to ensure the accuracy of both text and translation.

In the course of reading and thinking about "The Rise of Wisdom Moon," I have benefitted from conversations with many colleagues in the fields of Sanskrit and Indian Studies. In particular, I am grateful in this regard for the remarks of Yigal Bronner, Gary Tubb, and Alexis Sanderson. David Lorenzen did me the favor of sending me a copy of the fine Spanish version of the play that he co-translated with Mariela Álvarez, from which I have been happy to steal "Egoísmo" as my name for the character Ahan·kara.

At the University of Chicago Divinity School, two graduate research assistants have contributed to this work: Megan Doherty by tracking down and copying rare editions of the text and its commentaries, and Sonam Kachru by meticulously word-processing the Sanskrit texts of chapters three through six.

Special thanks are due to the noted contemporary philosopher Jitendranath Mohanty, Professor Emeritus at Temple University, for contributing the Foreword to this book.

## Dedication

Although in the past I have published translations of Sanskrit philosophical writings and several genres of Tibetan, this book is my first venture into Sanskrit dramatic literature. In the course of my efforts, assuredly insufficient, to find an appropriate style and tone, I was reminded time and again of the considerable impact two esteemed colleagues at the University of Chicago made upon my thinking on the whole risky business of translating South Asian literatures into contemporary English. It seems fitting, therefore, that I dedicate this work to the memory of Edward Dimock and A.K. Ramanujan.

## Notes

1 For the bibliographical details of the nineteenth-century editions and translations, in both India and Europe, see SCHUYLER (1906: 63–66).

2 TAYLOR 1893, p.v.

3 HULTZSCH (1888: 220), referring to Bílhana's *Vikramāṅkadeva-carita*, xviii.93.

4 SMITH (1908), the first and still influential attempt to provide a general synthesis of the data bearing on Chandélla history, proposed 1065 as a plausible date for Kirti·varman's restoration to the throne. BOSE (1956: 78) suggests the period 1060–64; MITRA (1977 [1958]: 100) favors "about 1070;" while DIKSHIT (1977: 107) regards the period 1059–64 as marking the reverse of Karna's fortunes in general. My remarks on Chandélla history in the paragraphs that follow are based upon the works mentioned here, together with MIŚRA (2000).

5 See in particular the discussion of this point in MITRA (1977 [1958]: 96–101).

6 Of course, the mention at the opening of the play of the intention that it be performed for Kirti·varman should not be taken to entail that it was in fact staged for the king, a nuance that has not been sufficiently appreciated. Despite this, the play's literary success and broad distribution suggest that the Chandélla rulers largely accepted its account of events.

7 AGRAVĀLA (1962), for instance, uses the latter term, and BAKHŚĪ (1993) the former.

8 KEITH (1924: 80–90) provides a still-useful summary of the Central Asian fragments of the early Buddhist plays. KRISHNAMACHARIAR (1970 [1937]: 676) implausibly seeks to link these works directly with the historical-cum-allegorical sixteenth-century play *Caitanyacandrodaya*, on which see below.

9 For an entertaining English translation, see LORENZEN (2000).

10 For a text and translation, refer to DEZSŐ (2005).

11 This question has been very widely discussed in work on classical Indian aesthetics since the first edition of RAGHAVAN (1975) was published in 1940 (and before that in a series of articles in the "Journal of Oriental Research," 1936–7). Refer in particular to MASSON & PATWARDHAN (1969, 1970). A useful summary will be found in DE (1988 [1960]: vol. 2, 274–82). The eight aesthetic sentiments that were universally recognized, before peace was

proposed as the ninth, were: the erotic (*śṛṅgāra*), heroic (*vīra*), ferocious (*raudra*), disgusting (*bībhatsa*), comic (*hāsya*), wondrous (*adbhuta*), pitiful (*karuṇa*), and terrible (*bhayānaka*).

12 As De (1988 [1960]: 275, n. 33) remarks, "This sentiment is also closely related to the sentiment of disgust; for it arises from an aversion to worldly things."

13 Bailey (1985) provides an excellent overview of the early use of these terms, though I disagree with his characterization of them as "ideologies." I believe, by contrast, that even in their early occurrences, they represent complementary facets of a common ideology.

14 *jānāmi dharmaṃ na ca me pravṛttiḥ; jānāmy adharmaṃ na ca me nivṛttiḥ.* I am grateful to Dr Csaba Dezső for identifying these lines, of which I had forgotten the source, as occurring in Vidyāraṇya, *Pañcadaśī*, 6.176, and Gopālabhaṭṭa, *Haribhaktivilāsa*, 3.94.

15 Thus, for instance, Sthira·mati, in his commentary on Vasu·bandhu's *Triṃśikā*, verse 6, writes, "If that afflicted thought engages (*pravartate*) indifferently in virtuous, afflicted, and indeterminate states, then there is no disengagement (*nivṛtti*) of it."

16 The authenticity of the attribution of this text to Shánkara has been contested. For a summary of the debate, refer to Potter (1981). Of course, the possibility that this work may be pseudepigraphical in no way diminishes the evident parallel of its outlook with that of "The Rise of Wisdom Moon."

17 Śaṅkarācārya, *Bhagavadgītābhāṣyam*, 1982 [1910]: 1–2.

18 Mitra 1977 [1958], chapter xiii.

19 For a comprehensive survey of the Khajuraho temple complex, refer to Deva (1990).

20 A fine survey of the history of the interpretation of erotic imagery at Khajuraho may be found in Guha-Thakurta (2004, ch. 8).

21 The temple is assigned to the reign of Yasho·varman during the early tenth century, so that it had been in existence for over a century during the period with which we are concerned.

22 Rabe (1996) provides a compelling analysis of the erotic elements of the iconography of Khajuraho that also turns on centrality of royal power. He concludes that the "metaphoric relationship between king and kingdom as that between lover and beloved(s) is certainly not unique to the Candella court, and perhaps the seemingly greater fixation on the theme at Khajuraho is unduly exaggerated by the comparatively greater devastation suffered by many of their contemporaries' monuments."

23 Agravāla (1962). However, even this does not cover the full extent of the legacy of "The Rise of Wisdom Moon" in Hindi and Braj. See McGregor (1986).

24 Sāyaṇamādhava (1978): *Cārvākadarśanam*, translated in Cowell & Gough (1894).

25 On the *Saṃkalpasūryodaya* in relation to Sanskrit allegory in general, see especially Bakhśī (1993). Lévi (1963 [1890]: 237–40) summarizes the *Caitanyacandrodaya.*

26 Keith (1924: 253–56) offers a useful synopsis.

27 Refer to Pollock (2003, 2006) on the process of vernacularization throughout the subcontinent during the second millennium.

28 Refer to Agravāla (1962) and McGregor (1986) above concerning Hindi and Braj renditions. Schuyler (1906: 65) mentions a number of Bengali and Hindustani (i.e. Urdu) versions. Reference to a Gujarati translation will be found in Pédraglio (1974: 114). Other examples include: *Pirapota cantirotayam: meyññana vilakkam* (in Tamil), by Kilmattur Tiruvenkatanatar (1623 –1700); *Prabodha candrodayamu* (Telugu), by Nandi Mallaya (fifteenth century); *Prabodhacandrodayam : bhasanatakam : tippanisahitam* (Malayalam), by Kumaran Asan.

29 On Dara Shikoh's efforts to find a meeting point between Hinduism and mystical Islam, see Shayegan (1979). The Persian

translation of the Upanishads became well known in Europe through the 1802–4 Latin translation of Antequil-Duperron under the title *Oupnek'hat*, wherein the German philosopher Arthur Schopenhauer found a marked resonance with his own thought.

30 Reprinted in COLEBROOKE (1873). He mentions "The Rise of Wisdom Moon" briefly on p. 94, noting that, "Among the persons of this drama are the passions and vices (pride, anger, avarice, etc.) with the virtues (as pity and patience), and other abstract notions, some of which constitute very strange personifications."

31 TAYLOR's career and contributions to Indology have not been so far studied at length. LEE (1898: 444) relates that he was "a member of the Asiatic Society of Bombay and of the Literary Society of Bombay, who was born in Edinburgh and obtained the degree of M.D. from the university in 1804. He entered the Bombay service, was appointed assistant-surgeon on 26 March 1809, and was promoted to the rank of surgeon in 1821. He was the author of several translations from the Sanscrit. He died on 6 Dec. 1821 at Shiraz in Persia, leaving a son John, born in 1804, who became a member of the Royal College of Physicians in Edinburgh, and died in that city on 14 July 1856." Besides his translation of the *Prabodhacandrodaya*, TAYLOR also published a work on Indian mathematics: "Lilawati: or a treatise on Arithmetic and Geometry by Bhascara Acharya" (Bombay: Courier Press, 1816).

32 NAMBIAR (1971). The author's 1960 dissertation at the University of Bonn was completed under her maiden name, SITA BHATT.

33 PÉDRAGLIO (1974), ÁLVAREZ & LORENZEN (1984), and PELLEGRINI (1987).

34 WOOLNER (1966) may be recommended as a handy introduction to the Prakrit languages and the various contexts of their use.

# Bibliography


## EDITIONS

Bhaṭṭācārya, Jīvānanda Vidyāsāgara (Ed.) 1874. *Prabodhacandrodayanāṭakam*. Kalikātā [Kolkata]: Kāvyaprakāśa.

Brockhaus, Hermann (Ed.) 1845. *Prabodha Chandrodaya. Krishna Misri Comoedia*. Leipzig: F.A. Brockhaus. Reprt. Hildesheim/New York: Georg Olms, 1979.

Miśra, Rāmacandra (Ed. and trans. [in Hindī]) 1968. *Prabodhacandrodayam*. Vidyābhavan Saṃskṛt Granthamālā 14. Vārāṇasī: Caukhambā.

Paṇśīkar, Vāsudevaśarma (Ed.) 1898. *Prabodhacandrodayam*. Mumbai: Nirṇaya Sāgara.

Sāmbaśiva Śāstrī, K. (Ed.) 1936. *The Prabodhacandrodaya of Kṛṣṇamiśrayati with the Commentary Nāṭakābharaṇa by Śrī-Govindāmṛtabhagavān*. Anantaśayanasaṃskṛtagranthāvaliḥ 122. Trivandrum: Government Press.

Tripāṭhī Śāstrī, Rāmanātha (Ed. and trans. [in Hindī]) 1977. *Prabodhacandrodayam*. Caukhambā Amarabhāratī Granthamālā 20. Vārāṇasī: Caukhambā.

## COMMENTARIES

*Candrikā* by Nāṇḍillagopa-Mantriśekhara. Ed. in Paṇśīkar 1898.

*Nāṭakābharaṇa* by Śrī-Govindāmṛtabhagavān. Ed. in Sāmbaśiva Śāstrī 1936.

*Prakāśa* by Rāmadāsa-Dīkṣita. Ed. in Brockhaus 1845 and Paṇśīkar 1898.

*Ṭīkā* by Bhaṭṭottarācārya-Maheśvara, also known as Maheśacandranyāyālaṅkāra. Ed. in Brockhaus 1845 and Bhaṭṭācārya 1874.

## TRANSLATIONS

Álvarez, Mariela and David Lorenzen. 1984. *Krishnamiśra, El anscenso de la luna de la illuminción*. Mexico City: El Colegio de México.

Chand, Tara and S. A. H. Abidi, eds. ca. 1961. *Gulzar-i-Hal, or Tulu'-i-qamar-i-ma'rifat: The Persian Translation of Prabodhachandrodaya*. Aligarh: Aligarh Muslim University.

Gulāb Siṅgh, kavi. 1905. *Prabodhacandrodayanāṭaka*. Ed. Paṇḍita Guruprasāda Udāsina. Bombay: Śrīvedakaṭeśvara yantrālaya.

Nambiar, Sita Krishna. 1971. *Prabodhacandrodaya of Kṛṣṇa Miśra*. Delhi: Motilal Banarsidass.

Pédraglio, Armelle. 1974. *Un drame allégorique Sanskrit: le Prabodhacandrodaya de Kṛṣṇamiśra*. Paris: Institut de Civilisation Indienne.

Pellegrini, Agata Sannino. 1987. *Kṛṣṇamiśra, La luna chiara della conoscenza*. Brescia: Paideia Editrice.

Taylor, J. 1893 [1812]. *Prabodha Chandrodaya or Rise of the Moon of Intellect: A Spiritual Drama and Âtma Bodha or the Knowledge of the Self*. Bombay.

## REFERENCES

Agravāla, Saroja. 1962. *Prabodhacandrodaya aur uskī Hindī paramparā* ["The Prabodhacandrodaya and its Hindī Tradition," in Hindī]. Prayāj: Hindī Sāhitya Sammelan.

Arnold, Daniel A. 2005. *Buddhists, Brahmins, and Belief: Epistemology in South Asian Philosophy of Religion*. New York: Columbia University Press.

Bailey, Greg. 1985. *Materials for the Study of Ancient Indian Ideologies; Pravṛtti and Nivṛtti*. Pubblicazioni di «Indologica Taurinensia» xix. Turin.

Bakhśī, Gāyatrī Devī. 1993. *Saṃskṛt ke pratīk nāṭak ke rūp meṃ śrī Vedāntadeśika kṛt Saṃkalpasūryodaya ek adhyayan* ["A Study of Śrī Vedāntadeśika's Saṃkalpasūryodaya, a Sanskrit Allegorical Drama in Form," in Hindī]. Jaipur/Udaipur: Saṃghī Prakāśan.

Banerjea, Jitendra Nath. 1956. *The Development of Hindu Iconography*. 2nd ed. Calcutta: University of Calcutta.

Bose, Nemai Sadhan. 1956. *History of the Candellas of Jejakabhukti*. Calcutta: K.L. Mukhopadhyay.

Bühler, G. 1886. *The Laws of Manu*. Sacred Books of the East xxv. Oxford: Clarendon Press.

COLEBROOKE, H.T. 1873. *Miscellaneous Essays*, vol. II. Ed. E.B. COWELL. London: Trübner.

COWELL, E.B. and A.E. GOUGH. 1894. *The Sarva-darśana-saṃgraha; or, Review of the different systems of Hindu philosophy*. London: Kegan Paul, Trench, Trübner and co.

DASGUPTA, SURENDRANATH, and SUSHIL KUMAR DE. 1962. *A History of Sanskrit Literature, Classical Period*, vol. I. 2nd ed. Calcutta: University of Calcutta.

DE, SUSHIL KUMAR. 1988 [1960]. *History of Sanskrit Poetics*. 2nd ed. Calcutta: Firma KLM Private Limited.

DEVA, KRISHNA. 1990. *Temples of Khajuraho*. 2 vols. New Delhi: Archaeological Survey of India.

DIKSHIT, R.K. 1977. *The Candellas of Jejākabhukti*. New Delhi: Abhinav Publications.

DEZSŐ, CSABA. 2005. *Much Ado About Religion by Bhatta Jayánta*. Clay Sanskrit Library. New York University Press/JJC Foundation.

DVIVEDI, MANILAL N. 1894. *The Māṇḍūkyopaniṣad with Gauḍapāda's Kārikās and the Bhāṣya of Śaṅkara*. Reprt. Freemont, Calif.: Asian Humanities Press.

ECK, DIANA. 1982. *Banāras: City of Light*. New York: Knopf.

GODE, P.K. and C.G. KARVE. 1957. *Prin. Vaman Shivaram Apte's The Practical Sanskrit-English Dictionary*. 3 vols. Poona: Prasad Prakashan.

GUHA-THAKURTA, TAPATI. 2004. *Monuments, Objects, Histories: Institutions of Art in Colonial and Postcolonial India*. New York: Columbia University Press.

HACKER, PAUL. 1965. "Relations of Early Advaitins to Vaiṣṇavism." *Wiener Zeitschrift für die Kunde Süd- und Ost-Asiens* IX (1965): 147–54.

HAMILTON, SUE. 2001. *Indian Philosophy: A Very Short Introduction*. Oxford/New York: Oxford University Press.

HULTZSCH, E. 1988. "A Chandella Inscription from Mahoba." *Epigraphica Indica* I (1888): 217–22.

JHA, GAṄGĀNĀTHA. 1978 [1911]. *The Prābhākara school of Pūrva Mīmāṃsā*. Delhi: Motilal Banarsidass.

KEITH, A. BERRIEDALE. 1924. *The Sanskrit Drama in its Origin, Development, Theory and Practice*. London: Oxford University Press.

KRISHNAMACHARIAR, M. 1970 [1937]. *History of Sanskrit Literature*. Delhi: Motilal Banarsidass.

LEE, SIDNEY, ed. 1898. *Dictionary of National Biography*, vol. LV. New York: Macmillan.

LÉVI, SYLVAIN. 1963 [1890]. *Le théatre indien*. Bibliothèque de l'École des Hautes Études, IVe section, Sciences Historiques et Philologiques 83. Paris: Collège de France.

LORENZEN, DAVID N. 2000. "A Parody of the Kāpālikas in the Mattavilāsa." In *Tantric Religions in Practice*, ed. DAVID WHITE. Princeton University Press, pp. 81–96.

MCGREGOR, R.S. 1986. "A Brajbhāṣā Adaptation of the Drama Prabodhacandrodaya, by Nanddās of the Sect of Vallabha." In PETER CONNOLLY, ed. *Perspectives in Indian Religion. Bibliotheca Indo-Buddhica* 30. New Delhi: Sri Satguru Publications, 135–44.

MASSON, J.L., and M.V. PATWARDHAN. 1969. *Śāntarasa and Abhinavagupta's Philosophy of Aesthetics*. Bhandarkar Oriental Series 9. Poona: Bhandarkar Oriental Research Institute.

———. 1970. *Aesthetic Rapture: The Rasādhyāya of the Nāṭyaśāstra*. Poona: Deccan College.

MAYEDA, SENGAKU. 1979. *A Thousand Teachings: The Upadeśasāhasrī of Śāṅkara*. Tokyo: University of Tokyo Press.

MIŚRA, KEŚAVACAṂDRA. 2000. *Caṃdel aur unkā rājatvakāl* ["The Candelas and the Age of Their Rule," in Hindī.] Vārāṇasī/New Delhi: Nāgarīpracāriṇī Sabhā.

MITRA, SISIR KUMAR. 1977 [1958]. *The Early Rulers of Khajurāho*. 2nd revised ed. Delhi: Motilal Banarsidass.

POLLOCK, SHELDON, ed. 2003. *Literary Cultures in History: Perspectives from South Asia*. Berkeley: University of California Press.

———. 2006. *The Language of the Gods in the World of Men: Sanskrit, Culture, and Power in Premodern India*. Berkeley: University of California Press.

POTTER, KARL, ed. 1981. *Advaita Vedānta up to Śaṃkara and his Pupils. Encyclopedia of Indian Philosophies* 3. Princeton: Princeton University Press.

RABE, MICHAEL. 1996. "Sexual Imagery on the 'Phantasmagorical Castles' at Khajuraho." International Journal of Tantric Studies (http://asiatica.org/ijts/) 2/2 (November 1996).

RADHAKRISHNAN, S. 1953. *The Principal Upaniṣads*. London: George Allen and Unwin.

RAGHAVAN, V. 1975. *The Number of Rasa-s*. 3rd ed. Madras: Adyar Library and Research Centre.

RENOU, LOUIS, and JEAN FILLIOZAT. 1985 [1947]. *L'Inde classique: manuel des études indiennes*. Vol. 1. Paris: École française d'Extrême-Orient.

ŚAṄKARĀCĀRYA. 1982 [1910], *Bhagavadgītābhāṣyam*, in *Śrīśaṅkaragranthāvaliḥ* 6. Chennai: Samata Books.

SĀYAṆAMĀDHAVA. 1978. *Sarvadarśanasaṅgraha*. Ed. Vasudev Abhayankar. Poona: Bhandarkar Oriental Research Institute.

SCHUYLER, MONTGOMERY, JR. 1906. *A Bibliography of Sanskrit Drama*. Columbia University Indo-Iranian Series III. New York: Columbia University Press, 1906.

SHAYEGAN, DARIUS. 1979. *Les relations de l'hindouisme et du soufisme: d'après le Majma' al-Bahrayn de Dârâ Shokûh*. Paris: Éditions de la différence.

SIVARAMAMURTI, C. 1955. *Sanskrit Literature and Art—Mirrors of Indian Culture*. Memoirs of the Archaeological Survey of India 73. New Delhi: Archaeological Survey of India.

SMITH, VINCENT A. 1908. "The History and Coinage of the Chandel (Chandella) Dynasty of Bundelkhand (Jejakabhukti) from 831 to 1203 A.D." *The Indian Antiquary* 37 (May, 1908): 114–48.

TABER, JOHN A. 2005. *A Hindu Critique of Buddhist Epistemology: Kumārila on Perception: the "Determination of Perception" Chapter of Kumārila Bhaṭṭa's Ślokavārttika*. New York: RoutledgeCurzon.

TÖRZSÖK, JUDIT. 2006. *Rama Beyond Price by Murári*. Clay Sanskrit Library. New York University Press/JJC Foundation.

WOODS, JAMES HAUGHTON. 1914. *The Yoga-system of Patañjali*. Harvard Oriental Series 17. Cambridge, Mass.: Harvard University Press.

WOOLNER, ALFRED C. 1966. *Introduction to Prakrit*. Varanasi: R.S. Panna Lal.

# Dramatis Personæ

In order of appearance

ACT 1

| | |
|---|---|
| SŪTRADHĀRA | Stage-manager |
| NAṬĪ | an actress, the Stage-manager's wife |
| KĀMA | (Lord) Lust, referred to also as Cupid and Cupidon |
| RATI | (Lady) Passion, the wife of Lord Lust |
| VIVEKA | Intuition, also called *rājā*, King. Although *viveka* is usually translated as discrimination or discernment, intuition both seems to work better as a name, and is closer in meaning to the use of *viveka* as that faculty is understood here. |
| MATI | (Lady) Intelligence, the wife of King Intuition |

ACT 2

| | |
|---|---|
| DAMBHA | Hypocrite, a grandson of Egoismo, and son of Craving and Greed, assigned by Magnus Nescience to take charge of the holy city of Varánasi |
| AHAṂKĀRA | Egoismo, son of Magnus Nescience |
| BAṬU | (a brahmin) lad in the service of Hypocrite |
| MAHĀMOHA | Magnus Nescience, the son of Thought by Eva Lucienne |
| CĀRVĀKA | Hedonist, the representative of worldly philosophy (Lokāyata) |
| ŚIṢYA | disciple (of Hedonist) |
| DAUVĀRIKA | gatekeeper in the service of Magnus Nescience |
| PURUṢA | a person from Orissa |
| KRODHA | (Sir) Anger |
| LOBHA | (Lord) Greed |
| TṚṢṆĀ | (Lady) Craving |

| | |
|---|---|
| HIṂSĀ | (Mistress) Harm |
| VIBHRAMĀVATĪ | Errancy |
| MITHYĀDṚṢṬI | Miss Conception. Note that while *mithyādṛṣṭi*, lit. "false views," is sometimes equated with heresy, this is inaccurate, as the false views found even among the adherents of orthodox schools must be included here. |

## ACT 3

| | |
|---|---|
| ŚĀNTI | Peace, daughter of Faith |
| KARUṆĀ | Mercy, companion of Peace, and sister of Love, Joy and Equanimity |
| DIGAMBARA | Naked (Jain) ascetic, also called *kṣapaṇaka,* "mendicant, ascetic" |
| ŚRADDHĀ | Faith (who appears in this act in a number of "false" forms) |
| BHIKṢU | (a Buddhist) monk |
| SOMASIDDHĀNTA | a Shaivite philosopher, also called *kāpālika,* "Skullman" |
| KĀPĀLINĪ | Skullgirl, the particular form of Faith accompanying Skullman |

## ACT 4

| | |
|---|---|
| MAITRĪ | Love, sister of Mercy, Joy and Equanimity |
| ŚRADDHĀ | Faith (now in her true form) |
| PRATĪHĀRĪ | (female) gatekeeper, also called *vedavatī*, "Veda-lady" |
| VASTUVICĀRA | Analyst, lit. "investigation of things" |
| KṢAMĀ | Patience |
| SANTOṢA | Contentment |
| PURUṢA | a person charged with relaying the King's commands to the army |
| PĀRIPĀRŚVAKA | an attendant |
| SĀRATHI | Intuition's charioteer |

## ACT 5

VIṢṆUBHAKTI Hail Vishnu, lit., "Vishnu-Devotion"

MANAḤ Thought, the son of the Supreme Lord and Illusion, and father of both Nescience and Intuition. He is sometimes referred to as Mind (*citta*).

SAṄKALPA Intention, Thought's aide-de-camp; in 6.18 [3], where he is clearly allied with Nescience, translated as Willfulness

SARASVATĪ daughter of the creator Brahma and the goddess who presides over speech and the arts.
Sometimes referred to here as *Vaiyāsikī Sarasvatī,* "Vyasa's Speech-Goddess," i.e. the muse of sage Vyasa, legendary author of the "Maha·bhárata"

VAIRĀGYA Dispassion, a long-lost son of Thought

## ACT 6

PURUṢA Inner Man, lit. the "Person," here also equivalent to the supreme self (*ātman*) and the "world soul" (*brahman*). As the latter, he is sometimes referred to in this play as the Supreme Lord (*parameśvara*). Referred to also on some occasions simply as the "Man" (*Puṃs*)

UPANIṢAT (Lady) Úpanishad, whose union with King Intuition gives birth to Scientia and Wisdom Moon

NIDIDHYĀSANA Contemplation, specifically, in Vedantic teaching, the contemplation whereby the message of the Upanishadic teaching is fully assimilated

PRABODHACANDRA Wisdom Moon, the offspring of Intuition and Úpanishad whose birth betokens the Inner Man's liberation. Sometimes also called "Wisdom's rise" (*prabodhodaya*)

## A SELECTION OF ADDITIONAL CHARACTERS AND PERSONS MENTIONED, WHO DO NOT ACTUALLY APPEAR:

| | |
|---|---|
| GOPĀLA, KĪRTIVARMAN & (LAKṢMĪ)KARṆA | Refer to the Introduction. |
| MĀYĀ | Illusion, the "wife" of the Inner Man and the creative power engendering the apparent world of experience. According to the philosophy of Adváita Vedánta, not only are *māyā*'s creations illusory, but so too *māyā* herself; for ultimately she is none other than the dynamic aspect of the supreme principle of *brahman*, and not a distinct being at all. |
| YAMA\|NIYAM'\|ĀDI | the eight limbs of the classical Yoga system, beginning with restraint (the "Restrainer") and regulation (the "Regulator"). See note on 1.39. |
| ŚAMA\|DAMA | Tranquility and Discipline, two of the qualities often heading the lists of the allies of Intuition |
| PRAVṚTTI | Eva Lucienne, the first wife of Thought and mother of Magnus Nescience and his faction |
| NIVṚTTI | Diva Lucienne, Thought's second wife; the mother of Intuition and his faction |
| VIDYĀ | Scientia, a daughter whose birth to Úpanishad is prophesied together with that of Wisdom Moon. She represents that aspect of dawning awakening, whose function it is to uproot mistaken beliefs and dispositions of all kinds, including those that in worldly terms are assumed to be positive. For that reason she is characterized by Lord Lust in |

| | |
|---|---|
| | Act One (1.58–72 [21]) as bringing destruction to the entire clan. |
| MADA | The term covers a range of meanings, including "intoxication, madness, overweening arrogance," hence here Drunkard, but on occasion also Self-Intoxication. Described in Act Two (2.107), with Pride (*māna*), as controlling the temple of Jagan·natha in Orissa |
| ANṚTA | Liar, son of Hypocrite |
| RĀGA, MĀTSARYA, PĀRUṢYA, ĀŚĀ, DAINYA, PAIŚUNYAVĀK, STEYA, ASATPARIGRAHA, DVEṢA, ASŪYĀ, MAMATĀ, SAṄGA | Desire, Envy, Abuse, Hope, Self-Pity, Slander, Theft, Fraud, Aversion, Jealousy, Selfishness, Attachment: kin and allies of Nescience |
| KALI | Craps, the fourth and last of the eons of the cosmic cycle, the degenerate age, named for the losing throw in the game of dice |
| DHARMA | Lex, the body of law and principle upholding the order of the world. He may be allied with either the faction of Nescience or that of Intuition, and is put out of work altogether once the Inner Man is securely on the path to liberation. |
| AHIṂSĀ | Harmlessness, or nonviolence. A positive moral principle particularly accentuated in Jainism. Here, a confidant of Mercy |
| ṚTAṂBHARĀ | Verity, a goddess on the side of Intuition |
| CATASRO BHAGINYAḤ | The Four Sisters: Mercy, Joy, Love and Equanimity. See 4.23 [5] and note thereof. |
| ANASŪYĀ, PAROTKARṢABHĀVANĀ, PARAGUṆĀDHIKYA, TARKA | Generosity, Altruism, Admiration-for-others, Reason: kin and allies of King Intuition |

| | |
|---|---|
| GĪTĀ | The "Bhágavad·gita," Úpanishad's daughter, who provides her mother with a refuge when the latter's message is no longer understood in the world |
| YAJÑAVIDYĀ | Sacrificial Science, the personification of the Vedic rites |
| KUMĀRILA | Kumárila, name of a famous teacher of the Mimánsaka school. The only historical philosopher who has an actual role (even if offstage) in the development of the story |
| MĪMĀṂSĀ | (Lady) Hermeneutics, the personification of the Mimánsa philosophy, translated here as "hermeneutics" in view of the special position of this school in the interpretation of the Veda. The name literally means, "examination, investigation." |

# THE RISE OF WISDOM MOON

# PRELUDE TO ACT ONE

1.1 MADHY'|ÂHN'|ârka|marīcikāsv iva payaḥ|
pūro yad a|jñānataḥ
khaṃ, vāyur, jvalano, jalaṃ, kṣitir iti
trailokyam unmīlati,
yat tattvaṃ viduṣāṃ nimīlati punaḥ
srag|bhogi|bhog'|ôpamaṃ,
sāndr'|ānandam upāsmahe tad a|malaṃ
sv'|ātm'|âvabodhaṃ mahaḥ. [1]

api ca:

antar|nāḍī|niyamita|marul|
laṅghita|brahma|randhraṃ,
sv'|ânte śānti|praṇayini samun-
mīlad ānanda|sāndram
pratyag|jyotir jayati Yaminaḥ
spaṣṭa|lālāṭa|netra|
vyāja|vyaktī|kṛtam iva jagad|
vyāpi candr'|ârdha|mauleḥ. [2]

*nāndy|ante tataḥ praviśati* SŪTRA|DHĀRAḤ.

1.5 SŪTRA|DHĀRAḤ: alam ati|vistareṇa! ādiṣṭo 'smi sakala|sāmanta|cakra|cūḍāmaṇi|marīci|mañjarī|nīrājita|caraṇa|kamalena, balavad|ari|nivaha|vakṣaḥ|sthala|kavāṭa|pāṭana|prakaṭita|Nṛsiṃha|rūpeṇa, prabalatara|narapati|kula|pralaya|mah"|ârṇava|nimagna|medinī|samuddharaṇ'|ôpanīta|mahā|Varāha|rūpeṇa, sakala|dig|vilāsinī|karṇapūrī|kṛta|kīrti|latā|pallavena, samast'|āśā|stamberama|karṇa|tāl'|āsphālana|bahala|pavana|sampāta|pravardhita|pratāp'|ânalena śrīmatā Gopālena, yathā khalv: «asya

Space, wind, fire, water, earth! 1.1
As a mirage-pond under noonday sun,
The triple world unfolds
in ignorance of what really is.
But, for those who know, it implodes once again,
like a serpent's shape in a garland.
We reverence, then, the taintless light, rich bliss,
the awareness of our true nature.*

What's more:

Revealing palpable bliss,
when one's spirit finds peace,
The divine aperture embraced by vital wind
restrained in the inner channel,
The soul's light excels, pervading the world,
as if made clear by that ruse,
The distinct middle eye,
of the crescent-moon-crowned Restrainer.*

*Following the benediction, enter the* STAGE-MANAGER.

STAGE-MANAGER: That's more than enough! I have been instructed by the honorable Gopála—the lotuses of whose feet are brightened by clustered light-beams from the crown jewels of the whole circle of his vassals; who appears as the Man-Lion* manifestly breaching the portal breasts of the host of his powerful rivals; who assumes the form of the Great Boar* come to uphold an earth sinking in the vast sea that is the dissolution of the mightiest kingly clans; the tendrils of whose fame fill lasses' ears in all quarters; and whose ardent flame swells as if struck by the great wind stirred by the rhythmic 1.5

sahaja|suhṛdo rājñaḥ Kīrtivarma|devasya digvijaya|vyāpār'|ântarita|para|brahm'|ānandair asmābhiḥ samunmīlita|vividha|viṣama|viṣaya|ras'|āsvāda|dūṣitā iv' âtivāhitā divasāḥ. idānīṃ tu kṛta|kṛtyā vayam. yataḥ—

nītāḥ kṣayaṃ kṣiti|vbhujo nṛ|pater vipakṣā;
  rakṣāvatī kṣitir abhūt prathitair amātyaiḥ.
sāmrājyam asya vihitaṃ kṣiti|pāla|mauli|
  māl'|ârpitaṃ bhuvi payonidhi|mekhalāyām. [3]

tad vayaṃ śānta|rasa|prayog'|âbhinayen' ātmānaṃ vinodayitum icchāmaḥ. tad yat pūrvam asmad|gurubhis, tatra| bhavadbhiḥ śrī|Kṛṣṇamiśraiḥ Prabodha|candr'|ôdayaṃ nāma nāṭakaṃ nirmāya bhavataḥ samarpitam āsīt, tad adya rājñaḥ śrī|Kīrtivarmaṇaḥ purastād abhinetavyaṃ bhavatā. asti c' âsya bhū|pateḥ sa|pariṣadas tad|avalokane kutūhalam» iti. tad bhavatu. gṛhaṃ gatvā, gṛhiṇīm āhūya, saṅgītakam anutiṣṭhāmi. *(parikramya, nepathy'|âbhimukham avalokya)* ārye! itas tāvat!

*(praviśya)*

NAṬĪ: ⌜esa mhi. āṇavedu ayya|utto, ko ṇioo aṇuciṭṭhīyadu tti.⌟

1.10 SŪTRA|DHĀRAḤ: ārye, viditam eva bhavatyā:

beat of the ears* of all the world-bearing elephants—as follows: "We, who have been deprived of divine bliss owing to the undertakings attending the victory of our natural ally and king, the lord Kirti·varman, have borne the passage of days that seem to have been wasted in savoring the rich flavors of all kinds of objects. So now we've done what we must. For—

Destroyed were the kings, our sovereign's foes;
The world was secured by his famed ministers.
His kingdom is worshipped by the procession of crowns
Of the kings on this sea-girdled earth.

Therefore, we'd like to be entertained by a play conveying the sentiment of peace.* Hence, as our guru, the honorable Sir Krishna·mishra has composed a drama entitled "The Rise of Wisdom Moon" and has had it delivered to you, you shall perform it today before the king, our sire Kirti·varman. The sovereign and his court are indeed eager to see it." So be it. I'll just go home, call the wife, and get the music going. *(He walks about, faces the backstage curtain and looks in.)* M'lady! here at once!

*She enters.*

ACTRESS: Here's me! Do tell, m'lord, what's on order?

STAGE-MANAGER: You must know, lady, that: 1.10

asti pratyarthi|pṛthvīpati|vipula|bal'|â-
raṇya|mūrcchat|pratāpa-
jyotir|jvāl"|âvalīḍha|tri|bhuvana|vivaro,
viśva|viśrānta|kīrtiḥ
Gopālo, bhūmi|pālān prasabham asi|latā|
mitra|mātreṇa jitvā,
sāmrājye Kīrtivarmā nara|pati|tilako
yena bhūyo 'bhyaṣeci. [4]

api ca:

ady' âpy unmada|yātudhāna|taruṇī|
cañcat|kar'|āsphālana|
vyāvalgan|nṛ|kapāla|tāla|raṇitair
nṛtyat|piśāc'|âṅganāḥ
udgāyanti yaśāṃsi yasya vitatair
nādaiḥ pracaṇḍ'|ânila|
prakṣubhyat|kari|kumbha|kūṭa|kuhara|
vyaktai raṇa|kṣoṇayaḥ. [5]

tena ca śānta|patha|prasthiten' ātmano vinod'|ârthaṃ Prabodha|candr'|ôday'|âbhidhānaṃ nāṭakam abhinetum ādiṣṭo 'smi. tad ādiśyantāṃ bharatā varṇikā|parigrahāya!

1.15 NAṬĪ *(sa|vismayam)*: ⌜accariaṃ, accariaṃ! jeṇa taha ṇia|bhua|bala | vikkam' | ekka | ṇibbhacchia | saala | rāa | maṇḍaleṇa ākaṇṇ' | ākiṭṭha | kaṭhiṇa | koaṇḍa | daṇḍa | bahala | ghaṇa | varisanta | santaa | sara | dhārā | ṇiara | jajjarijjanta | turaṃga |

His fame reaches everywhere,
  sweeping through the three worlds' vale,
  flames of ardent fire flattening
  vast, jungly ranks of hostile kings.
Gopála struck down the earth's sovereigns
  with but his blade as a friend;
  and then, in imperial dominion,
  he consecrated once again
  Kirti·varman, the best lord of men.

And also:

Today demon dames are dancing
  to the rhythmic beat
  of skull-drums a-shaking
  in the swaying hands
  of crazy vampire vixens.
Battlegrounds resound
  with fame sung in strident sounds
  from hot winds a-howling
  through fissures in the piles
  of elephant heads.

But he who is now set upon the path of peace has commanded that for his amusement I stage the play called "The Rise of Wisdom Moon." So let the actors be ordered to don their costumes!

ACTRESS *(excitedly)*: It's simply amazing, m'lord! That he 1.15
with the surpassing force of his own arms single-handedly defeated the whole array of kings and quite stirred up the ocean of Karna's army: its crashing waves were the shattered horses upon which volleys of arrows

taraṃga | mālaṃ, ṇirantara | ṇivaḍanta | tikkha | khagga | vikkhitta|sa|hattha|sattha|paliatt'|ôttuṅga|māaṅga|mahā| mahīhara | sahassaṃ, bhamanta | bhua | daṇḍa | Mandal' | âhihāda|ghuṇṇanta|saala|patti|salila|saṅghāaṃ, kaṇṇa| seṇṇa | sāaraṃ ṇimmahia, Mahumahaṇeṇa vva khīra | samuddaṃ, āsādiā samara|vijaa|lacchī. tassa saṃpadaṃ saala|muṇi|aṇa|silaṇijjo kahaṃ īriso uvasamo saṃvutto?⌋

SŪTRA|DHĀRAḤ: ārye! nisarga|saumyam eva brāhmaṃ jyotiḥ, kuto 'pi kāraṇāt prāpta|vikriyam api, punaḥ svabhāva ev' âvatiṣṭhate. yataḥ sakala|bhūpāla|kula|pralaya|kāl'| âgni|rudreṇa Cedi|patinā samunmūlitaṃ candr'|ânvaya| pārthivānāṃ pṛthivyām ādhipatyaṃ sthirī|kartum ayam asya saṃrambhaḥ. paśya tathā—

kalp'|ânta|vāta|saṃkṣobha|
  laṅghit'|â|śeṣa|bhūbhṛtaḥ
dhairya|prasāda|maryādās
  tā eva hi mah"|ôdadheḥ. [6]

api ca, bhagavan | Nārāyaṇ' | âṃśa | saṃbhūtā bhūta | hitāya tathā|vidha|pauruṣa|bhūṣaṇāḥ puruṣāḥ kṣitim avatīrya, niṣpādita | kṛtyāḥ punaḥ śāntim eva prapadyante. tathā hi Paraśurāmam ev' ākalayatu bhavatī tāvat—

rained plentifully from his mighty bow-shaft drawn all the way back to the ear, its myriad lofty mountains were the huge elephants scattered by the great missiles that he lanced, sharp shafts falling incessantly, and its waters were all the foot-soldiers whirling about when struck with the Mándara mountain* of his churning arms. He was like the slayer of Madhu* who stirred up the ocean of milk; and that's how he obtained the glory of victory in battle. So how is it now that he has turned to such peace as is extolled by all the sages?

STAGE-MANAGER: Lady! The divine light is by nature pacific, so that, if for whatever reason it suffers modification, it abides once more as it is in its essence. In this way, he undertook to shore up on this earth the rule of the princes of the lunar line, when they were uprooted by the Chedis' lord,* the terrible holocaust of the kingly clans at the end of days. Behold, then—

Though all the mountains be submerged,
after it is stirred by epoch-ending winds,
The flooding ocean, too, recedes
to enduring, sure embankments.

What is more, such persons, ornaments of manliness, who are of a piece with Lord Naráyana,* descend to earth for the sake of beings and when they have completed their tasks attain peace once again. As in the tale of Axman Rama,* whom you, Lady, should consider—

yena triḥ|sapta|kṛtvo
nṛpa|bahula|vasā|māṃsa|mastiṣka|paṅka|
prāgbhāre 'kāri bhūri|
cyuta|rudhira|sarid|vāri|pūre 'bhiṣekaḥ,
yasya strī|bāla|vṛddh'|â-
vadhi|nidhana|vidhau nirdayo viśruto 'sau
rājany'|ôcc'|âṃsa|kūṭa|
truṭana|paṭu|raṭad|ghora|dhāraḥ kuṭhāraḥ. [7]

1.20 so 'pi sva|vīryād avatārya, bhūmer
bhāraṃ samutkhāya kulaṃ nṛpāṇām,
praśānta|kopa|jvalanas tapobhiḥ
śrīmān punaḥ śāmyati Jāmadagnyaḥ. [8]

tath" âyam api kṛta|kartavyaḥ saṃprati parāṃ śāntiṃ prapannaḥ. yena ca—

Viveken' êva nirjitya
Karṇaṃ Moham iv' ōrjitam,
śrī|Kīrtivarma|nṛpater
Bodhasy' êv' ôdayaḥ kṛtaḥ. [9]

NEPATHYE: āḥ pāpa śailūṣ'|âdhama! katham, asmāsu jīvatsu, svāmino Mahāmohasya Viveka|sakāśāt parājayam udāharasi?

Twenty-one times he took his bath
in waters filled by streams of free-flowing blood,
in reservoirs of slime—
kings' copious fat, flesh and brains.
His ax was well-famed, ruthless in murder's means,
sparing not women, children or elders,
and so fearsomely sharp that it brilliantly
screamed
as it lopped heads off the necks of the rulers.

But even he, the glorious sage, Jamad·agni's son,* 1.20
grew calm,
the flames of wrath stilled by austerity,
After the earth's burden was heroically put down
by exterminating the race of nobility.

So it was that he, too, having completed his task, now attained peace as his highest end. Similarly, in the present instance—

Having defeated Karna, powerful like Nescience,
as if by Intuition,
He effected the rise of our glorious king,
Kirti·varman,
as if that of Wisdom.

BACKSTAGE: O damn stinking actor! How, while we live, dare you speak of our master Magnus Nescience's defeat before Intuition?

SŪTRA|DHĀRAḤ *(sa|saṃbhramaṃ vilokya)*: ārye, itas tāvat!

1.25 uttuṅga|pīvara|kuca|dvaya|pīḍit'|âṅgam,
āliṅgitaḥ pulakitena bhujena Ratyā,
śrīmāñ, jaganti madayan, nayan'|âbhirāmaḥ
Kāmo 'yam eti mada|ghūrṇita|netra|padmaḥ. [10]

mad|vacanāc c' âyam upajāta|krodha iva lakṣyate. tad apasaraṇam ev' âsmākam itaḥ śreyaḥ.

*niṣkrāntau.*

*prastāvanā.*

STAGE-MANAGER *(looking about distractedly)*: M'lady, get over here!

Embraced by Lady Passion, his body pressed 1.25
by her two firm, full breasts,
the hairs of her arms all a-quiver,
Here comes Lord Lust, lotus-eyes rolling
like a drunk's,
but glorious, a delight to behold,
inflicting his madness on whomsoever.

It seems my words made him angry. So it would be best if we got out of here.

*Exeunt ambo.*

*Thus the prologue.*

# INTERLUDE

*tataḥ praviśati yathā|nirdiṣṭaḥ* KĀMO RATIŚ *ca.*

1.30 KĀMAḤ *(sa|krodham, «āḥ pāp'!» êti pūrv' ôktam eva paṭhitvā)*: nanu re re, bharat'|âdhama!

prabhavati manasi Viveko
  viduṣām api śāstra|saṃbhavas tāvat,
nipatanti dṛṣṭi|viśikhā
  yāvan n' êndīvar'|âkṣīṇām. [11]

api ca:

ramyaṃ harmya|talaṃ, navāḥ su|nayanā,
  guñjad|dvirephā latāḥ,
 pronmīlan|nava|mallikā, surabhayo
  vātāḥ, sa|candrāḥ kṣapāḥ—
ity etāni jayanti hanta paritaḥ
  śastrāṇy amoghāni me,
 tad, bhoḥ, kīdṛg asau Viveka|vibhavaḥ,
  kīdṛk Prabodh'|ôdayaḥ? [12]

RATIḤ: ⌜ajja|utta! garuo kkhu mahā|rāa|Mahāmohassa paḍivakkho Viveo, tti takkemi.⌟

1.35 KĀMAḤ: priye, kutas tav' êdaṃ strī|svabhāva|sulabhaṃ Vivekād bhayam utpannam? paśya—

api yadi viśikhāḥ śarāsanaṃ vā
kusumamayaṃ, sa|sur'|âsuraṃ tath|āpi
mama jagad akhilaṃ, var'|ōru, n' ājñām
idam atilaṅghya dhṛtiṃ muhūrtam eti. [13]

*Then enter* LORD LUST, *as depicted, with* LADY PASSION.

LUST *(angrily, repeatedly saying, "O damn!")*: Listen up, vile 1.30
actor!

> Intuition, book-based, may well be solid
> in the minds of the scholars,
> Just so long as they've not yet been felled
> by the shafts
> of lily-eyed damsels' glances.

And what's more:

> Pleasing palace pavilions,
> young beauties, vines buzzing with bees,
> fresh jasmine blossoms,
> moonlit night, perfumed breeze—
> If these, my unfailing weapons,
> win me the world by conquest,
> of what use then is Wisdom's rise,
> what use Intuition's bequest?

PASSION: M'lord! It seems to me that our chief Magnus Nescience's rival Intuition is something of a heavy.

LUST: Why, dear, though it suits your feminine nature, are 1.35
you so frightened of Intuition? Look—

> Though my arrows and bow be but flower-formed,
> m'lady of thighs beauty-blessed!
> Should any one, god or titan, within this world,
> my commandments transgress,
> he'll not find a moment's rest.

tathā hi—

Ahalyāyā jāraḥ
    Surapatir abhūd, ātma|tanayāṃ
  Prajānātho 'yāsīd,
    abhajata Guror Indur abalām.
iti prāyaḥ ko vā
    na padam a|pade 'kāryata mayā?
  śramo mad|bāṇānāṃ
    ka iva bhuvan'|ônmātha|vidhiṣu? [14]

RATIḤ: ⌜ajja|utta, evvaṃ edaṃ. taha vi mahā|sahāa|saṃpaṇṇo saṅgidavvo arādī. jado ssa Jama|Ṇiama|ppamuhā amaccā mahā|balā suṇīandi.⌟

1.40 KĀMAḤ: priye, yān etān rājño Vivekasya balavato Yam'|ādīn aṣṭāv amātyān paśyasi, ta ete niyatam asmābhir abhiyukta|mātrād drāg eva vighaṭiṣyante. tathā hi—

ahiṃsā k" âiva kopasya?
  brahmacary'|ādayo mama?
lobhasyaurataḥ ke 'mī
  saty'|âstey'|âparigrahāḥ? [15]

yama|niyam'|āsana|prāṇāyāma|pratyāhāra|dhyāna|dhāraṇā|samādhayas tu nirvikāra|citt'|âika|sādhyatvād īṣat|kara|samunmūlanā eva. api ca striya ev' âmīṣāṃ kṛtyās, ten' âite 'smad|gocarā eva na vartante? yataḥ—

And in a similar vein:

Indra became Ahályа's lover,
  Brahma came to his own daughter,
  while Moon-god played with the wife of Guru.*
Just whom haven't I caused to step clear out of line?
  Who can equal my arrows' work
  in ways to churn up the world?

PASSION: That may be so, m'lord. But still let's be careful about enemies who have major backing. I've heard he's got some strong-armed lieutenants: the "Restrainer" and the "Regulator,"* for starters.

LUST: My dear, the eight lieutenants who you regard as boss Intuition's bouncers, the "Restrainer" and the others, will certainly crumble just as soon as we attack. As we say— 1.40

What is harmlessness before anger?
  chastity before me?
And before greed what are these:
  truth, detachment, non-thievery?

Self-restraint, regulation, posture, breath-control, withdrawal, meditation, concentration and absorption can be uprooted for a trifle, as they may be attained only by an undisturbed mind. Moreover, they're subject to the enthrallment of women and in this way don't they also come under my sway? So—

santu vilokana|bhāṣaṇa|
vilāsa|parihāsa|keli|parirambhāḥ!
smaraṇam api kāminīnām
alam iha manaso vikārāya. [16]

viśeṣataś c' âite Mada|Māna|Mātsarya|Dambha|Stambha|Lobh'|ādibhir asmat|svāmi|vallabhair abhiyujyamānā nara|pati|mantriṇo '|dharmam ev' āśrayiṣyante.

1.45 RATIḤ: ⌜sudaṃ mae, tumhāṇaṃ Sama|Dama|Vivea|ppahudīṇaṃ ca ekkaṃ uppatti|tthāṇaṃ ti.⌟

KĀMAḤ: āḥ, priye, kim ucyata, «ekam utpatti|sthānam» iti, nanu janaka ev' âsmākam a|bhinnaḥ. tathā hi—

saṃbhūtaḥ prathama|Maheśvarasya saṅgān
Māyāyāṃ Mana iti viśrutas tanūjaḥ.
trailokyaṃ sakalam idaṃ visṛjya bhūyas,
ten' âtho janitam idam kula|dvayaṃ naḥ. [17]

tasya ca Pravṛtti|Nivṛttī dve dharma|patnyau. tayoḥ Pravṛttyāṃ samutpannaṃ Mahāmoha|pradhānam ekaṃ kulam. Nivṛttyāṃ ca dvitīyaṃ Viveka|pradhānam iti.

RATIḤ: ⌜ajja|utta, jaï evvaṃ, tā kiṃ|ṇimittaṃ tumhāṇaṃ s'|ôarāṇaṃ vi īrisaṃ veram?⌟

1.50 KĀMAḤ: priye,

Let there be glances, chit-chat, entertainment,
 laughter, games and then petting!
For even the memory of lovesick girls
 is enough to distort one's thinking.

In particular, his royal ministers should be attacked by our boss's pals—Drunkard, Conceit, Pride, Envy, Hypocrite, Stubbornness, Greed, whoever—and then they'll be partners in crime.

PASSION: But I've heard that you and they—Tranquility, 1.45
Discipline, Intuition, and the others—have common origins.

LUST: Yes, my dear, one may speak of "common origins," but in truth we have a single father. Thus—

Thought emerged as the famed son
 of the First Great Lord's tryst with Illusion.
He in turn created all the three worlds
 and then engendered these, our paired clans.

It's said that he had two lawful wives: Eva Lucienne and Diva Lucienne.* Of them, Eva gave birth to one clan, of which Magnus Nescience was chief. Diva's was the second, led by Intuition.

PASSION: Then, m'lord, why is it that you hate each other so, even though you're blood relations?

LUST: My dear, 1.50

ek'|āmiṣa|prabhavam eva mahī|patīnām
ujjṛmbhate jagati vairam, iti prasiddham.
pṛthvī|nimittam abhavat Kuru|Pāṇḍavānāṃ
tīvras tathā hi bhuvana|kṣaya|kṛd virodhaḥ. [18]

sarvam ev' âitaj jagad asmākaṃ pitryam upārjanaṃ, tac c' âsmābhis tāta|vallabhatayā sarvam ev' ākrāntam, teṣāṃ tu viralaḥ pracāraḥ. ten' âite pāpāḥ sāṃprataṃ pitaram asmāṃś c' ônmūlayitum udyatāḥ!

RATIḤ: ⌜sāntaṃ pāvaṃ, sāntaṃ pāvaṃ! ajja|utta, kiṃ edaṃ pāvaṃ viddesa|matteṇa tehiṃ āraddhaṃ? aha vā uvāo vi ko vi ettha mantido?⌟

KĀMAḤ: priye, asty atra kiṃ cin nigūḍhaṃ bījam.

1.55 RATIḤ: ⌜ajja|utta, tā kiṃ ṇa ugghāḍīadi?⌟

KĀMAḤ: priye, bhavatī strī|svabhāvād bhīrur, iti na dāruṇa|karma pāpīyasām udāhriyate!

RATIḤ *(sa|bhayam)*: ⌜ajja|utta, kerisaṃ tam?⌟

KĀMAḤ: priye, na bhetavyaṃ, na bhetavyam. hat'|āśānāṃ mano|ratha|mātram ev' âitat. asti kil' âiṣā kiṃ|vadantī: «asmākaṃ kule kāla|rātri|kalpā Vidyā nāma rākṣasī samutpatsyata» iti.

RATIḤ *(sa|bhayam)*: ⌜haddhi! kadhaṃ uṇa amhāṇaṃ kule rakkhasi—tti vevadi me hiaam!⌟

Among kings, enmity born
from a single token yawns wide in the world
—it's common opinion.
Thus, for the sake of the earth,
Kuru and Pándava* waged
fierce, world-destroying contention.

This whole world was the endowment of our father, for which reason we, being dad's darlings, overran everything, while their territory was a patchwork. That's why these criminals are now trying to overturn us and dad!

PASSION: Let them damn well rest in peace! Tell me, m'lord, are they into their crimes owing only to hatred? Or is there a recommended remedy or not?

LUST: There is a concealed secret in all this, dear.

PASSION: Why don't you let it out, m'lord? 1.55

LUST: Owing to your feminine nature, my dear, you're fearful, so I'm not going to utter aloud the awful misdeed of those criminals!

PASSION *(frightened)*: What could it be, m'lord?

LUST: Don't be afraid, dear, don't be afraid. It's merely the last hope of those who are hopeless. There's just this saying: "Here, in our family, a demoness named Scientia, like unto black night,* will arise."

PASSION *(frightened)*: O hell! How could there be a demoness in our family? It makes my heart shudder!

1.60 KĀMAḤ: priye, na bhetavyaṃ, na bhetavyaṃ. kiṃ|vadantī|mātram etat.

RATIḤ: ⌜aha tāe rakkhasīe kiṃ kādavvam?⌟

KĀMAḤ: priye, asti kil' âiṣā Prājāpatyā sarasvatī:

Puṃsaḥ saṅga|samujjhitasya gṛhiṇī
    Māy" êti, ten' âpy asāv
  a|spṛṣṭ" âpi Manaḥ prasūya tanayaṃ,
    lokān asūta kramāt.
tasmād eva janiṣyate punar asau
    Vidy" êti kanyā, yayā
  tātas, te ca sah'|ôdarāś ca, jananī—
    sarvaṃ ca bhakṣyaṃ kulam. [19]

RATIḤ *(sa|trās'|ôtkampam)*: ⌜ajja|utta! parittāāhi, parittāāhi!⌟ *(iti bhartāram āliṅgati.)*

1.65 KĀMAḤ *(sparśa|sukham abhinīya, sva|gatam)*:

sphurad|rom'|ôdbhedas
    taralatara|tār'|ākula|dṛśo
  bhay'|ôtkamp'|ôttuṅga|
    stana|yuga|bhar'|āsaṅga|subhagaḥ
a|dhīr'|âkṣyā guñjan|
    maṇi|valaya|dor|valli|racitaḥ
  parīrambho modaṃ
    janayati ca saṃmohayati ca. [20]

*(prakāśam, dṛḍhaṃ pariṣvajya)* priye, na bhetavyaṃ, na bhetavyam. asmāsu jīvatsu kuto Vidy"|ôtpattiḥ?

LUST: Don't be afraid, dear, don't be afraid. It's just a saying. 1.60

PASSION: So what's this demoness going to do?

LUST: My dear, there is also this dictum of the Creator:

His housewife was Illusion, though she never
consummated with her Man,*
but still, untouched by him, bore Thought,
her son;
then worlds were engendered in turn.
From him the girl Scientia will too be born,
and she'll devour all the clan:
father, mother, and sibling kin.

PASSION *(trembling with terror)*: Save me, m'lord! Save me! *(So saying, she embraces her husband.)*

LUST *(acting pleased with her touch, aside)*: 1.65

Her eyes darting so the pupils seem to vibrate,
the pleasing pressure of her two firm breasts,
trembling with expectation,
is exciting right down to the pores.
Eyes unsteady, she's decked out
with a chiming jewel necklace and bangles;
her embrace both delights and deludes.

*(aloud, hugging her tightly)* Don't be afraid, dear, don't be afraid. While I yet live, where's Scientia going to come from?

RATIḤ: ⌜ajja|utta, kiṃ tāe rakkhasīe uppattī amhāṇaṃ paḍivakkhāṇaṃ sammadā?⌟

KĀMAḤ: bāḍham! sā khalu Viveken' Ôpaniṣad|devyāṃ Prabodha|candreṇa bhrātrā samaṃ janayitavyā. tatra sarva ev' âite Śama|Dam'|ādayaḥ pratipann'|ôdyogāḥ.

1.70 RATIḤ: ⌜kahaṃ puṇa appaṇo viṇāsa|kāriṇīe Vijjāe uppattī tehiṃ duv|viṇīdehiṃ silāhijjaï?⌟

KĀMAḤ: priye, kula|kṣaya|pravṛttānāṃ pāpa|kāriṇāṃ kutaḥ sva|para|pratyavāya|gaṇanā? paśya—

sahaja|malina|vakra|bhāva|bhājāṃ
   bhavati bhavaḥ prabhav'|ātma|nāśa|hetuḥ.
jala|dhara|padavīm avāpya dhūmo
   jvalana|vināśam anuprayāti nāśam. [21]

NEPATHYE: āḥ pāpa! dur|ātman! katham asmān eva «pāpa|kāriṇa» ity ākṣipasi! nanu re!

guror apy avaliptasya, kāry'|â|kāryam a|jānataḥ,
utpathaṃ pratipannasya parityāgo vidhīyate. [22]

1.75 iti paurāṇikīṃ gāthāṃ purāṇa|vida udāharanti! anena c' âsmākaṃ janaken' Âhaṅkār'|ânuvartinā Jagat|patiḥ pit" âiva tāvad baddhaḥ! Moh'|ādibhiś ca sa eva bandhaḥ su|dṛḍhatāṃ nītaḥ.

PASSION: So then, m'lord, how do your rivals think that the demoness'll be born?

LUST: Well! she's supposed to be begotten, along with her brother Wisdom Moon, upon Lady Úpanishad by Intuition. The whole lot of them—Tranquility, Discipline and the others—have gone to work for that.

PASSION: So why, m'lord, are these scoundrels so eager for the birth of Scientia if she's going to destroy them too? 1.70

LUST: Just why, my dear, should a bunch of criminals who are set upon terminating the clan take into account their own and others' obliteration? Just look—

> 'Tis the nature of those inherently tainted and bent,
> to destroy themselves, their origins too.
> Smoke following the clouds quenches the blaze
> and thereby stifles itself.

BACKSTAGE: O damn! scoundrel! How dare you slander us as "criminals!" But hey!

> It is ordained that one renounce even a guru,
> who sets out on errant trails,
> Knows not what's obliged or forbidden,
> and whose arrogance prevails.

This is a traditional verse recited by those who know their tradition! Indeed, our father, taken in by Egoismo, has imprisoned his own father, the Lord of the World! Nescience and others, too, then tightened the bonds. 1.75

KĀMAḤ *(samantād avalokya)*: priye, ayam asmākaṃ kule jyāyān Matyā devyā saha Viveka ita ev' âbhivartate. ya eṣaḥ—

Rāg'|ādibhiḥ sva|rasa|cāribhir ātta|kāntir,
  nirbhartsyamāna iva māna|dhanaḥ, kṛś'|âṅgaḥ,
Matyā nitānta|kaluṣī|kṛtayā śaś'|âṅkaḥ
  kānty" êva sāndra|tuhin'|ântarito vibhāti. [23]

tan na yuktam ih' âsmākam avasthātum.

*iti niṣkrāntau.*

1.80 *viṣkambhakaḥ.*

LUST *(looking about)*: In our clan, dear, that's the elder—Intuition—who's arrived here with Lady Intelligence. He's—

> Sagacious, but weak and despised so it seems
> by Desire and others, who do what they please;
> they've stolen his luster,
> Lady Intelligence, quite the adulteress:
> with her he shines like the moon,
> its radiance dimmed by a dense frosty fog.

So it's no use for us to hang around here.

*Exeunt.*

*Thus the interlude.*

# ACT ONE

# ILLUSION'S GAME

*tataḥ praviśati rājā* VIVEKO MATIŚ *ca.*

RĀJĀ *(vicintya)*: priye, śrutaṃ tvay” âsya dur|vinītasya Kāma|baṭor mada|visphūrjitaṃ vaco, yad asmān eva «pāpa|kāriṇa» ity ākṣipati?

MATIḤ: ⌜ajja|utta, kiṃ appaṇo dosaṃ loo viāṇādi?⌟

RĀJĀ: paśya—

1.85 asāv Ahaṅkāra|parair dur|ātmabhir
nibadhya taiḥ pāpa|śaṭhair Mad’|ādibhiḥ,
ciraṃ cid|ānanda|mayo nirañjano
Jagat|patir dīna|daśām anīyata. [24]

ta ete puṇya|kāriṇo, vayaṃ tu tan|muktaye pravṛttāḥ pāpa|kāriṇa! ity aho jitaṃ dur|ātmabhiḥ!

MATIḤ: ⌜ajja|utta, jado so saha’|āṇanda|sundara|sahāvo ṇicca|ppaāsa|pphuranta|saala|ttihuaṇa|ppaāro Parames-saro suṇīadi. tā kahaṃ edehiṃ duv|viaḍḍhehiṃ baṃdhia mahāmoha|sāare ṇikkhitto?⌟

RĀJĀ: priye,

satata|dhṛtir apy,
uccaiḥ śānto ’py, avāpta|mah”|ôdayo ’py,
adhigata|nayo ’py,
antaḥ|svaccho ’py, udīrita|dhīr api
tyajati sahajaṃ
dhairyaṃ strībhiḥ pratārita|mānasaḥ

*Then enter* KING INTUITION *with* INTELLIGENCE.

KING* *(thoughtfully)*: Did you hear, my dear, the mad, bellowing voice of this scoundrel, that brat Lust, slandering us as "criminals?"

INTELLIGENCE: Since when, m'lord, do worldlings recognize their own faults?

KING: Look—

The spotless Lord of the World, by nature spirit and bliss, 1.85
has long been dragged down to a wretched state,
Bound by bad souls, Egoismo first,
together with Drunkard and all his damned mates.

So they're a bunch of saints and we, who've set about to liberate that One, are the sinners! O how we've been brought down by these crooks!

INTELLIGENCE: M'lord, the way I've heard it, the Lord Supreme* is essentially beautiful owing to innate bliss, eternally radiant, his dominion illuminating all the three worlds. So how is it that he's been bound up by these rogues and then tossed into the great sea of unknowing?

KING: My dear,

Be he always resolute, distinguished,
tranquil, most prosperous,
mannered, good-hearted,
apt to realize his intentions,
He'll still lose his inner composure when
his mind's got befuddled by women.

svam api yad ayaṃ
Māyā|saṅgāt Pumān—iti vismṛtaḥ? [25]

1.90 MATIḤ: ⌜ajja | utta, ṇaṃ andhakāra | lehāe sahassa | rassiṇo tirak | kāro jaṃ Māāe taha papphuranta | maha | ppaāsa | sāarassa devassa vi ahihavo.⌟

RĀJĀ: priye, a | vicāra | siddh" êyaṃ veśyā | vilāsin" îva Māyā a | sato 'pi bhāvān upadarśayantī Puruṣaṃ vañcayati. paśya—

sphaṭika|maṇi|vad bhāsvān devaḥ
pragāḍham an|āryayā
vikṛtim anayā nītaḥ kām apy
a|saṅgata|vikriyaḥ.
na khalu tad|upaśleṣād asya
vyapaiti rucir manāk,
prabhavati tath" âpy eṣā Puṃso
vidhātum a|dhīratām. [26]

MATIḤ: ⌜ajja | utta, kiṃ puṇa kālaṇaṃ, jeṇa taha udāra | caridaṃ duv|vaḍḍhā paāredi?⌟

RĀJĀ: na khalu prayojanaṃ kāraṇaṃ vā vilokya Māyā pravartate. svabhāvaḥ khalv asau strī|piśācīnāṃ. paśya—

1.95 saṃmohayanti, madayanti, viḍambayanti,
nirbhartsayanti, ramayanti, viṣādayanti.
etāḥ praviśya sa|dayaṃ hṛdayaṃ narāṇāṃ,
kiṃ nāma vāma|nayanā na samācaranti? [27]

asti c' âparam api kāraṇam.

For is this not said of the Man* himself,
thanks to the embrace of Illusion?

INTELLIGENCE: Certainly, m'lord, it is just as when the sun is obscured by lines of darkness, that Illusion overcomes even that god who is a vibrant vast ocean of radiance. 1.90

KING: Dear one, Illusion, frisky as a playmate, though not established by reason, conjures up visions of unreal things and so fools the Man. Look—

The god shining like crystal has been dragged down,
undone by this wretch,
without quite being deformed by her contact.
His luster declines through her embrace not a bit,
though she still makes the Man lose his wits.

INTELLIGENCE: Why is it, m'lord, that this fishwife takes one so eminent for a sucker?

KING: Illusion proceeds without any regard to purpose or reason. Her nature is just that of a she-devil. Look—

They make you dumb, make you mad, 1.95
then they ridiculize you;
They put you to shame, make you glad,
then they just depress you.
What is it these foxy-eyed beauties won't start,
once they've entered a man's gentle heart?

But there's another reason, too.

MATIḤ: ⌜ajja|utta, kiṃ ṇāma taṃ kālaṇam?⌟

RĀJĀ: evam anayā dur|ācārayā vicintitaṃ, yad «ahaṃ tāvad gata|yauvanā, varṣīyasī jātā. ayaṃ ca purāṇa|Puruṣaḥ sv-abhāvād eva viṣaya|rasa|vimukhaḥ. tataḥ sva|tanayam eva Pārameśvara|pade niveśayām'» îti. tam eva mātur abhiprāyam āsādya nitānta|tat|pratyāsannatayā tad|rūpatām iv' āpannena Manasā nava|dvārāṇi purāṇi racayitvā,

eko 'pi bahudhā teṣu vicchidy' êva niveśitaḥ.
sva|ceṣṭitam atho tasmin nidadhāti maṇāv iva. [28]

1.100 MATIḤ *(vicintya)*: ⌜jārisī mādā, putto vi tāriso jevva jādo.⌟

RĀJĀ: tato 'sāv Ahaṃkāreṇa Cittasya jyeṣṭha|putreṇa naptrā pariṣvaktaḥ. tataś c' âsāv Īśvaraḥ—

«jāto 'haṃ; janako mam' âiṣa, jananī,
kṣetraṃ, kalatraṃ, kulaṃ,
putrā, mitram, arātayo, vasu, balaṃ,
vidyā, suhṛd, bāndhavāḥ.»
citta|spandita|kalpanām anubhavan
vidvān a|vidyā|mayīṃ
nidrām etya vighūrṇito bahu|vidhān
svapnān imān paśyati. [29]

INTELLIGENCE: What's that other reason, m'lord?

KING: Here's what this bad girl thinks: "I'm no longer young, but aging. This Old Man is by nature disinclined to the delights of the senses. So I'm going to install my own son in the place of the Lord Supreme." And Thought, on discovering his mother's wish, and owing to his great proximity to Him, borrows, as it were, His likeness and so fabricates the nine-gated citadels.* Then,

> Though one, he enters them,
> many times, it seems, divided.
> Thus, within Him, as in a gemstone,
> each one's actions are projected.

INTELLIGENCE *(thoughtfully)*: Like mother, like son. 1.100

KING: And then He's embraced by His grandson, Egoismo, Mind's* eldest son. As to what then befalls the Lord—

> "Born am I, and these are my
> dad, mum, fields, body, kin, kids, enemies, friends,
> riches, talents, knowledge, dear ones and
> relations."
> The Wise One, thus subject to concepts mind-made,
> born of unknowing,
> falls into REM sleep,
> and beholds diverse things he is dreaming.

MATIḤ: ⌜ajja|utta, evvaṃ dīha|dīhatara|ṇiddā|viddāvia|ppabohe Paramessare kahaṃ Paboh|uppattī bhavissadi?⌟

RĀJĀ *sa|lajjam adho|mukhas tiṣṭhati.*

1.105 MATIḤ: ⌜kitti guruara|lajjā|bhara|ṇamida|seharo tūṇhīṃ|bhūdo 'si?⌟

RĀJĀ: priye, s'|ērṣyaṃ prāyeṇa yoṣitāṃ bhavati hṛdayam. tena s'|âparādham iv' ātmānaṃ śaṅke.

MATIḤ: ⌜aṇṇāo tāo itthiāo, jāo sa|rasa|ppaüttassa vā dhamma|paha|vāvāra|ppavuttassa vā bhattuṇo hiaa|tthidaṃ vihaṇandi.⌟

RĀJĀ: priye—

māninyāś cira|viprayoga|janit'|â-
  sūy'|ākulāyā bhavec
chānty|āder anukūlanād Upaniṣad|
  devyā mayā saṃgamaḥ,
tūṣṇīṃ ced viṣayān apāsya bhavatī
  tiṣṭhen muhūrtaṃ, tato
jāgrat|svapna|suṣupti|dhāma|virahāt
  prāptaḥ Prabodh'|ôdayaḥ. [30]

1.110 MATIḤ: ⌜ajja|utta, jadi evaṃ kula|ppahuṇo diḍha|gaṃthi|ṇiṭṭhāvia bandha|mokkho bhodi, tado tāe ṇicc'|âṇubaddho jevva ajja|utto bhodu! suṭṭhu me piam.⌟

INTELLIGENCE: And so, m'lord, while the Lord Supreme remains far from awakening from His prolonged sleep, how will Wisdom's birth take place?

KING *stands with his face down-turned in embarrassment.*

INTELLIGENCE: Why is it that you stand silent, your crown bent with the heavy burden of shame? 1.105

KING: Women's hearts, my dear, are generally given to jealousy. I therefore suspect that I will seem culpable.

INTELLIGENCE: Such are other women, who oppose the heartfelt intent of a husband who pursues his own fulfillment or is engaged in his rightful business.

KING: My dear—

If I may know union with Lady Úpanishad,
in concert with Peace and the rest,
though she's proud and put out by jealousy
born of our long separateness,
And if you, Lady, would stay silent just a minute,
letting objects go,
Then Wisdom's rise will be obtained
in relinquishing wakefulness, dream, and sleep,
and even transic repose.*

INTELLIGENCE: M'lord, if it's a question of liberating the head of the clan, who's all tied up in knots, from his bonds, then by all means, m'lord should be always tied down with her! It's just fine with me. 1.110

RĀJĀ: yady evaṃ prasann" âsi, siddhās tarhy asmākaṃ mano|rathāḥ. tathā hi—

baddhv" âiko bahudhā vibhajya jagatām
ādiḥ prabhuḥ śāśvataḥ
kṣiptvā yaiḥ Puruṣaḥ pureṣu paramo
mṛtyoḥ padaṃ prāpitaḥ,
teṣāṃ Brahma|bhidāṃ vidhāya vidhivat
prāṇ'|ântikaṃ Vidyayā
prāyaś|cittam idaṃ mayā punar asau
Brahm'|âikatāṃ nīyate. [31]

tad bhavatu. prastuta|vidhānāya Śam'|ādīn udyojayāmaḥ.

*niṣkrāntau.*

1.115 *iti śrī|Kṛṣṇamiśra|yati|racite Prabodhacandrodaye Māyā|vilasitaṃ nāma prathamo 'ṅkaḥ.*

KING: If this pleases you, my dear, then our wishes are as good as accomplished. Just so—

> The eternal, first lord of the world, though one,
> was bound and broken into many:
> the supreme Man was thus thrown into bodies,
> and made mortal by Brahman's breakers*.
> When Scientia, as ordained, has them breath
> their last,
> then, to purge the sin,
> I shall restore this one
> to Brahman's oneness again.

So be it, then. Let's set Tranquility and the others to work as planned.

*Exeunt ambo.*

*Thus concludes the First Act, 'Illusion's Game,'* in "The Rise of Wisdom Moon," composed by the eminent Krishna·mishra·yati.* 1.115

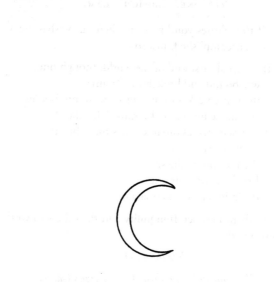

# INTERLUDE INTRODUCING ACT TWO

2.1 *tataḥ praviśati* DAMBHAḤ.

DAMBHAḤ: ādiṣṭo 'smi mahā|rāja|Mahāmohena yathā: «vatsa Dambha, pratijñātaṃ s'|âmātyena Vivekena Prabodh'|ôdayāya, preṣitāś ca teṣu teṣu tīrtheṣu Śama|Dam'|ādayaḥ. sa c' âyam asmākam upasthitaḥ kula|kṣayo bhavadbhir avahitaiḥ pratikartavyaḥ. tatra pṛthivyāṃ paramaṃ mukti|kṣetraṃ Vārāṇasī nāma nagarī. tad bhavāṃs tatra gatvā caturṇām apy āśramāṇāṃ niḥśreyasa|vighnāya prayatatāṃ» iti. tad idānīṃ vaśī|kṛta|bhūyiṣṭhā mayā Vārāṇasī, saṃpāditaś ca svāmino yathā|nirdiṣṭa ādeśaḥ. tathā hi mad|adhiṣṭhitair idānīm—

veśyā|veśmasu sīdhu|gandhi|lalanā|
vaktr'|āsav'|āmoditair
nītvā nirbhara|Manmath'|ôtsava|rasair
unnidra|candrāḥ kṣapāḥ,
«sarva|jñā» iti, «dīkṣitā» iti, «cirāt
prāpt'|âgni|hotrā» iti,
«brahma|jñā» iti, «tāpasā» iti divā
dhūrtair jagad vañcyate. [1]

*(vilokya)* ko 'py ayaṃ pāntho Bhāgīrathīm uttīrya sāmpratam ita ev' âbhivartate? yathā c' âyaṃ—

2.5 jvalann iv' âbhimānena,
grasann iva jagat|trayīm,
bhartsayann iva vāg|jālaiḥ,
prajñay" ôpahasann iva. [2]

*Enter* HYPOCRITE. 2.1

HYPOCRITE: I received the order of our chief Magnus Nescience as follows: "My dear Hypocrite, Intuition with his henchmen has promised Wisdom's rise, and has therefore dispatched Tranquility, Discipline and the others to the various shrines.* As he is thus set upon the destruction of our family, you must oppose him with vigilance. The supreme field for liberation on earth is the city called Varánasi. Hence, it is there that you must go to apply yourself to obstructing the highest good in each of the four stations of life."* So now Varánasi is mostly my territory and I've fulfilled the boss's order as he commanded. And, thanks to my minions—

Led into loose ladies' lairs
  on moonlit nights,
  lapping liquor from wine-perfumed lovers' lips,
  and really juiced at Cupid's love-feast,
These rogues by day deceive the whole world:
  "I'm omniscient," "...an initiate,"
  "...long-skilled in fiery oblation,"
  "...a god-knower," or "... an adept austere."

*(looking about)* And now who is this pilgrim who arrives here having just crossed the Ganges? It appears that he's—

Blazing, it seems, with arrogance, 2.5
  gobbling, it seems, the three worlds,
Hurling abuse, it seems, with a webwork of words,
  and laughing, it seems, at his own jokes.*

tathā tarkayāmi nūnam ayaṃ dakṣiṇa|Rāḍhā|pradeśād āgataḥ. tad asmād āryasy' âhaṃkārasya vṛttāntam avagacchāmi. *(iti parikrāmati.)*

*tataḥ praviśaty* AHAṄKĀRO *yathā|nirdiṣṭaḥ.*

AHAṄKĀRAḤ: aho! mūrkha|bahulaṃ jagat! tathā hi—

n' âiv' âśrāvi Guror mataṃ, na viditaṃ
Kaumārilaṃ darśanaṃ,
tattva|jñānam aho na Śālika|girāṃ,
Vācaspateḥ kā kathā?
sūktaṃ nāpi Mahodadher adhigataṃ,
Māhāvratī n' ēkṣitā
sūkṣmā vastu|vicāraṇā. nṛ|paśubhiḥ
sva|sthaiḥ kathaṃ sthīyate? [3]

2.10 *(vilokya)* ete tāvad arth'|âvadhāraṇa|vidhurāḥ; svādhyāy'|âdhyayana|mātra|niratā veda|viplāvakā eva. *(punar anyato gatvā)* ete ca bhikṣā|mātraṃ gṛhīta|yati|vratā, muṇḍita|muṇḍāḥ paṇḍitam|manyā Vedānta|śāstraṃ vyākulayanti. *(vihasya)*

pratyakṣ'|ādi|pramā|siddha|
viruddh'|ârth'|âbhidhāyinaḥ
Vedāntā yadi śāstrāṇi,
Bauddhaiḥ kim aparādhyate? [4]

So I suppose that he must be someone who comes from down south, from the area around Radha.* So I'll get the news of don Egoismo from him. *(He walks around.)*

*Enter* EGOISMO *as described.*

EGOISMO: Yes, indeed! the world's full of fools. Just so—

> Don't know much about Guru's thought,
> haven't learned what Kumárila taught,
> no real knowledge of Shálika's speech,
> what's then left of Vachas·pati?
> They've not mastered the Great Sea's gnomes,
> nor beheld the Great Vow's tomes,*
> subtle in analysis of reality.
> How is it, then, that these man-beasts,
> manage even to stand on their feet?

*(looking about)* These guys are nowhere when it comes to grasping the meaning; they're just blasphemers of the Veda, attached solely to repeating their rote lessons. *(He moves elsewhere.)* They've taken their mendicant-vows only to get alms, and with their shaven pates and scholars' conceits they make a real hash of the Vedánta system. *(laughing)* 2.10

> Given their contradictions in sense
> with proofs of perceptual evidence,
> If Vedantic texts could count as science,
> what fault is there in the Buddhists' compliance?*

tad etad vāṅ|mātra|śravaṇam api gurutara|durit'|ôdayāya! *(punar anyato gatvā)* ete ca Śaiva|Pāśupat'|ādayo dur|abhyast'|Âkṣapāda|matāḥ paśavaḥ pāṣaṇḍāḥ! amīṣāṃ saṃbhāṣaṇād api narā narakaṃ yānti. tad ete darśana|pathād dūrataḥ pariharaṇīyāḥ. *(punar anyato gatvā)* ete ca—

Gaṅgā|tīra|taraṅga|śītala|śilā|
vinyasta|bhāsvad|bṛsī|
saṃviṣṭāḥ, kuśa|muṣṭi|maṇḍita|mahā|
daṇḍāḥ, karaṇḍ'|ôjjvalāḥ,
paryāya|grathit'|âkṣa|sūtra|valaya|
pratyeka|bīja|graha|
vyagr'|âgr'|âṅgulayo haranti dhaninām
vittāny, aho dāmbhikāḥ! [5]

*(anyato gatvā, vilokya)* ete tri|daṇḍa|vyapadeśa|jīvino dvait'|âdvaita|mārga|paribhraṣṭā eva! aye! kasy' âitad dvār'|ôpānta|nikhāt'|âtiprāṃśu|vaṃśa|kāṇḍa|tāṇḍavita|dhauta|sita|sūkṣm'|âmbara|sahasram, itas tato vinyasta|kṛṣṇ'|âjina|dṛṣad|upala|samic|caṣāl'|ôlūkhala|musalam, an|avarata|hut'|ājya|gandhī|dhūma|śyāmalita|gagana|maṇḍalam amara|sarito n' âtidūre vibhāty āśrama|maṇḍalam? nūnam idaṃ kasy' âpi gṛha|medhino gṛhaṃ bhaviṣyati.

And their clinging to mere verbiage, too, leads to grave error! *(Again he moves elsewhere.)* And these, the Páshupatas and other Shaivites, who have to put up with the study of Aksha·pada's system,* are beasts, heretics! Just speaking with them leads men to hell. So they should be excluded from the path of philosophy altogether. *(Again he moves elsewhere.)* Moreover—

Poised on gleaming grass mats
spread on stones cooled
by waves on the Ganges' shores,
Their great staffs adorned
with tufts of sacred straws,
their mendicant-baskets seem to glow,
While their fingers tremble over each bead
of their chaplets
for counting their prayers—
Con-men they are!
picking the pockets
of those with the wherewithal.

*(He moves elsewhere, looking around.)* These guys who make their living with this gimmick of a trident have broken with both the dualist and nondualist paths!* Hey, hey! And whose is this ashram-center that gleams not far from the divine river? Near the gate they've set up tall bamboo staffs, on which thousands of clean white and fine cloths are fluttering. All over the place there are hides of black antelope, mill-stones, kindling wood,

bhavatu, yuktam asmākam atipavitram etad dvi|tri|divasa|nivāsa|sthānam. *(praveśaṃ nāṭayati, vilokya ca)* aye!

2.15 mṛd|bindu|lāñchita|lalāṭa|bhuj'|ôdar'|ôraḥ|
kaṇṭh'|oṣṭha|pṛṣṭha|cibuk'|ōru|kapola|jānuḥ,
cūḍ''|âgra|karṇa|kaṭi|pāṇi|virājamāna|
darbh'|âṅkuraḥ sphurati mūrta iv' âiṣa dambhaḥ. [6]

bhavat', ûpasarpāmy enam. *(upasṛtya)* kalyāṇam bhavatu bhavatām!

DAMBHO *huṃkāreṇa nivārayati.*

*praviśati* BAṬUḤ.

BAṬUḤ *(sa|saṃbhramam)*: brahman, dūrata eva sthīyatām! yataḥ pādau prakṣālya etad āśrama|padaṃ praveṣṭavyam!

2.20 AHAṄKĀRAḤ *(sa|krodham)*: āḥ pāpa! Turuṣka|deśaṃ prāptāḥ smaḥ, yatra śrotriyān atithīn āsana|pādy'|ādibhir api gṛhiṇo n' ôpatiṣṭhanti!

DAMBHAḤ *hasta|saṃjñayā samāśvāsayati.*

BAṬUḤ: evam ārādhya|pādā ājñāpayanti, dūra|deśād āgatasy' āryasya kula|śīl'|ādikaṃ na samyag asmābhir viditam.

rings for the sacrificial post, mortars and pestles, and fragrant smoke from offerings of ghee continuously blackens the whole sky. It must be the home of some householder-priest. Well, then, it should pass as a sufficiently hallowed residence for us to spend two or three days. *(He acts out an entrance and looks about.)* Hey, there!

Forehead, arms, belly, chest, throat and lips, 2.15
back, chin, cheeks, thighs and knees,
all marked with earthen spots;
Crest, ears, hands and ass
brightened up with fresh *kusha*-grass:
O, how he glows! the hypocrite in bodily presence.

Well, then, I'll approach him. *(He approaches.)* Good fortune to you, sir!

HYPOCRITE *repulses him with a "humph!"**

*A brahmin* LAD *enters.*

LAD *(agitatedly)*: Stand your distance, brahmin! Only after washing your feet can you come into this ashram!

EGOISMO *(angrily)*: O damn! I've landed in Turkestan,* where the householders don't even treat learned guests to cushions, a footwash and all! 2.20

HYPOCRITE *reassures him with a wave of the hand.*

LAD: My respected master makes it known that we were not rightly aware of the familial customs and such of the gentleman who has come from afar.

AHAṄKĀRAḤ: āḥ! katham asmākam api kula|śīl'|ādikam idānīṃ parīkṣitavyam? śrūyatām!

> Gauḍaṃ rāṣṭram an|uttamaṃ;
> nirupamā tatr' âpi Rāḍhā|purī.
> Bhūri|śreṣṭhika|nāma dhāma paramaṃ;
> tatr' ôttamo naḥ pitā.
> tat|putrāś ca mahā|kulā na viditāḥ
> kasy' âtra teṣām api,
> prajñā|śīla|viveka|dhairya|vinay'|ā-
> cārair ahaṃ c' ôttamaḥ. [7]

2.25 DAMBHO BAṬUṂ *paśyati.*

BAṬUḤ *(tāmra|ghaṭīṃ gṛhītvā)*: brahman! pāda|śaucaṃ vidhīyatām!

AHAṄKĀRAḤ: bhavatu. ko 'tra virodhaḥ? evaṃ kriyate. *(tathā kṛtv" ôpasarpati.)*

DAMBHO *dantān sampīḍya* BAṬUṂ *paśyati.*

BAṬUḤ: dūre tāvat sthīyatām! vāt'|āhatāḥ prasveda|kaṇikāḥ prasaranti!

2.30 AHAṄKĀRAḤ: aho! a|pūrvaṃ idaṃ brāhmaṇyam!

BAṬUḤ: brahman, evam etat! tathā hi—

> a|spṛṣṭa|caraṇā hy asya cūḍā|maṇi|marīcibhiḥ
> nīrājayanti bhūpālāḥ pāda|pīṭh'|ânta|bhūtalam. [8]

EGOISMO: Ah-hah! Why is it just now that our family, customs and what have you have come under scrutiny? Listen up!

> Gauda* is the greatest land,
> and, there, best of all is Radha city,
> Where, in the household called "Biggest Best,"
> my father was the big cheese.
> No one here has ever seen the likes
> of the great clan of his sons,
> Among whom, in learning, manners, insight,
> courage, comportment, and conduct,
> it is I who am number one.

HYPOCRITE *eyes the* LAD. 2.25

LAD *(grasping a copper vessel)*: Brahmin! by all means, bathe your feet!

EGOISMO: So be it. What harm is there? Let it be done. *(Thus having done, he approaches.)*

HYPOCRITE *eyes the* LAD *while clenching his teeth.*

LAD: Stay over there! Your drops of sweat are being dispersed by the wind!

EGOISMO: Hey-ho! This Brahmanical purity is unprecedented! 2.30

LAD: So it is, brahmin! Just so—

> The rulers of the earth illuminate
> the ground beneath his foot stool,
> With their crown-jewels' radiant glows,
> but not daring to touch his toes.

AHAṄKĀRAḤ *(sva|gatam)*: aye! dambha|grāhyo 'yaṃ deśaḥ! *(prakāśam)* bhavatu. asminn āsane upaviśāmi! *(tathā kartum icchati.)*

BAṬUḤ: m" âivam! n' ārādhya|pādānām anyair āsanam ākramyate!

2.35 AHAṄKĀRAḤ: āḥ pāpa! asmābhir api dakṣiṇa|Rāḍhā|pradeśa|prasiddha|viśuddhibhir n' ākramaṇīyam idam āsanam! śṛṇu, re mūrkha—

n' âsmākaṃ jananī tath" ôjjvala|kulā,
sac|chrotriyāṇāṃ punar
vyūḍhā kā cana kanyakā khalu mayā,
ten' âsmi tāt'|âdhikaḥ.
asmat|syālaka|bhāgineya|dayitā
mithy"|âbhiśastā, yatas
tat|saṃparka|vaśān mayā sva|gṛhiṇī
preyasy api projjhitā. [9]

DAMBHAḤ: brahman, yady apy evaṃ, tath" âpy a|vidit'|âsmad|vṛttānto bhavān. tathā hi—

sadanam upagato 'haṃ pūrvam Ambhoja|yoneḥ,
sapadi munibhir uccair āsaneṣ' ûjjhiteṣu,
sa|śapatham anunīya Brahmaṇā gomay'|âmbhaḥ|
parimṛjita|nij'|ōrāv āśu saṃveśito 'smi. [10]

EGOISMO *(aside)*: Uh-oh! This place is in hypocrisy's clenches! *(aloud)* So be it. I'll plonk myself down on this seat! *(He makes to do just that.)*

LAD: No, no! Others may not transgress the seat of my worshipful master!

EGOISMO: O damn! Even those of us who are pure according to the famous standards of the region of Radha down south can't transgress this seat! Listen up, dumb-bell— 2.35

Though my mum was not of exalted clan,
I married a girl
from a true priestly line
and in that way excelled my dad.
But the wife of my brother-in-law's sister's son
was wrongfully accused,
and, through guilt by association,
my own wife, though dear, I recused.

HYPOCRITE: That may be so, brahmin, but you, sir, know nothing of our own story. Here it is—

On my ascending to the realm of the Lotus-born god,
where the highest sages at once arose from their thrones,
I was embraced straightaway in Brahma's lap,
clean with cowstuff and water, and thus given repose.*

AHAṄKĀRAḤ *(sva|gatam)*: aho! dāmbhikasya brāḥmaṇasy' âtyuktiḥ! *(vicintya)* atha vā ... Dambhasy' âiva! bhavatv evaṃ tāvat! *(prakāśam)* āḥ, kim evaṃ garvāyase? *(sa|krodham)*

2.40 are! ka iva Vāsavaḥ?
kathaya, ko nu Padmodbhavo?
vada, prabhava|bhūmayo
jagati kā ṛṣīṇām api?
avehi tapaso balaṃ
mama Purandarāṇāṃ śataṃ,
śataṃ ca Parameṣṭhināṃ;
patatu vā munīnāṃ śatam. [11]

DAMBHAḤ *(vilokya s'|ānandam)*: aye! āryaḥ pitā|maho 'smākam Ahaṅkāraḥ! ārya! Dambho Lobh'|ātmajo 'haṃ, bho, abhivādaye!

AHAṄKĀRAḤ: vatsa, āyuṣmān bhava! bālaḥ khalv asi mayā Dvāpar'|ânte dṛṣṭaḥ! saṃprati cira|kāla|viprakarṣād vārdhakya|grastatayā ca na samyak pratyabhijānāmi! api tvat|kumārasy' Ânṛtasya kuśalam?

DAMBHAḤ: atha kim? so 'py atr' âiva Mahāmohasy' ājñayā vartate. na hi tena vinā mūhurtam apy ahaṃ prabhavāmi.

AHAṄKĀRAḤ: atha tava mātā|pitarau Tṛṣṇā|Lobhāv api kuśalau?

2.45 DAMBHAḤ: tāv api rājño Mahāmohasy' ājñay" âtr' âiva vartete. tayor vinā kṣaṇam api na tiṣṭhāmi. ārya|miśraiḥ punaḥ kena prayojanen' âtra prasādaḥ kṛtaḥ?

EGOISMO *(aside)*: O wow! the exaggerations of this hypocritical brahmin! *(thinking)* Or else … he's Hypocrite! That's it! *(aloud)* Ah, why so arrogant? *(angrily)*

Oh, yeah! Who's like Indra? 2.40
Tell me just who's Lotus-born?
Say, where in the world
are the birthplaces of the sages?
Know that I have the austerity and powers
of a hundred Indras, a hundred Brahmas too;
and let a hundred sages fall before me.

HYPOCRITE *(gazing joyfully)*: O my! It's our blessed grandpa, Egoismo! Good sir! it's me, Greed's son Hypocrite, and I salute you!

EGOISMO: May you live long, my boy! You were just a child when I last saw you, at the end of the Age of Snake-eyes!* Now that a long time has passed and you're quite grown-up, I hardly recognize you. Is your son Liar keeping well?

HYPOCRITE: How else? He's here, too, at Magnus Nescience's order. I couldn't get by for a minute without him.

EGOISMO: And your parents Lady Craving and Lord Greed are quite hale?

HYPOCRITE: They're here too, as boss Magnus Nescience 2.45
directed. Without the two of them, I couldn't stand for a second. But for what reason do you, honored sir, grace us here?

AHAṄKĀRAḤ: vatsa, mayā Mahāmohasya Viveka|sakāśād atyāhitaṃ śrutam. tena tad vṛttāntaṃ pratyetum āgato 'smi.

DAMBHAḤ: tarhi sv|āgatam ev' āryasya. yato mahā|rājasy' âp' Îndralokād atr' āgamanaṃ śrūyate. asti ca kiṃ|vadantī, yad devena Vārāṇasī rāja|dhānī vastuṃ nirūpit" êti.

AHAṄKĀRAḤ: kiṃ punar Vārāṇasyāṃ sarv'|ātmanā Mohasy' âvasthāna|kāraṇam iti?

DAMBHAḤ: ārya, nanu Vivek'|ôparodha eva. tathā hi—

2.50 Vidyā|Prabodhodaya|janma|bhūmir
Vārāṇasī Brahma|purī dur|atyayā.
asau kul'|ôccheda|vidhiṃ cikitsur
nirvastum atr' êcchati nityam eva. [12]

AHAṄKĀRAḤ *(sa|bhayam)*: yady evam, a|śakya|pratīkāra ev' âyam arthaḥ. yataḥ—

paramam a|viduṣāṃ padaṃ narāṇāṃ
  Puravijayī karuṇā|vidheya|cetāḥ
kathayati bhagavān ih' ânta|kāle
  bhava|bhaya|kātara|tārakaṃ prabodham. [13]

DAMBHAḤ: satyam etat, tath" âpi n' âitat Kāma|Krodh'|âbhibhūtānāṃ sambhāvyate! tathā hy udāharanti tairthikāḥ—

EGOISMO: My boy, I've heard something from Intuition himself that could be quite dangerous to Magnus Nescience. I've come to apprise him of the news.

HYPOCRITE: Then, honored sir, you are most welcome. For I've heard that our sovereign is on his way here from the world of Indra. There's a rumor about that the master has cased Varánasi as the capital where he'll live.

EGOISMO: But why is it that Nescience is getting set up all over in Varánasi?

HYPOCRITE: Well, sir, it's to put a stop to Intuition. So—

Varánasi, the birthplace of Scientia and 2.50
Wisdom's rise,
is the unassailable city of Brahma.
This one, to remedy the annihilation of his clan,*
now wishes to dwell here forever.

EGOISMO *(frightened)*: If that's the case, his purpose is a remedy that's futile. For—

The Conqueror of the City,* his thoughts bent
on compassion,
the lord in this end of time proclaims
The highest truth to foolish men,
the wisdom that frees
those frightened by worldly fears.

HYPOCRITE: That's true, but it's not possible so long as they're overcome by Lust and Anger! As the cultists* here say—

«yasya hastau ca, pādau ca,
manaś c' âiva su|saṃyatam,
vidyā, tapaś ca, kīrtiś ca,
sa tīrtha|phalam aśnute.» iti. [14]

2.55 NEPATHYE: bho bhoḥ! paurāḥ! eṣa khalu saṃprāpto devo Mahāmohaḥ! tena—

niṣyandaiś candanānāṃ
sphaṭika|maṇi|śilā|vedikāḥ saṃskriyantāṃ,
mucyantāṃ yantra|mārgāḥ,
pracaratu parito vāri|dhārā gṛheṣu!
ucchrīyantāṃ samantāt
sphurad|uru|maṇayaḥ śreṇayas toraṇānāṃ,
dhūyantāṃ saudha|mūrdhasv
amara|pati|dhanur|dhāma|citrāḥ patākāḥ. [15]

DAMBHAḤ: ārya! pratyāsanno 'yaṃ mahā|rājaḥ! tat praty-udgamanena saṃbhāvyatām āryeṇa.

AHAṄKĀRAḤ: evaṃ bhavatu.

*niṣkrāntau.*

2.60 *viṣkambhakaḥ.*

"Whose hands, feet and mind are well-restrained,
  is learned, ascetic, and famed,*
The reward of the pilgrimage does obtain."

OFFSTAGE: Hear, hear! Citizens! Lord Magnus Nescience has arrived! Therefore— 2.55

Arrange crystal gemstone altars with sandal-streams,
  turn on the fountains,
  let waters flow 'round your homes!
Raise arched gateways all about
  with strings of glowing rich jewels,
And on palace roofs hoist up flags
  resplendent with rainbow hues.

HYPOCRITE: Sir! the sovereign approaches! You should show your respects by advancing to meet him.

EGOISMO: So be it.

*Exeunt ambo.*

*Thus the interlude.* 2.60

# ACT TWO

# WHERE MAGNUS NESCIENCE IS CHIEF

*tataḥ praviśati* MAHĀMOHO *vibhavataś ca parivāraḥ.*

MAHĀMOHAḤ *(vihasya)*: aho! niraṅkuśā jaḍa|dhiyaḥ!

«ātm" âsti dehād vyatirikta|mūrtir,
bhoktā sa lok'|ântaritaḥ phalānām.»—
āś" êyam ākāśa|taroḥ prasūnāt
prathīyasaḥ svādu|phala|prasūtau. [16]

idaṃ ca sva|kalpanā|vinirmita|padārth'|âvaṣṭambhena jagad eva dur|vidagdhair vañcyate. tathā hi—

2.65 «yan n' âsty eva, tad asti vastv» iti mṛṣā
jalpadbhir ev' āstikair
vācālair bahubhis tu satya|vacaso
nindyāḥ kṛtā nāstikāḥ.
haṃ ho! paśyata! tattvato yadi punaś
chinnād ito varṣmaṇo
dṛṣṭaḥ kiṃ pariṇāma|rūṣita|citer
jīvaḥ pṛthak kair api? [17]

api ca, na kevalaṃ jagad, ātm" âiva tāvad amībhir vañcyate! tathā hi—

tulyatve vapuṣāṃ mukh'|ādy|avayavair
varṇa|kramaḥ kīdṛśo?
yoṣ" êyaṃ vasu vā parasya—tad amuṃ
bhedaṃ na vidmo vayam.
hiṃsāyām, atha vā yath"|êṣṭa|gamane
strīṇāṃ, parasva|grahe

*Then enters* MAGNUS NESCIENCE *with his retinue by order of rank.*

MAGNUS NESCIENCE *(laughing)*: Ho-ho! What hopeless dim-wits!

"There's a Self, not body but embodied,
the enjoyer of extra-worldly reward."—
So does hope spring like ripened fruit
grown on the great tree of spaced-out thought.

This is how crooks sucker the world with the prop of fancies cooked up in their own imaginations. And as a result—

Defamed are truthful nihilists* 2.65
by multitudes of fantasists,
affirmers, who lie with this prattle:
"what is not, that thing exists."
Hey ho! Look and see! If what they say is true,
then who's seen life come anew
from the body cut down,
though confected consciousness once was in it?

What's more, they deceive not just the world, but also themselves! So I say:

If there's bodily equality
in terms of face and other parts,
then what's the sense of caste hierarchy?
This woman and that wealth
belong to someone else—
it's a distinction we don't understand.
Whether in matters of harm,
taking pleasure with the ladies,

kāry'|âkārya|kathāṃ tath" âpi yad amī
nispauruṣāḥ kurvate. [18]

*(vicintya, sa|ślāgham)* sarvathā lok'|āyatam eva śāstraṃ, yatra pratyakśam eva pramāṇaṃ; pṛthivy|ap|tejo|vāyavas tattvāni; artha|kāmau puruṣ'|ârthau; bhūtāny eva cetayante. n' âsti para|lokaḥ; mṛtyur ev' âpavargaḥ. tad etad asmad|abhiprāy'|ânubandhinā Vācaspatinā praṇīya Cārvākāya samarpitam. tena ca śiṣy'|ôpaśiṣya|dvāreṇ' âsmil loke bahulī|kṛtaṃ tantram.

*tataḥ praviśati* CĀRVĀKAḤ ŚIṢYAŚ *ca.*

2.70 CĀRVĀKAḤ: vatsa, jānāsi, daṇḍa|nītir eva vidyā! atr' âiva vārt" ântar|bhavati. dhūrta|pralāpas trayī! svarg'|ôtpādakatvena viśeṣ'|âbhāvāt. paśya—

svargaḥ kartṛ|kriyā|dravya|
vināśe yadi yajvanām,
tato dāv'|âgni|dagdhānāṃ
phalaṃ syād bhūri bhūruhām. [19]

api ca—

or seizing others' goods,
This preoccupation
with what's right and what's not
is the concern of the impotent.

*(thinking, then pedantically)* In all events, materialism* is the philosophy! Where perception is the criterion; earth, water, fire and wind are what's real; profit and pleasure are our personal ends; and the elements are what form consciousness. There's no next life, for it's death that's salvation. Accordingly, Vachas·pati*, who was devoted to these our intentions, systematized them and transmitted them to Hedonist. Thanks to his disciples and their disciples in turn, it's a system that has proliferated throughout this world.

*Then enter* HEDONIST *and his* DISCIPLE.

HEDONIST: As you know, Poli Sci's* what's worthy knowing, my boy! Business belongs here as well. But the three Vedas are crooks' patter! For they make no difference when it comes to reaching heaven. Look— 2.70

If those who perform the sacrifice,
find their way to paradise
once agent, act, and object are destroyed,
Then plentiful fruit there ought to be
after the fire has burned up the trees!

Moreover—

nihatasya paśor yajñe svarga|prāptir yad' îṣyate,
sva|pitā yajamānena tatra kasmān na hanyate? [20]

api ca—

2.75 mṛtānām api jantūnāṃ
śrāddhaṃ cet tṛpti|kāraṇam,
nirvāṇasya pradīpasya
snehaḥ saṃvardhayec chikhāṃ. [21]

ŚIṢYAḤ: ⌜ācālia, jaï eso evva pulu'|attho jaṃ khajjae pijjaea, tā kitti edehiṃ titthiehiṃ saṃsāla | sokkhaṃ palihalia appā ghola|gholehiṃ palāa|sāṃtavaṇa|saṭṭha|kāl'|âsaṇa|ppahudihiṃ dukkhehiṃ khavijjadi?⌟

CĀRVĀKAḤ: dhūrta|praṇīt'|āgama|pratāritānām mūrkhāṇām āśā|modakair ev' êyaṃ tṛptir! paśya, paśya,

kv' āliṅganaṃ bhuja|nipīḍita|bāhu|mūla|
bhagn'|ônnata|stana|manoharam āyat'|âkṣyāḥ,
bhikṣ"|ôpavāsa|niyam'|ârka|marīci|dāhair
deh'|ôpaśoṣaṇa|vidhiḥ ku|dhiyāṃ kva c' âiṣaḥ? [22]

ŚIṢYAḤ: ⌜ācālia, evaṃ khu titthiā ālavanti, dukkha|missidaṃ saṃsāla|sokkhaṃ palihalaṇijjaṃ tti.⌟

If he holds that heaven is attained
by the beast that's sacrificed,
Then why does not the sacrificer
slaughter as well his own father?*

And also—

If funeral rites brought contentment 2.75
even to creatures quite dead,
The oil might well sustain the flame
of the lamp once it's quenched.

DISCIPLE: Teacher! If eating and drinking were indeed man's highest truth, then why is it that these cultists reject worldly pleasures and wear themselves out with the horrible troubles of penance, self-mortification, fasting* and what not?

HEDONIST: The dopes duped by cults contrived by crooks are satisfied with cakes from Never Never Land! Look, look,

How can fools' emaciating restrictions—
alms, fasting, rites of contrition,
and mortification under the sun—
Compare with the embrace,
arms pressed by arms entwined,
of a sloe-eyed lass,
pleasing you with firm, swollen nipples?

DISCIPLE: But, Teacher, the cultists say that you should abandon worldly pleasures that involve suffering.

2.80 CĀRVĀKAḤ *(vihasya)*: āḥ! dur|buddhi|vilasitam idaṃ nara|paśūnām!

> «tyājyaṃ sukhaṃ viṣaya|saṃgama|janma puṃsāṃ
> duḥkh'|ôpasṛṣṭam»—iti mūrkha|vicāraṇ" âiṣā.
> vrīhīn jihāsati sit'|ôttama|taṇḍul'|āḍhyān
> ko nāma bhos tuṣa|kaṇ'|ôpahitān hit'|ârthī? [23]

MAHĀMOHAḤ: aye, cireṇa khalu pramāṇavanti vacanāni karṇa|sukham upajanayanti! *(vilokya, s'|ānandam)* hanta! priya|suhṛn me Cārvākaḥ!

CĀRVĀKAḤ *(vilokya)*: eṣa mahā|rāja|Mahāmohaḥ! upasarpāmi. *(upasṛtya)* jayatu, jayatu mahā|rājaḥ! eṣa Cārvākaḥ praṇamati.

MAHĀMOHAḤ: Cārvāka, sv|āgataṃ te! ih' ôpaviśyatām.

2.85 CĀRVĀKAḤ *(upaviśya)*: deva! Kaler asāv aṣṭ'|âṅga|pātaḥ praṇāmaḥ.

MAHĀMOHAḤ: atha Kaler bhadram a|vyāhatam.

CĀRVĀKAḤ: deva|prasādena Kaler bhadram! nirvartita|kartavya|śeṣaś ca deva|pāda|mūlaṃ draṣṭum icchati. yataḥ—

> ājñām avāpya mahatīṃ
> dviṣatāṃ nikhātān
> nirvartya tāṃ, sapadi lab-
> dha|sukha|prasādaḥ,

HEDONIST *(laughing)*: Ah yes! the man-beasts play this game with the feeble-minded! 2.80

> "Pleasures from contact with objects bring pains,
> hence men should cast them off"—
> so runs the idiot's gaff.
> For what profit-seeker renounces rice
> with its white, tender grains
> just because they are covered with chaff?

MAGNUS NESCIENCE: Yes, indeed, after a long spell, these well-reasoned words give pleasure to my ears! *(looking about, then joyfully)* Hey! It's my dear friend, Hedonist!

HEDONIST *(looking about)*: It's His Majesty Magnus Nescience! I shall approach. *(approaching)* Victory, victory unto His Majesty! This Hedonist salutes you.

MAGNUS NESCIENCE: And greetings to you, Hedonist! Sit down over here.

HEDONIST *(sitting down)*: M'lord! Such is the eight-limbed salute of the Age of Craps!* 2.85

MAGNUS NESCIENCE: Craps, indeed, brings unbroken blessings.

HEDONIST: By our lord's grace, Craps grants blessings! I wish to see my lord's feet, having completed the entire assignment. For—

> Having received your great command,
> and fulfilled it through the downfall of your foes,
> all at once I am graced with joy.

uccaiḥ pramodam anumo-
dita|darśanaḥ san,
dhanyo namasyati pad'|âm-
buruhaṃ prabhūṇām. [24]

MAHĀMOHAḤ: atha tatra kiyat saṃpannam?

2.90 CĀRVĀKAḤ: deva—

vyatīta|Ved'|ârtha|pathaḥ prathīyasīṃ
yath"|êṣṭa|ceṣṭāṃ gamito mahā|janaḥ.
tad atra hetur na Kalir na c' âpy ahaṃ,
prabhu|prasādo hi tanoti pauruṣam. [25]

tatr' ôttarāḥ pathikāḥ pāścātyāś ca trayīm eva tyājitāḥ. Śama|Dam'|ādīnāṃ k" âiva kathā? anyatr' âpi prāyaśo jīvikā|mātra|phal" âiva trayī. yath" āh' ācāryaḥ—

agni|hotraṃ, trayo Vedās,
tri|daṇḍaṃ, bhasma|guṇṭhanam—
buddhi|pauruṣa|hīnānāṃ
jīvik", êti Bṛhaspatiḥ. [26]

tena Kurukṣetr'|ādiṣu tīrtheṣu tāvad devena svapne 'pi Vidyā|Prabodh'|ôdayo n' āśaṅkanīyaḥ.

2.95 MAHĀMOHAḤ: sādhu! saṃpāditam! mahat khalu tat tīrthaṃ vyarthī|kṛtam.

With happiness supreme, favored by your sight,
thus enriched,
I do homage at my lord's lotus-feet.

MAGNUS NESCIENCE: So just what's transpired there?

HEDONIST: My lord— 2.90

The great folk* from the path of Vedic meaning
have strayed,
and hence broadly indulge in all that they crave.
The reason for this is neither me nor Craps,
for my lord's favor is up to the task.

As matters stand, the northerners and westerners have already abandoned the Three Vedas.* So what's left to say about Tranquility, Discipline and their kind? Elsewhere, too, the Three Vedas just ensure a bare livelihood. As the Teacher says—

Fire oblation, triple Veda, trident staff,
smearing the body all over with ash—
These are, Brihas·pati declares,
trades for those lacking brains and panache.

Hence, in Kuru·kshetra* and the other shrines, not even in a dream need my lord fear the rise of Scientia and Wisdom.

MAGNUS NESCIENCE: Excellent! It's done! Though great be 2.95
the holyplace, it's been rendered useless.

CĀRVĀKAḤ: deva, anyac ca vijñāpyam asti.

MAHĀMOHAḤ: kiṃ tat?

CĀRVĀKAḤ: asti Viṣṇubhaktir nāma mahā|prabhāvā yoginī. sā tu Kalinā yady api virala|pracārā kṛtā, tath" âpi tad|anugṛhītān vayam ālokayitum api na prabhavāmaḥ. tad atra deven' âvadhātavyam iti.

MAHĀMOHAḤ *(sa|bhayam, ātma|gatam)*: āḥ! prasiddha|mahā|prabhāvā sā yoginī, sva|bhāvād vidveṣiṇī c' âsmākaṃ. dur|ucchedā sā. *(prakāśam)* bhadra, alam anayā śaṅkayā. Kāma|Krodh'|ādiṣu pratipakṣeṣu kutr' êyam udeṣyati? tath" âpi laghīyasy api ripau n' ân|avahitena jigīṣuṇā bhavitavyam. yataḥ—

2.100 vipāka|dāruṇo rājñāṃ
ripur alpo 'py aruṃ|tudaḥ,
udvejayati sūkṣmo 'pi
caraṇaṃ kaṇṭak'|âṅkuraḥ. [27]

*(nepathy'|âbhimukham avalokya)* ko 'tra bhoḥ?

*praviśya* DAUVĀRIKAḤ.

DAUVĀRIKAḤ: jayatu, jayatu! ājñāpayatu devaḥ!

MAHĀMOHAḤ: bho! a|sat|saṅga! ādiśyantāṃ Kāma|Krodha|Lobha|Mada|Mātsary'|ādayo yathā: «yoginī Viṣṇubhaktir bhavadbhir ev' âvahitair vihantavy"» êti.

HEDONIST: There's something else you should know, lord.

MAGNUS NESCIENCE: What's that?

HEDONIST: There's a most powerful *yógini* named Hail Vishnu. Although Craps has interrupted her scope for action, nonetheless we are unable to perceive those whom she favors. So my lord should take this into consideration.

MAGNUS NESCIENCE *(frightened, aside)*: Ah! That *yógini* is well-known to be most powerful, and by nature she hates us. She'll be hard to eliminate. *(aloud)* Well, then, let's lay aside our doubts. So long as Lust, Anger and the others are on hand to oppose her, just where will she emerge? Still, even if the opponent's a lightweight, one who wishes victory should not be inattentive. Thus—

Even the king's minor enemy, 2.100
  becomes a major pain in the ass,
Just as the foot is quite agonized
  by the thorn's subtle lance.

*(facing offstage and looking around)* Who's there, man?

*Enter the* GATEKEEPER.

GATEKEEPER: Victory, victory! Your command, my lord?

MAGNUS NESCIENCE: Boo! lout! Pass this order to Lust, Anger, Greed, Drunkard, Envy and the others: "You guys have got to kill the *yógini* Hail Vishnu, but do the job carefully."

2.105 DAUVĀRIKAḤ: yad ājñāpayati devaḥ. *(iti niṣkrāntaḥ.)*

*tataḥ praviśati patra|hastaḥ* PURUṢAḤ.

PURUṢAḤ: ⌜ahake Ukkala|desādo āado mhi. tattha sāala|tīla|saṇṇivese Pulisottama|saggidaṃ devad"|āadaṇam. tassiṃ Mada|Māṇehiṃ bhaṭṭakehiṃ mahā|lāa|saāsaṃ pesido mhi.⌟ *(vilokya)* ⌜esā Vālāṇasī. edaṃ lāa|ulam. jāva ppavisāmi.⌟ *(praviśya)* ⌜eso bhaṭṭako Cavvākeṇa satthaṃ kiṃ vi mantaanto ciṭṭhadi. bhodu, uvasappāmi ṇam.⌟ *(upasṛtya)* ⌜jedu, jedu bhaṭṭako! edaṃ pattaṃ ṇilūpañjadū bhaṭṭako.⌟ *(iti patram arpayati.)*

MAHĀMOHAḤ *(patraṃ gṛhītvā)*: kuto bhavān?

PURUṢAḤ: ⌜bhaṭṭaka! Pulisottamādo.⌟

2.110 MAHĀMOHAḤ *(sva|gatam)*: kāryam atyāhitaṃ bhaviṣyati. *(prakāśam)* Cārvāka! gaccha! kartavyeṣv avahitena bhavatā bhavitavyam.

CĀRVĀKAḤ: yad ājñāpayati devaḥ. *(iti niṣkrāntaḥ.)*

MAHĀMOHAḤ *(patraṃ vācayati.)*: «svasti! śrī|Vārāṇasyāṃ mahā|rāj'|âdhirāja|param'|ēśvara|Mahāmoha|pādān Puruṣottam'|āyatanād Mada|Mānau s'|âṣṭ'|âṅga|pātaṃ praṇamya vijñāpayataḥ. yathā bhadram a|vyāhatam! anyac ca, devī Śāntir mātrā Śraddhayā saha Vivekasya dautyam āpannā Viveka|saṃgamāya devīm Upaniṣadam ahar|niśaṃ pratibodhayati. api ca Kāma|sahacaro 'pi

GATEKEEPER: As my lord commands. *(Exit.)* 2.105

*Then enters a* PERSON *with a letter in hand.*

PERSON: I've come from Orissa. There, by the shores of the sea, is the temple of a divinity renowned as the Ultimate Person.* There, the distinguished gentlemen Drunkard and Pride have dispatched me to the sovereign's presence. *(looking around)* This is Varánasi. It's the royal household. I'll just go in. *(Enters.)* Here's the master, dictating some orders together with Hedonist. I'll just approach him. *(Approaches.)* Victory, victory, distinguished gentleman! May the distinguished gentleman examine this letter. *(He delivers the letter.)*

MAGNUS NESCIENCE *(taking the letter)*: And where are you from, sir?

PERSON: Master! I've come from the Ultimate Person.

MAGNUS NESCIENCE *(aside)*: There is an exceedingly odi- 2.110
ous deed to be done. *(aloud)* Hedonist! get going! You should be careful in your undertakings.

HEDONIST: As my lord commands. *(Exit.)*

MAGNUS NESCIENCE *(reciting the letter)*: "Benediction! Saluting, with the eight points prostrate, the feet of the great sovereign emperor and supreme lord, Magnus Nescience, in glorious Varánasi, we, Drunkard and Pride, from the temple of the Ultimate Person, bring this before your attention. May blessings be unbroken! As for the other business, Lady Peace, accompanied by her mother Faith, has become the go-between for Intuition, beseeching

Dharmo Vairāgy'|ādibhir upajapta iva lakṣyate. yataḥ Kāmād vibhidya kutaś cin nigūḍhaḥ pracarati. tad etaj jñātvā, tatra devaḥ pramāṇam» iti.

MAHĀMOHAḤ *(sa|krodham)*: āḥ! kim evam atimugdhau Śānter api bibhītaḥ? Kām'|ādiṣu pratipakṣeṣu kuto 'syāḥ saṃbhavaḥ? tathā hi—

Dhātā viśva|visṛṣṭi|mātra|nirato;
devo 'pi Gaurī|bhuja|
śleṣ'|ānanda|vighūrṇamāna|nayano
Dakṣ'|âdhvara|dhvaṃsanaḥ;
Daity'|âriḥ Kamalā|kapola|makarī|
lekh''|âṅkit'|ôraḥ|sthalaḥ
śete 'bdhāv. itareṣu jantuṣu punaḥ
kā nāma Śānteḥ kathā? [28]

2.115 (PURUṢAṂ *prati vadati)* jālma, gaccha! Kāmaṃ sa|tvaram upety' ādeśam asmākaṃ pratipādaya, yathā: «dur|āśayo Dharma, ity asmābhir avagatam. tad asmin muhūrtam api na viśvasitavyam. dṛḍhaṃ baddhvā dhārayitavya» iti.

Lady Úpanishad day and night to enter into union with Intuition. Lex,* moreover, though he is a companion of Lust, seems to have been brought over by Dispassion and the others. Hence, he is traveling somewhere in disguise, having broken with Lust. Knowing this, may our lord be authoritative with respect to it."

MAGNUS NESCIENCE *(angrily)*: Oh! how can these two jerks be frightened even by Peace? Where's she going to come from while Lust and the others stand in opposition? Just so—

The Creator was preoccupied only with producing
the world;
even the god who wrecked Daksha's sacrifice
was mad-eyed with bliss
when wrapped in the pale goddess's embrace;
And Daitya's foe, whose breast has a serpentine
mark,
where pressed by Lakshmi's cheek,
now reclines upon the sea.
So what's there left to say of Peace
among those merely ordinary?*

*(addressing the* PERSON*)* Get moving, deadbeat! Go quickly to Lust and deliver this order to him: "We know that Lex is a scoundrel. Therefore you must not trust him for even a second. He is to be bound tightly and kept in custody." 2.115

PURUṢAḤ: ˹jaṃ devo āṇavedi.˼ *(iti niṣkrāntaḥ.)*

MAHĀMOHAḤ *(sva|gatam, vicintya)*: Śānteḥ ko 'bhyupāyaḥ? atha vā alam upāy'|ântareṇa! Krodha|Lobhāv eva tāvad atra paryāptau. *(prakāśam)* kaḥ ko 'tra bhoḥ?

*praviśya* DAUVĀRIKAḤ.

DAUVĀRIKAḤ: ājñāpayatu devaḥ.

2.120 MAHĀMOHAḤ: tāvad āhūyatāṃ Krodho Lobhaś ca.

DAUVĀRIKAḤ: yad ājñāpayati devaḥ. *(iti niṣkrāntaḥ.)*

*tataḥ praviśati* KRODHO LOBHAŚ *ca.*

KRODHAḤ: śrutaṃ mayā, Śānti | Śraddhā | Viṣṇubhaktayo mahā|rājasya pratipakṣam ācarant' îti. aho! mayi jīvati katham āsām ātma|nirapekṣitaṃ ceṣṭitam? tathā hi—

andhī|karomi bhuvanaṃ, badhirī|karomi.
dhīraṃ sa|cetanam a|cetanatāṃ nayāmi.
kṛtyaṃ na paśyati, na yena hitaṃ śṛṇoti
dhīmān, adhītam api na pratisaṃdadhāti. [29]

2.125 LOBHAḤ: are! mad | upagṛhītā mano | ratha | sarit | paramparām api tāvan na tariṣyanti, kiṃ punaḥ Śānty|ādīṃś cintayiṣyanti. paśya—

santy ete mama dantino mada|jala|
pramlāna|gaṇḍa|sthalā.
vāta|vyāyata|pātinaś ca turagā—
bhūyo 'pi lapsye 'parān!

PERSON: As my lord commands. *(Exit.)*

MAGNUS NESCIENCE *(aside, thoughtfully)*: What's the method to deal with Peace? But why bother with other methods! Anger and Greed should be up to the mark here. *(aloud)* Who's there, dammit?

*Enter the* GATEKEEPER.

GATEKEEPER: Your order, my lord?

MAGNUS NESCIENCE: Just send for Anger and Greed. 2.120

GATEKEEPER: As my lord commands. *(Exit.)*

*Enter* ANGER *and* GREED.

ANGER: I've heard that Peace, Faith and Hail Vishnu are acting up in opposition to our sovereign. Hey-ho! While I live, how can they behave with such self-neglect? Indeed—

> I blind the world, I deafen it.
> The mindful wise, I make mindless.
> The learned see not what's to be done,
> nor hear advice from anyone,
> nor recall at all their learning.

GREED: Aye! Those I've grasped can't ford the stream of their 2.125
own imaginations, much less bother about Peace and her kind. Look—

> These are my tusked elephants,
> their cheeks moist with madness-juice.*
> My horses dash, overtaking the wind—
> I'll get me some more of them!

etal labdham, idaṃ labhe; punar idaṃ
labdhv" âdhikaṃ dhyāyatāṃ
cintā|jarjara|cetasāṃ bata nṛṇāṃ
kā nāma Śānteḥ kathā? [30]

KRODHAḤ: sakhe, viditas tvayā mat|prabhāvaḥ—

Tvāṣṭraṃ Vṛtram aghātayat sura|patiś,
candr'|ârdha|cūḍo 'cchinad
devo Brahma|śiro, Vasiṣṭha|tanayān
āghātayat Kauśikaḥ. [31*ab*]

api c' âhaṃ—

2.130 vidyāvanty api, kīrtimanty api, sad|ā-
cār'|āvadātāny api,
proccaiḥ pauruṣa|bhūṣaṇāny api
kulāny uddhartum īśaḥ kṣaṇāt. [31*cd*]

LOBHAḤ: Tṛṣṇe! itas tāvat!

*praviśya* TṚṢṆĀ.

TṚṢṆĀ: ⌜ajja|utta āṇavedu!⌟

LOBHAḤ: priye, śrūyatām—

2.135 kṣetra|grāma|van'|âdri|pattana|pura|
dvīpa|kṣamā|maṇḍala|
pratyāś"|āyata|sūtra|baddha|manasāṃ
labdh'|âdhikaṃ dhyāyatāṃ,
Tṛṣṇe devi, yadi prasīdasi, tanoṣy
aṅgāni tuṅgāni cet,
tad bhoḥ prāṇa|bhṛtāṃ kutaḥ śama|kathā
brahm'|âṇḍa|lakṣair api? [32]

That obtained, I acquire this;
  for those who think to get even more,
Men whose minds indeed are worry-worn,
  What's left for Peace to implore?

ANGER: You've witnessed my force, friend—

The gods' lord terminated Vritra, Tvashtri's son,
  the crescent-crested god cut off Brahma's head,
  and Káushika slaughtered Vasíshtha's sons.*

And so far as I'm concerned—

Though they be learned, though they be famed, 2.130
  though they be moral paragons,
Exalted adornments among even the manly,
  in a flash they're able to uproot families.

GREED: Lady Craving! get over here!

*Enter* CRAVING.

CRAVING: Your command, m'lord!

GREED: Listen, dear—

As for those contemplating gain, 2.135
  with minds tied up in hopes
  for fields, villages, groves,
  mountains, parks, isles, towns,
  the world all around,
If it please you, Lady Craving,
  and you fatten up their limbs,
  then where among those who live
  in a hundred thousand worlds
  will the word "tranquility" be found?*

TṚṢṆĀ: ⌜ajja|utta, saaṃ jevva dāva ahaṃ edassiṃ atthe ṇiccaṃ ahijuttā. saṃpadaṃ ajja|uttassa aṇṇāe bamh'|aṇḍa|koḍīhiṃ pi ṇa me udaraṃ pūraïssadi!⌟

KRODHAḤ: Hiṃse! itas tāvat!

*praviśya* HIṂSĀ.

HIṂSĀ: ⌜esa mhi! āṇavedu ajja|utto!⌟

2.140 KRODHAḤ: priye, saha|dharma|cāriṇyā tvayā mātṛ|pitṛ|vadho 'pi mam' ēṣat|kara eva! tathā hi—

k" êyaṃ mātā? piśācī!
ka iva hi janako? bhrātaraḥ ke 'tra? kīṭā!
vandhyo 'yaṃ bandhu|vargaḥ.
kuṭila|viṭa|suhṛc|ceṣṭitā jñātayo 'mī. [33*ab*]

*(hastau niṣpīḍya)*

ā garbhaṃ yāvad eṣāṃ
kulam idam a|khilaṃ n' âiva niḥśeṣayāmi.
sphūrjantaḥ krodha|vahner
na dadhati viratiṃ tāvad aṅge sphuliṅgāḥ. [33*cd*]

*(vilokya)* eṣa svāmī! tad upasarpāmaḥ!

2.145 SARVE *(upasṛtya)*: jayatu, jayatu, devaḥ!

MAHĀMOHAḤ: Śraddhāyās tanayā Śāntir asmad|dveṣiṇī. sā bhavadbhir avahitair nigrāhyā.

CRAVING: I, too, chief, am also always set upon this goal. Right now, if you give the order, chief, even a billion galaxies wouldn't fill up my belly!

ANGER: Lady Harm! come over here!

*Enter* HARM.

HARM: It's me! Command me, my chief!

ANGER: My dear, together with you as my help-mate, even 2.140
matricide and patricide are small work for me! Thus—

> Who is this mother? A ghoul!
> And who, it seems, the father?
> Who are these brothers? Worms!
> Sterile is this family rabble.
> Relations are but crooks and cons
> made out to be friends.

*(clapping his hands)*

> This, their whole clan,
> even down to the womb
> I'll not spare.
> The flaming tongues of anger's fire
> will not cease
> so long as sparks burn within my limbs.

*(looking about)* Here is our master! Let us approach him!

ALL *(approaching)*: Victory, victory, lord! 2.145

MAGNUS NESCIENCE: Faith's daughter Peace is our hateful enemy. You, ladies and gentlemen, must cautiously restrain her.

SARVE: yad ādiśati devaḥ. *(iti niṣkrāntāḥ.)*

MAHĀMOHAḤ: «Śraddhāyās tanayā»—ity upakṣepeṇ' ôpāy'|ântaram api hṛdayam ārūḍham. tathā hi, Śānter mātā Śraddhā, sā ca para|tantrā. tat ken' âpy upāyen' Ôpaniṣat|sakāśāt tāvac Chraddh"|âpakarṣaṇaṃ kartavyam. tato mātṛ|viyoga|duḥkhād atimṛdulatarā Śāntir uparatā bhaviṣyati, avasīdantī vā viraṃsyati. Śraddhāṃ c' ākarṣṭuṃ Mithyādṛṣṭir eva vilāsinī pragalbh", êti tasmin viṣaye s" âiva niyojyā. *(pārśvato vilokya)* Vibhramāvati! sa|tvaram āhūyatāṃ Mithyādṛṣṭi|vilāsinī!

VIBHRAMĀVATĪ: ⌜jaṃ devo āṇavedi.⌟ *(niṣkramya* MITHYĀDṚṢṬYĀ *saha praviśati.)*

2.150 MITHYĀDṚṢṬIḤ: ⌜sahi, cira|diṭṭhassa mahā|rāassa kahaṃ muhaṃ pekkhissaṃ? ṇaṃ mahā|rāo maṃ uvālambhissadi.⌟

VIBHRAMĀVATĪ: ⌜sahi, tuha daṃsaṇe appāṇaṃ pi mahā|rāo ṇa cedaïssadi, tado kahaṃ uvālambhissadi?⌟

MITHYĀDṚṢṬIḤ: ⌜kīsa maṃ alīa|sohaggaṃ saṃbhāvia viḍambesi?⌟

VIBHRAMĀVATĪ: ⌜sahi, saṃpadaṃ jevva pekkhissaṃ aliattaṇaṃ sohaggassa! aṇṇaṃ ca ghuṇṇanta|ṇidd"|āulaṃ via pia|sahīe loaṇaṃ pekkhāmi. tā kiṃ khu ppia|sahīe viṇiddadāe kālaṇam?⌟

ALL: As our lord orders. *(Exeunt.)*

MAGNUS NESCIENCE: "Faith's daughter"—the implications of this call to mind another means. So, Peace's mother is Faith, which makes her a dependent. By some means, then, Faith must be drawn away from the presence of Lady Úpanishad. In that way, softened up by the pain due to her being deprived of her mother, Peace will expire, or being depressed she'll waste away. And to lure out Faith that playgirl Miss Conception is most capable, indeed, so let her be assigned to this task. *(looking to the side)* Errancy! call that playgirl Miss Conception and make it snappy!

ERRANCY: As my lord commands. *(Exits and reenters with* MISS CONCEPTION.*)*

MISS CONCEPTION: But, my friend, how can I gaze upon 2.150
the face of the sovereign whom I've not seen for days? The monarch will no doubt scold me.

ERRANCY: My friend, once he sees you the king won't even recognize himself, so how's he going to scold you?

MISS CONCEPTION: Why? do you think me unfortunate, so that you are mocking me?

ERRANCY: Friend, now I'll see about the fickleness of your luck! Another thing that I see is that my dear friend's eyes are distracted and rolling with sleep. So why are you, dear friend, sleep-deprived?

MITHYĀDṚṢṬIḤ: ⌜eka|vallahā vi jā itthiā hoi, tāe vi ṇiddā dul|lahā ṇāma. kiṃ uṇa amhāṇaṃ saala|vallahāṇam?⌟

2.155 VIBHRAMĀVATĪ: ⌜ke uṇa pia|sahīe vallahā?⌟

MITHYĀDṚṢṬIḤ: ⌜mahā|rāo, tado uvari Kāmo, Koho, Loho a. aha va alaṃ viseseṇa! ettha ule jo jādo hiaa|ṇihidae ratti|diahāiṃ ahiramaï mae ṇa viṇā—bālo, ṭhaviro, juvāṇo a.⌟

VIBHRAMĀVATĪ: ⌜ṇaṃ Kāmassa Raī, Kohassa Hiṃsā, Lohassa Tiṇhā parama|ppia tti suṇiadi. tāsaṃ kadhaṃ pia|jaṇaṃ ṇiccaṃ ramaantī issaṃ ṇa jāṇesi?⌟

MITHYĀDṚṢṬIḤ: ⌜issa tti kiṃ bhaṇiadi? tāo vi mae viṇā muhuttaṃ vi ṇa tussanti!⌟

VIBHRAMĀVATĪ: ⌜ado jevva bhaṇāmi, tuha sarisī suhaā iha puhivīe ṇ' atthi tti, jāe sohagga|veragg'|vijaria|hiaāo sa|vattīo vi sampasādaṃ paḍicchanti. sahi, aṇṇaṃ vi bhaṇāmi. evaṃ ṇidd"|āula|hiaā visaṃṭhula|kkhalanta|calaṇa|neura|jhaṃkāra|muharāe gadīe mahā|rāaṃ saṃbhāvaaṃtī saṃkida|hiaaṃ karissadi pia|sahi, tti takkemi.⌟

2.160 MITHYĀDṚṢṬIḤ: ⌜kiṃ ettha saṃkidavvaṃ? ṇaṃ amhāṇaṃ mahā|rāa|ṇiuttāṇaṃ jevva eso a|viṇao. avi a, daṃsaṇa|matta|ppasādia|purusāṇaṃ juvaīṇaṃ kerisaṃ bhaam?⌟

MISS CONCEPTION: My friend, a woman with just one partner finds it hard to get her sleep. What about me, then, as I'm the darling of all the world?

ERRANCY: Who indeed are all my dear friend's partners? 2.155

MISS CONCEPTION: There's the sovereign, and then Lust, Anger, and Greed. But I've said enough about the particulars! Whoever gets born into this family—whether child, elder, or youth—enjoys not a day or night without me, once I've gotten into his heart.

ERRANCY: But Lord Lust's sweetheart is Lady Passion, Anger's is Mistress Harm, and Greed's is Lady Craving, or so I've heard. As you're always playing with their boyfriends, how is that you don't make them jealous?

MISS CONCEPTION: How can you even speak of jealousy, my friend? The girls are also unhappy after a minute without me!

ERRANCY: Then I say that on this earth there is none so fortunate as you, whose favor is sought even by your co-wives, whose hearts do not burn with aversion to your good luck. I'll tell you something else, my friend. With the jingle-jangle of your ankle-bracelets that shake so because your sleepy heart makes you unsteady as you walk, you're imagining that you'll make our sovereign suspicious, dear friend, or so it seems to me.

MISS CONCEPTION: What's for him to suspect? For this 2.160
impropriety is indeed in the service of our great king. Moreover, friend, what do girls have to fear before men who are satisfied with a mere glimpse?

MAHĀMOHAḤ *(vilokya)*: aye! saṃprāpt" êva priyā me Mithyādṛṣṭiḥ. y" âiṣā—

śroṇī|bhāra|bhar'|ālasā, dara|galan|
mâly'|ôpavṛtti|cchalāl
līl"|ôtkṣipta|bhuj'|ôpadarśita|kuc'|ôn-
mīlan|nakh'|âṅk'|āvaliḥ,
nīl'|êndīvara|dāma|dīrghatarayā
dṛṣṭyā dhayantī mano,
dor|āndolana|lola|kaṅkaṇa|jhaṇat|
kār'|ôttaraṃ sarpati. [34]

VIBHRAMĀVATĪ: ⌜eso mahā|rāo. uvasappadu pia|sahī.⌟

MITHYĀDṚṢṬIḤ *(upasṛtya)*: ⌜jaadu, jaadu mahā|rāo!⌟

2.165 MAHĀMOHAḤ: priye—

dalita|kuca|nakh'|âṅkam aṅka|pālīṃ
racaya mam' âṅkam upetya, pīvar'|ōru.
anuhara, hariṇ'|âkṣi, Śaṅkar'|ârdha-
sthita|Himaśaila|sutā|vilāsa|lakṣmīm. [35]

MITHYĀDṚṢṬIḤ *sa|smitaṃ tathā karoti.*

MAGNUS NESCIENCE *(looking her over)*: My, my! it seems that dear Miss Conception has arrived. She, well—

She slithers hither:
slowed by the big burden of her booty,
and revealing by a little trick
of her flowing garland's pose,
pressed by playful arms,
breasts marked with lovers' scratches;
With glances as long as strings of blue lotuses
she drinks up your mind
while jingling her bangles
with the languid movements of her wrists.

ERRANCY: This is our sovereign. Do approach, dear friend.

MISS CONCEPTION *(approaching)*: Victory, victory, O king!

MAGNUS NESCIENCE: My dear, 2.165

What full thighs!
Come and sit on my knees,
embrace me until
your swollen breasts are marked with scratches.
Give to me, doe-eyed girl,
splendid love-play
like Himálaya's daughter,*
poised upon Shiva's lap.

MISS CONCEPTION *does so with a smile.*

MAHĀMOHAḤ *(āliṅgana|sukham abhinīya)*: aho, priyāyāḥ pariṣvaṅgāt parāvṛttaṃ nava|yauvanam. tathā hi—

yaḥ prāg āsīd abhinava|vayo|
vibhram'|âvāpta|janmā,
citt'|ônmāthī, vigata|viṣay'|ô-
paplav'|ānanda|sāndraḥ,
vṛttīr antas tirayati tav' ā-
śleṣa|janmā sa ko 'pi
prauḍha|premā nava iva punar
mānmatho me vikāraḥ. [36]

2.170 MITHYĀDṚṢṬIḤ: ⌜mahā|rāa, ahaṃ vi saṃpadaṃ ṇava|jovvaṇā saṃvuttā. ṇa khu bhāv'|āṇubandho ppemā kāleṇ' âvi vihaḍaï. āṇavedu bhaṭṭā, kiṃ|ṇimittaṃ bhaṭṭiṇā sumarida mhi?⌟

MAHĀMOHAḤ: priye—

smaryate sā hi, vām'|ōru, cyutā yā hṛdayād bahiḥ;
mac|citta|bhittau bhavatī śāla|bhañj" îva rājate. [37]

MITHYĀDṚṢṬIḤ: ⌜maha|ppasādo!⌟

MAHĀMOHAḤ: yath" âiva prakāśitair aṅgaiḥ sarvatra vicarasi, tath" âiva pravartitavyam. anyac ca: dāsyāḥ putrī Śraddhā Vivekena sah' Ôpaniṣadaṃ saṃyojayituṃ kuṭṭinī|bhāvaṃ pratipannā. tataḥ—

MAGNUS NESCIENCE *(acting out the bliss of her embrace)*: Oh-ho! Your embrace, my dear, brings a return of new youth. Just so—

The birth obtained through youthful love
as it was before,
Rich bliss flowing about objects of all sorts,
churning thought,
That heavy love,
as if new again,
a cupidic alteration,
A state somehow born from your embrace,
dispels turmoil within.

MISS CONCEPTION: My king, I've also now found new youth. 2.170
For heartfelt love never diminishes with the passage of time. Tell me, lord, how is it that my master recalls me?

MAGNUS NESCIENCE: My dear—

She is recalled, pretty thighs!
who's fallen outside one's heart;
But you, lady, shine
in the recess of my mind
as does a sculpted image.*

MISS CONCEPTION: Great is your favor!

MAGNUS NESCIENCE: As you show off everywhere with your limbs in plain view, just so should you continue to do. But there is another thing: that daughter of a slave Faith has become the go-between to bring about the union of Lady Úpanishad with Intuition. Hence—

2.175 pratikūlām, a|kula|jāṃ, pāpāṃ, pāp'|ânuvartinīm keśeṣv ākṛṣya tāṃ raṇḍāṃ pāṣaṇḍeṣu niveśaya. [38]

MITHYĀDṚṢṬIḤ: ⌜eddaha|mettae visae alaṃ bhaṭṭiṇo ahiṇivesẹṇa! vaaṇa|matteṇa vva bhaṭṭiṇo dāsa vva savvo aṇṇāṃ karissadi. sā khu mae mitthā dhammo, mitthā mokkho, mitthā vea|maggo, mitthā suha|viggha|arāiṃ sattha|ppalavidāiṃ, mitthā sagga|phalaṃ ti bhaṇiantī vea|maggaṃ jevva parihalissadi, kiṃ uṇa Uvaṇisadam. avi a—⌟

⌜visa'|āṇanda|vimukke
mokkhe dosāṇa daṃsaantīe
Uvaṇisaā hi virattā
jhatti karijjaï mae Saddhā.⌟ [39]

MAHĀ|RĀJAḤ: yady evaṃ, suṣṭhu priyaṃ me saṃpāditaṃ priyayā. *(punar āliṅgya cumbati.)*

MITHYĀDṚṢṬIḤ: ⌜hanta! paāse evvaṃ paütteṇa bhattuṇā lajjemi.⌟

2.180 MAHĀMOHAḤ: tad bhavatu! sv'|āgāram eva praviśāmaḥ.

*iti niṣkrāntāḥ sarve.*

*iti śrī|Kṛṣṇamiśra|yati|viracite Prabodhacandrodaye Mahāmoha|pradhāno nāma dvitīyo 'ṅkaḥ.*

She opposes us, is outside our clan, 2.175
a sinner multiplying her sins—
That wench should be seized by the hair
and sent among outcastes to live.

MISS CONCEPTION: My master has worried enough about this trivial affair! At a mere word she will obey my master's commands as does every slave. I'll make her to repeat, "false is the law, false liberation, false the Veda's path, false the joy-killing babble in the treatises, false the fruit of heaven!"* and so to reject even the Veda's way, not to speak of Úpanishad. What's more—

Seeing that freedom's flawed
without the pleasures of the senses,
I'll fix it soon so that Faith,
becomes an Úpanishad-rejecter.

MAGNUS NESCIENCE: If it be so, then you, my dear, will have well fulfilled what is dear to me. *(Again embraces and kisses her.)*

MISS CONCEPTION: Oh gracious! I am embarrassed by such ostentation on the part of my honored master.

MAGNUS NESCIENCE: So be it, then! Let us return to our quarters. 2.180

*Exeunt omnes.*

*Thus concludes the Second Act, 'Where Magnus Nescience is Chief,'* in "The Rise of Wisdom Moon," composed by the eminent Krishna·mishra·yati.*

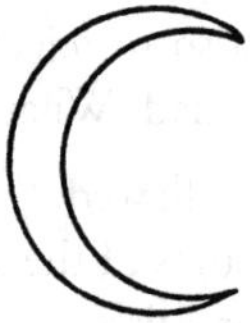

# ACT THREE

# CHARLATANS' CHARADES

3.1 *tataḥ praviśati* ŚĀNTIḤ KARUṆĀ *ca.*

ŚĀNTIḤ *(s'|âsram)*: mātar, mātaḥ! kv' âsi? dehi me prativacanam.

> mukt'|ātaṅka|kuraṅgakā vana|bhuvaḥ,
> śailāḥ skhalad|vārayaḥ,
> puṇyāny āyatanāni, santata|tapo|
> niṣṭhāś ca vaikhānasāḥ—
> yasyāḥ prītir amīṣu, s" âdya bhavatī
> caṇḍāla|veśm'|ôdaraṃ
> nītā gauḥ kapil" êva jīvati kathaṃ
> pāṣaṇḍa|hastaṃ gatā? [1]

atha v" âlaṃ jīvita|saṃbhāvanayā! yataḥ,

> 3.5 mām an|ālokya na snāti,
> na bhuṅkte, na pibaty apaḥ.
> na mayā rahitā Śraddhā
> muhūrtam api jīvati. [2]

tad vinā Śraddhayā muhūrtam api Śānter jīvitaṃ viḍambanam eva. tat, sakhi Karuṇe, mad|arthaṃ citām āracaya! yāvad a|ciram eva hut'|âśana|praveśena tasyāḥ saha|carī bhavāmi.

KARUṆĀ *(s'|âsram)*: ⌜sahi, evvaṃ visama|jjolaṇa|jjāl"|āvalī|tikkhāiṃ akkharāiṃ jappantī savvahā vilutta|jīviaṃ maṃ karesi. tā pasīda muhuttaaṃ, dhāredu jīviaṃ pia|sahī. jāva ido tado puṇṇesu assamesu muṇi|aṇa|samāulesu Bhāīrahī|tīresu su|ṇiuṇaṃ ṇirūvamha. sā kadā i vi Mahāmoha|bhīdā kahaṃ vi pacchaṇṇaṃ ṇivasaï.⌟

*Then enter* PEACE *and* MERCY. 3.1

PEACE *(tearfully)*: Mother, mother! Where are you? Give me your response.

Forest lands where antelope fearless roam,
mountains with rushing streams,
auspicious, holy places,
anchorites whose austerity ever reigns supreme—
In these does this lady find pleasure.
How, today, does she fare in infidel hands,
as if she were a tawny cow
consigned to an outcaste's shanty?

But enough of false hopes of life! For,

Without sight of me, she'll neither bathe, 3.5
nor eat, nor drink water.
Without me, indeed, Faith cannot live
for even a moment longer.

And without Faith, for just a minute, the life of Peace, too, is a joke. Therefore, Mercy, my friend, prepare the cremation pyre for me! In this way I'll soon be her companion on entering the sacrificial fire.

MERCY *(tearfully)*: My friend, your sobbing, sharp words like firebrands blazing with distress brings me altogether to despair of life. So sit down for a moment and pull yourself together, dear friend. In a while we two are going to search thoroughly among the auspicious ashrams on the banks of the Ganges, where the holy men gather together. At some point or another she must have gone into hiding from fear of Magnus Nescience.

ŚĀNTIḤ: sakhi, kiyad anviṣyate?

nīvār'|âṅkita|saikatāni saritāṃ,
kūlāni vaikhānasair
ākrāntāni, samic|caṣāla|camasa|
vyāptā gṛhā yajvanām—
pratyekaṃ ca nirūpitāḥ pratipadaṃ
catvāra ev' āśramāḥ,
Śraddhāyāḥ kva cid apy aho sakhi mayā
vārt" âpi n' ākarṇitā. [3]

3.10 KARUṆĀ: ⌜sahi, evvaṃ bhaṇāmi. jaï sattaī Saddhā, tado ṇa tāe īrisīṃ duggaïṃ saṃbhāvemi. ṇa khu tārisīo puṇṇa-maīo tārisaṃ a|saṃbhāvaṇijjaṃ vipattiṃ aṇuhondi.⌟

ŚĀNTIḤ: sakhi, kin nu pratikūle vidhātari na saṃbhāvyate? tathā hi—

śrīr devī Janak'|ātmajā daśa|mukhasy'
āsīd gṛhe rakṣaso;
nītā c' âiva rasā|talaṃ bhagavatī
pūrvaṃ Trayī dānavaiḥ;
gandharvasya Madālasāṃ ca tanayāṃ
Pātālaketuś chalād
daity'|êndro 'pajahāra—hanta! viṣamā
vāmā vidher vṛttayaḥ. [4]

tad bhavatu! pāṣaṇḍ'|ālayeṣv eva tāvad anusarāvaḥ.

PEACE: My friend, what's the use of more searching?

River banks where the sands are scattered with grains
and where the forest-sages descend,
The homes of priests
with sacred tinder, posts, and implements—
I've searched in each and every place
where the four stages* are upheld,
And no news at all have I heard, my friend,
of Faith's present whereabouts.

MERCY: Here's what I say, my friend. If it's indeed true Faith,* then I can't imagine that she'll have so much hardship. For those born of such merits as hers are not subject to this sort of unimaginable misfortune. 3.10

PEACE: When fate is adverse, friend, what can't be imagined? Just so—

The glorious goddess, Jánaka's daughter,
was brought to the home of the ten-faced ogre;
Her Excellence Three was once dragged down
to the underworld by the titans;
And the fairies' daughter Madálasa,
by the cunning of Patála·ketu,
Was kidnapped by the *daitya* lord—
what folly! fate's twisted, misshapen ways.*

So be it! We'll just have to take up our search in the dwellings of infidels.

KARUṆĀ: ⌜sahi, evaṃ hodu.⌟

3.15 *iti parikrāmataḥ.*

KARUṆĀ *(sa|trāsam)*: ⌜sahi, rakkhaso, rakkhaso!⌟

ŚĀNTIḤ: kv' âsau rākṣasaḥ?

KARUṆĀ: ⌜pekkha, pekkha! jo eso galanta|mala|paṅka|picchila|bībhaccha|duppekkhe|deha|cchaī, ulluṃchia|ciura|bharo, mukka|vasaṇa|vesa|duddaṃsaṇo, sihi|sihaṇḍa|piṃcchiā|hattho ido jevva ahivaṭṭadi.⌟

ŚĀNTIḤ: sakhi, n' âyaṃ rākṣasaḥ. nirvīryaḥ khalv ayam.

3.20 KARUṆĀ: ⌜tā ko eso bhavissadi?⌟

ŚĀNTIḤ: sakhi, «piśāca» iti śaṅke.

KARUṆĀ: ⌜sahi, evvaṃ papphuranta|maūha|māl"|ôbbhāsia|bhuaṇ'|antarāe jalanta|ppacaṇḍa|maccaṇḍa|maṇḍale diaha|muhe kahaṃ pisāāṇaṃ avaāso?⌟

ŚĀNTIḤ: tarhi an|antaram eva naraka|vivarād uttīrṇaḥ ko 'pi nārakī bhaviṣyati! *(vilokya vicintya ca)* āḥ, jñātam! Mahāmoha|pravartito 'yaṃ digambara|siddhāntaḥ. tat sarvathā dūre pariharaṇīyam asya darśanam. *(iti parāṅ|mukhī|bhavati.)*

KARUṆĀ: ⌜sahi, muhuttakaṃ ciṭṭha, jāva ido Saddhāṃ aṇṇesāmi.⌟ *(ubhe tathā sthite.)*

3.25 *tataḥ praviśati yathā|nirdiṣṭo* DIGAMBARA|SIDDHĀNTAḤ.

MERCY: Then it's settled, my friend.

*The two walk about.* 3.15

MERCY *(fearfully)*: There's an ogre, my friend, an ogre!

PEACE: Just where's this ogre?

MERCY: Look, look! There's one skulking about over here: slimy and oozing with filth, his complexion is so scary that he's hard to look at! He's got no hair and he's not wearing any clothing at all—really ugly! And he's got this fan of peacock feathers in his hand.

PEACE: Then, friend, it's no ogre. He's quite harmless.

MERCY: So then who might he be? 3.20

PEACE: I think, friend, he's what's called a "ghost."

MERCY: But how, my friend, can ghosts appear in broad daylight, while the blazing solar disk burns in the midst of a sky that's bright with the current of pulsating rays?

PEACE: So it must be some infernal creature that's just escaped from the pit of hell! *(looking about thoughtfully)* I've got it! This one's into the nudist cult* that Magnus Nescience started. That's a philosophy to stay far from in every respect. *(She turns away.)*

MERCY: Hold on for a minute, my friend, while I look for Faith hereabouts. *(The two remain there.)*

*Then enter the* ADHERENT OF THE NAKED ASCETICS, *as indicated.* 3.25

DIGAMBARAḤ: ⌜ṇamo aluhantāṇam, aluhantāṇam! ṇava|duvāla|ghara|majjhe appā dīva vva palittae. ese jiṇa|vala|bhāsido palam'|attho mokkha|sukha|do dhammo!⌟ *(iti parikrāmati. ākāśe)* ⌜le le sāvaā! suṇāha, suṇāha!⌟

⌜mala|maa|puggala|piṇḍe
  saala|jalehiṃ vi kelisī suddhī?
appā vimala|sahāvo
  lisi|palicalaṇehi jāṇavvo.⌟ [5]

⌜kiṃ bhaṇāha, kelisaṃ lisi|palicalaṇaṃ ti? taṃ suṇāha!⌟

⌜dūle calaṇa|paṇāmo,
  kida|sakkālaṃ ca, bhoaṇam miṭṭham,
issā|malaṃ ṇa kajjaṃ
  lisiṇaṃ dālaṃ lamantāṇam.⌟ [6]

3.30 *(nepathy'|âbhimukham avalokya)* ⌜Saddhe! ido dāva!⌟

*ubhe sa|bhayam ālokayataḥ. tataḥ praviśati tad|anurūpa|veṣā* ŚRADDHĀ.

ŚRADDHĀ: ⌜kiṃ āṇavei lāa|ulaṃ?⌟ (ŚĀNTIR *mūrcchitā patati.)*

DIGAMBARA|SIDDHĀNTAḤ: ⌜sāvaāṇaṃ kuḍumbaṃ muhuttaṃ pi mā paliccaa.⌟

ŚRADDHĀ: ⌜jaṃ āṇavei lāa|ulaṃ.⌟ *(iti niṣkrāntā.)*

NAKED ASCETIC: Hail the saints, yes, the saints!* The soul burns like a lamp in the midst of the city of nine gates.* The absolute truth that was proclaimed by the supreme Victor* is the way to the joys of freedom! *(So saying, he walks about. Aloud)* Hey, disciples! Listen up, listen up!

> How might all the waters cleanse
> the soiled individual mass?*
> Rather know the Self, of taintless nature,
> by following the Sage's path.

Now tell me, how is it to follow the Sage's footsteps? Listen up!

> You offer salutation from afar to their feet,
> loyal service and foodstuffs sweet,
> But ever avoid envy's taint,
> if the Sages play with your mate.*

*(looking offstage)* Faith! Get over here! 3.30

*The two look on in horror. Then enter* FAITH *costumed as he is.*

FAITH: What does my royal master command? *(*PEACE *falls unconscious.)*

NAKED ASCETIC: That you not depart for even an instant from the company of us disciples.

FAITH: As my royal master commands. *(Exit.)*

3.35 KARUṆĀ: ⌜samassasaü pia|sahī. ṇa hu ṇāma|matteṇa pia|sahīe bhedavvaṃ. jado sudaṃ mae Ahiṃsāe saāsādo, jaṃ atthi pāsaṇḍāṇaṃ vi Tamassa sudā «Saddh"» êti. teṇa esā Tāmasī Saddhā bhavissadi.⌟

ŚĀNTIḤ *(samāśvasya)*: sakhi, evam ev' âitat. tathā hi,

dur|ācārā sad|ācārāṃ, dur|darśā priya|darśanām,
ambām anusaraty eṣā dur|āśā na kathaṃ cana. [7]

tad bhavatu. tāvat saugat'|ālayeṣv apy asāv anviṣyatām. *(*ŚĀNTI/KARUṆE *parikrāmataḥ.)*

*tataḥ praviśati pustaka|hasto* BHIKṢU*/rūpo Buddh'|āgamaḥ.*

3.40 BHIKṢUḤ *(vicintya)*: bho bhoḥ! upāsakāḥ!

sākṣāt kṣaṇa|kṣayina eva, nirātmakāś ca
yatr' ârpitā bahir iva pratibhānti bhāvāḥ,
s" âiv' âdhunā vigalit'|âkhila|vāsanatvād
dhī|santatiḥ sphurati nirviṣay'|ôparāgā. [8]

*(parikramya, punaḥ sa|ślāgham)* aho! sādhur ayaṃ saugata|dharmo, yatra saukhyaṃ mokṣaś ca! tathā hi—

MERCY: Courage, dear friend. Don't be upset, my friend, by just a name. For I heard it from Harmlessness* herself that among the infidels there is one called "Faith," who is the daughter of Darkness.* This must be that Faith, born of Darkness. 3.35

PEACE *(with a sigh of relief)*: So it is, friend. Thus,

> Not her bad manners mother's good,
> nor her ugliness mother's beauty,
> For her bad faith will never at all
> follow the way of my mommy.

Let it be, then. We should look for her, too, in the dwelling-places of the Buddhists. *(*PEACE *and* MERCY *walk about.)*

*Then enter a Buddhist in the form of a* MONK *holding a book.*

MONK *(thinking)*: Hey, hey! lay followers! 3.40

> Visibly evaporating in an instant,
> and devoid of substantial self,
> Entities appear as external
> where they are so projected.
> The stream of consciousness is vibrant,
> free from objects and attachments,
> When as now one lets go
> of all latent dispositions.*

*(walking about, and then boastfully)* Wow! Excellent indeed is this Buddhist teaching, where we have happiness and freedom! For—

āvāso layanaṃ manoharam, abhi-
prāy'|ânukūlā vaṇiṅ|
nāryo, vāñchita|kālam iṣṭam aśanaṃ,
śayyā mṛdu|prastarāḥ.
śraddhā|pūrvam upāsikā|yuvatibhiḥ
kḷpt'|âṅga|dān'|ôtsava|
krīḍ"|ānanda|bharair vrajanti vilasaj|
jyotsn"|âṅkurā rātrayaḥ. [9]

KARUṆĀ: ⌜sahi, ko eso? taruṇatara|tāla|talu|pallavo lambanta| kasāa|pisaṅga|cīra|cīvaro sa|cūḍa|muṇḍia|muṇḍa|veso ido jevva ahiacchadi.⌟

3.45 ŚĀNTIḤ: sakhi, Buddh'|āgama eṣaḥ.

BHIKṢUḤ *(ākāśe)*: bho, bho! upāsakāḥ! bhikṣavaś ca! śrūyatāṃ bhagavataḥ Sugatasya vāky'|âmṛtam! *(pustakaṃ vācayati.)* paśyāmy ahaṃ divyena cakṣuṣā lokānāṃ su|gatiṃ durgatiṃ ca. kṣaṇikāḥ sarve saṃskārāḥ. n' âsty ātmā sthāyī. tasmād bhikṣuṣu dārān ākramatsu n' ērṣitavyam. citta|malaṃ hi tad yad īrṣyā nāma. *(nepathy'|âbhimukham avalokya)* Śraddhe! itas tāvat!

*praviśya* ŚRADDHĀ.

ŚRADDHĀ: ⌜āṇavedu lāa|ulam.⌟

BHIKṢUḤ: upāsakān bhikṣūṃś ca nirbharam āliṅgya sthīyatām!

Our dwellings are pleasant homes
where merchants' wives ply to our needs,
Where the food we want's there when we want it,
and we have broad beds, so comfy.
As an expression of their faith,
by young laywomen we are served
with festive play, great bliss,
their willing bodies' gift,
Thus do pass our nights,
with dancing flames of delight.

MERCY: Now who's this, my friend? Here he comes, a shiny bald-pate, like a fresh palm frond draped with dirty red robes.

PEACE: He's a Buddhist, my friend. 3.45

MONK *(aloud)*: Hey, hey! Laymen and monks! Listen to the immortal words of the Blessed Lord Buddha! *(He recites from the book.)* With the divine eye I see the favorable and evil destinies of the worlds. All conditioned things are momentary. There is no enduring self. So don't get jealous when the monks screw your wives. For what is called "jealousy" is a taint of the mind. *(He looks offstage.)* Faith! Get over here!

*Enters* FAITH.

FAITH: I await my royal master's command.

MONK: May you remain firmly in the embrace of the laymen and monks!

3.50 ŚRADDHĀ: ⌜jaṃ āṇavedi lāa|ulam.⌟ *(iti niṣkrāntā.)*

ŚĀNTIḤ: sakhi, iyam api Tāmasī Śraddhā.

KARUṆĀ: ⌜evvaṃ edaṃ.⌟

KṢAPAṆAKAḤ (BHIKṢUM *āloky' ôccaiḥ|śabdam)*: ⌜alele! bhikkhua! ido dāva! kiṃ pi pucchissam.⌟

BHIKṢUḤ *(sa|krodham)*: āḥ! pāpa piśāc' | ākṛte! kim evaṃ pralapasi?

3.55 KṢAPAṆAKAḤ: ⌜ale, muñca koham. saccha|gadaṃ pucchāmi.⌟

BHIKṢUḤ: are, kṣapaṇaka, śāstra|kathām api vetsi! bhavatu. pratīmas tāvat. *(upasṛtya)* kiṃ pṛcchasi?

KṢAPAṆAKAḤ: ⌜bhaṇa dāva, kkhaṇa|viṇāsiṇā tue kassa kide vadaṃ dhālīadi?⌟

BHIKṢUḤ: are, śrūyatām! asmat|saṃtati|patitaḥ kaś cid vijñāna|lakṣaṇaḥ, samucchinna|vāsano, mokṣyate.

KṢAPAṆAKAḤ: ⌜ale! mucca|lajja! kassiṃ vi Maṇṇ|antale ko vi mukko bhavissadi? tado de saṃpadaṃ ṇaṭṭhassa kīrisaṃ uvaālaṃ kalissadi? aṇṇaṃ vi pucchāmi: keṇa de īriso dhammo saṃdiṭṭho?⌟

3.60 BHIKṢUḤ: nūnaṃ sarva | jñena bhagavatā Buddhen' ôkto 'yam eva dharmaḥ.

FAITH: As my royal master commands. *(Exit.)* 3.50

PEACE: My friend, this too is Faith the daughter of Darkness.

MERCY: So she is.

ASCETIC* *(looking at the* MONK, *and in a sharp voice)*: Hey! monklet! get over here! I have something to ask.

MONK *(angrily)*: Ah! damn shadow of a ghost! what have you got to say?

ASCETIC: Hey, let go of your anger. I'll ask you something about doctrine. 3.55

MONK: So, ascetic, you know doctrinal talk! OK. We'll soon see. *(approaching)* What's your question?

ASCETIC: Tell me, then, just for whose sake do you maintain your vows, given that you dissolve in each instant?*

MONK: Well, just listen! It is something of the nature of consciousness, running through the stream of our existence, that, when its latent dispositions are eradicated, attains liberation.*

ASCETIC: Oh! how shameless! So at some point at the end of the eon someone's going to get free? And how's that going to be of any use to you, who is liable to dissolution right now? I have another question: who is it that taught this doctrine of yours?

MONK: Of course, it was the omniscient lord Buddha* who pronounced this doctrine. 3.60

KṢAPAṆAKAḤ: ⌜ale! savva|ṇṇo Buddho tti kadhaṃ tue ṇādam?⌟

BHIKṢUḤ: nanu re, tad|āgamair eva prasiddho Buddhaḥ sarva|jña iti.

KṢAPAṆAKAḤ: ⌜ale! ujjia|buddhae! jaï tassa bhāsideṇa savva|ṇṇattaṃ paḍivajjesi, tā ahaṃ vi savvaṃ jāṇāmi. tumaṃ pi pidu|pidāmahehiṃ satta|pulisehiṃ me dāso tti!⌟

BHIKṢUḤ *(sa|krodham)*: āḥ pāpa! piśāca mala|paṅka|dhara! kiṃ tāvad ahaṃ dāsaḥ?

3.65 KṢAPAṆAKAḤ: ⌜ale! vihāla|dāsī|bhuaṅga! duṭṭha|palivvajia, diṭṭhaṃdo mae daṃsido. tā piaṃ de vissaddhaṃ bhaṇāmi: Buddh'|âṇusāsaṇaṃ palihalia alihant'|âṇusāsaṇaṃ jevva aṇusalidu bhavam. diambala|madaṃ ācaledu bhavam!⌟

BHIKṢUḤ: āḥ pāpa! svayaṃ naṣṭaḥ, parān api nāśayitum icchasi.

svārājyaṃ prājyam utsṛjya loke nindyām a|ninditaḥ,
abhivāñchati ko nāma bhavān iva piśācatām? [10]

api ca, arhato 'pi dharma|vedanaṃ kaḥ śraddadhāti?

ASCETIC: Hah! And how do you know of the omniscience of this Buddha?

MONK: Well, of course, his own scriptures clearly proclaim the omniscience of the Buddha.

ASCETIC: Hah! you must be out of your mind! If you understand omniscience owing just to what he said, then I too know everything. There, then, I say that you, with your father and ancestors for seven generations, are my slaves!

MONK *(angrily)*: Oh damn! you dirty, filthy ghost! how's it that I'm your slave?

ASCETIC: Hah! you dildo for the monastery's slavegirls! what 3.65
a sorry excuse for a mendicant! I used that as an example. And now I'll say something that you're sure to like: you should get out of this Buddhist racket and follow the teaching of the Saint. Join us in our naked asceticism, my man!

MONK: Oh damn! Defeated yourself, you just wish to defeat others.

> Having renounced one's liberty supreme,
> what blameless person would seek,
> In this world, sir, as you must,
> the despicable state of a ghost?

And just who believes in your Saint's doctrinal knowledge, anyway?

KṢAPAṆAKAḤ: ⌜gaha | ṇakkhatta | cāla | canda | sull' | ôpalāa | dukkhala|palama|lahassāṇaṃ ādesa|saṃvāda|daṃsaṇeṇa ṇilūvidaṃ savvaṇṇattaṇaṃ bhaavado alihantassa.⌟

3.70 BHIKṢUḤ: are! an|ādi|pravṛttena jyotiṣ'|âtīndriya|jñānena pratāritena bhavat" êdam atikaṣṭaṃ vratam āśritam? tathā hi—

> jñātuṃ vapuḥ|parimitaḥ kṣamate tri|lokīṃ
> jīvaḥ kathaṃ, kathaya, saṃgatim antareṇa?
> śaknoti kumbha|nihitaḥ su|śikho 'pi dīpo
> bhāvān prakāśayitum apy udare gṛhasya? [11]

tasmāl loka|dvaya|viruddhād ārhata|matād varaṃ Sugata|matam eva, sākṣāt sukh'|āvaham atiramaṇīyam paśyāmaḥ.

ŚĀNTIḤ: sakhi, anyato gacchāvaḥ.

KARUṆĀ: ⌜evaṃ bhodu.⌟ *(iti parikrāmataḥ.)*

3.75 ŚĀNTIḤ *(puro vilokya)*: eṣa purastāt Soma|siddhāntaḥ. bhavatu, atr' âpi tāvad anusarāvaḥ.

*tataḥ praviśati* KĀPĀLIKA*|rūpa|dhārī* SOMA|SIDDHĀNTAḤ.

ASCETIC: The omniscience of the Blessed Lord, the Saint, is adduced by instruction, dialectic and theory concerning the paths of planets and stars, lunar and solar eclipses, and difficult, most esoteric matters.*

MONK: Ha! So you adhere to your harsh austerity because 3.70
you've been taken in by the extra-sensory knowledge of astrology that's been around forever? If so—

Tell me, how it is that the vital soul,
whose dimension is that of the body,
Can know the three world-realms
in the absence of further connections?*
For can the lamp, though well-lit,
but concealed within a pot,
Illuminate many things
in the house, or not?

Therefore, we find that the philosophy of the Buddha, which visibly delivers the most pleasant happiness, is superior to that of your Saint, which is at odds with both this world and the next.

PEACE: Let's move on, my friend.

MERCY: So be it. *(They walk about.)*

PEACE *(looking ahead)*: Here's a Shaivite philosopher,* just 3.75
in front of us. Alright, let's follow him as well.

*Enter the* SHAIVITE PHILOSOPHER *in the guise of a* SKULLMAN.

SOMA|SIDDHĀNTAḤ *(parikramya)*:

nar'|âsthi|mālā|kṛta|cāru|bhūṣaṇaḥ,
śmaśāna|vāsī, nṛ|kapāla|bhojanaḥ
paśyāmi yog'|âñjana|śuddha|cakṣuṣā
jagan mitho bhinnam, a|bhinnam īśvarāt. [12]

KṢAPAṆAKAḤ: ⌜ale! ko eso kāvālaṃ vadaṃ dhāledi puliso? tā eṇaṃ pucchissaṃ.⌟ *(upasṛtya)* ⌜alele, Kāvālia! ṇal'|atthi|muṇḍa|dhāi! kīliso tuha sokkho? kīliso tuha mokkho?⌟

3.80 KĀPĀLIKAḤ: are, Kṣapaṇaka! dharmaṃ tāvad asmākam avadhāraya!

mastiṣk'|ântra|vas"|âbhidhārita|mahā|
māṃs'|āhutīr juhvatāṃ
vahnau brahma|kapāla|kalpita|surā|
pānena naḥ pāraṇā.
sadyaḥ|kṛtta|kaṭhora|kaṇṭha|vigalat|
kīlāla|dhār"|ôjjvalair
arcyo naḥ puruṣ'|ôpahāra|balibhir
devo Mahābhairavaḥ. [13]

BHIKṢUḤ *(karṇau pidhāya)*: Buddha! Buddha! aho dāruṇā dharma|caryā!

SHAIVITE *(walking about)*:

Dwelling in the graveyard,
eating from a skull,
prettily adorned
with strings of human bone,
I see with eyes cleansed by yoga's balm
that the world divided is a lie,
but from my Lord knows no divide.*

ASCETIC: Hey! Who's this guy maintaining the Skullman's vow? I'm going to ask him. *(Approaches.)* Hey, Skullman! you there with the human bones and skull! What's your pleasure? and what's your liberation?

SKULLMAN: What's up, Ascetic! You should be upholding 3.80
our law!

Oblations of Great Meat,
replete with brains, guts, and marrow!
Offered in the flames,
with liquor measured in a brahmin's skull,
are the feast fulfilling our ritual vow.
Let our god, the Great Terror, be worshipped
with humans sacrificed,
brilliant with streaming blood that spurts
from thick necks as they are sliced.*

MONK *(stopping up his ears)*: Oh Buddha! Oh Buddha! What a terrible religion!

KṢAPAṆAKAḤ: ⌜alihanta! alihanta! aho gholaṃ pāvaṃ! kāvālieṇa keṇa vi vippaladdho eva eso, tti takkemi!⌟

KĀPĀLIKAḤ *(sa|krodham)*: āḥ pāpa pākhaṇḍ'|âpaśada! muṇḍita|muṇḍa! caṇḍāla|veśa! keśa|luñcaka! are! vipralambhakaḥ kila catur|daśa|bhuvan'|ôtpatti|sthiti|pralaya|pravartako Vedānta|siddhānta|prasiddha|vibhavo bhagavān Bhavānī|patiḥ? darśayāmas tarhi dharmasy' âsya mahimānam?

3.85 Hari|Hara|sura|jyeṣṭha|śreṣṭhān
surān aham āhare.
viyati vahatāṃ nakṣatrāṇāṃ
ruṇadhmi gatīr api.
sa|naga|nagarīm ambhaḥ|pūrṇāṃ
vidhāya mahīm imāṃ,
kalaya sakalaṃ bhūyas toyaṃ
kṣaṇena pibāmi tat. [14]

KṢAPAṆAKAḤ: ⌜ale, Kāvālia! ṇaṃ ado jevva bhaṇāmi: keṇa vi endajālieṇa māāṃ daṃsia vippaladdho tti!⌟

KĀPĀLIKAḤ: āḥ pāpa! punar api Parameśvaram aindrajālikam ity ākṣipasi? tan na marṣaṇīyam asya daurātmyam! *(khaḍgam ākṛṣya)* tad aham asya...

etat|karāla|karavāla|nikṛtta|kaṇṭha|
nāl'|ôccalad|bahula|phenila|budbud'|âughaiḥ
sārdhaṃ ḍamaḍ|ḍamaru|ḍāṃkṛti|hūta|bhūta|
vargeṇa Bharga|gṛhiṇīṃ rudhirair dhinomi. [15]

ASCETIC: Oh Saint! Oh Saint! What horrible sin! I think he must have been duped by some skull-master!

SKULLMAN *(angrily)*: O you damn miserable outcaste! hairless baldhead! pariah impersonator! plucked pate! Damn! The Lord, Párvati's Master,* who creates, maintains, and destroys the fourteen worlds,* and who is exalted in the renowned philosophy of the Vedánta, is a con artist? Do we need to demonstrate to you the glory of his law?

I coerce the gods: 3.85
  Vishnu, Shiva, the eldest and best of deities.
I arrest in space
  the paths of wandering stars.
Filling this whole world with water,
  the mountains, cities, and all,
Know that I'll drink in an instant
  the entire flood once more.

ASCETIC: Hey, Skullman! I'll say this: you've been duped by a magic show put on by some wizard!

SKULLMAN: Oh damn! Again you curse the Supreme Lord as a wizard? I can't put up with his villainy! *(Draws a sword.)* I'll give it to him...

To my Lord's Lady* I give pleasure with torrents
  of frothing, bubbling blood,
  flowing from the quivering reeds of the neck
  severed by this fearsome sword;
The host of the spirits will join me,
  summoned by the ta-dum-dum
  tapped out by my *dámaru*-drum.

*iti khaḍgam udyacchati.*

3.90 KṢAPAṆAKAḤ *(sa|bhayam)*: ⌜mahā | bhāa! a | hiṃsā palamo dhammo! hiṃsā palamo a|dhammo!⌟ *(iti* BHIKṢOR *aṅkaṃ praviśati.)*

BHIKṢUḤ *(*KĀPĀLIKAṂ *vārayan)*: bho, bho, mahā | bhāga! kautuka|prayukta|vāk|kalahen' â|yuktam etasmiṃs tapasvini prahartum.

KĀPĀLIKAḤ *khaḍgam pratisaṃharati.*

KṢAPAṆAKAḤ *(samāśvasya)*: ⌜mahā|bhāo jaï saṃhalida|ghola|los' | āveso saṃvutto, tado ahaṃ kiṃ vi pucchiduṃ icchemi.⌟

KĀPĀLIKAḤ: pṛccha, pṛccha.

3.95 KṢAPAṆAKAḤ: ⌜sudo tumhāṇaṃ palamo dhammo. adha keliso sokkha|mokkho tti?⌟

KĀPĀLIKAḤ: śṛṇu!

dṛṣṭaṃ kv' âpi sukhaṃ vinā na viṣayair.
ānanda|bodh'|ôjjhitā
jīvasya sthitir eva muktir upal"|â-
vasthā kathaṃ prārthyate?
Pārvatyāḥ pratirūpayā dayitayā
s'|ānandam āliṅgito
muktaḥ krīḍati candra|cūḍa|vapur. ity
ūce Mṛḍānī|patiḥ. [16]

*So saying, he brandishes the sword.*

ASCETIC *(frightened)*: Good sir! Harmlessness is the highest law! Injury is the greatest crime! *(Hides besides the* MONK.*)* 3.90

MONK *(warding off the* SKULLMAN*)*: Please, please, good sir! It's unworthy of you to strike this ascetic because of his joking word-games.

SKULLMAN *resheathes the sword.*

ASCETIC *(catching his breath)*: If the good sir has now restrained the rage that possessed him, then there is something that I would like to ask.

SKULLMAN: Ask, ask.

ASCETIC: I've heard about your highest teaching. So what's this "blissful freedom" all about? 3.95

SKULLMAN: Listen up!

> Joy is nowhere without objects.
> How can one yearn for freedom
> as life that just goes on and on,
> rock-like, not knowing bliss?
> Free, in the form of the Moon-crested god,
> one sports in ecstatic embrace
> with a lover in Párvati's guise.
> For this is what we've been taught
> by that glad goddess's lord.*

BHIKṢUḤ: mahā|bhāga, a|śraddh" êyam etad a|vīta|rāgasya muktir iti.

KṢAPAṆAKAḤ: ⌜ale, Kāvālia! jaï ṇa lussasi, tado bhaṇāmi. salīlī sa|lāgī mukko a, tti viluddham.⌟

3.100 KĀPĀLIKAḤ *(sva|gatam)*: aye! a | śraddh" | ākṣiptam anayor antaḥ | karaṇam. bhavatv. evaṃ tāvat. *(prakāśam)* Śraddhe! itas tāvat!

*tataḥ praviśati* KĀPĀLINĪ*|rūpa|dhāriṇī* ŚRADDHĀ.

KARUṆĀ: ⌜sahi, pekkha! Rajassa sudā Saddhā. sā esā—⌟

⌜viphulla|ṇīl'|uppala|lola|loaṇā,
ṇar'|atthi|mālā|kida|cālu|bhūsaṇā,
ṇiamba|pīṇa|tthaṇa|bhāla|manthalā,
vihādi puṇṇ'|êndu|muhī vilāsiṇī. [17]⌟

ŚRADDHĀ *(parikramya)*: ⌜esa mhi! āṇavedu sāmī.⌟

3.105 KĀPĀLIKAḤ: priye, enaṃ dur|abhimāninaṃ bhikṣuṃ tāvad gṛhāṇa!

ŚRADDHĀ BHIKṢUM *āliṅgati.*

BHIKṢUḤ *(s'|ānandaṃ pariṣvajya, rom'|âñcam abhinīya, jan| āntikam)*: aho! sukha|sparśā Kāpālinī. tathā hi—

MONK: Good sir, it's said that we should not place our faith in a liberation that's not dispassionate.

ASCETIC: Yes, indeed, Skullman! If you don't become vexed, I have something to say. The very notion of an embodied, impassioned liberation is a contradiction.

SKULLMAN *(aside)*: Wow! The brains of these two have fallen 3.100
among the faithless. Alright, then. *(aloud)* Faith! get over here!

*There enters* FAITH *in the guise of a* SKULLGIRL.

MERCY: Look! my friend, it's Faith, daughter of Desire!* And she—

> Her eyes darting about
> resemble blossomed blue lotuses,
> She's charmingly adorned
> with strings of human bone,
> Her hips and heavy breasts
> slow her graceful steps,
> With a full, moon-like face
> she seems quite the playmate.

FAITH *(walking about)*: Here I am! Command me, m'lord!

SKULLMAN: My dear, give a little hug to this ill-disposed 3.105
monk!

FAITH *hugs the* MONK.

MONK *(joyfully embracing, acting delighted, then whispering)*: Yes, indeed! She feels good, this Skullgirl! So—

raṇḍāḥ pīna|payodharāḥ kati mayā
caṇḍ'|ânurāgād bhuja|
dvandv'|āpīḍita|pīvara|stana|bharaṃ
no gāḍham āliṅgitāḥ?
buddhebhyaḥ śataśaḥ śape, mayi punaḥ
kutr' âpi Kāpālinī|
pīn'|ôttuṅga|kuc'|âvagūhana|bhavaḥ
prāptaḥ pramod'|ôdayaḥ! [18]

aho! puṇyaṃ Kāpālika|caritam! aho! ślāghyaḥ Soma|siddhāntaḥ! āścaryo 'yaṃ dharmaḥ! bho, mahā|bhāga! sarvathā Buddh'|ânuśāsanam asmābhir utsṛṣṭam, praviṣṭāḥ smaḥ Pārameśvaraṃ siddhāntam! tad ācāryas tvaṃ, śiṣyo 'ham. praveśaya māṃ Pārameśvarīṃ dīkṣām!

3.110 KṢAPAṆAKAḤ: ⌜ale, bhikkhua! Kāvāliṇī|phalasaṇeṇa dūsido tumam. tā dūlaṃ apasala!⌟

BHIKṢUḤ: āḥ pāpa! vañcito 'si re Kāpālinyāḥ parirambha|mah"|ôtsavena!

KĀPĀLIKAḤ: priye, kṣapaṇakaṃ gṛhāṇa.

KĀPĀLIṆĪ KṢAPAṆAKAM *āliṅgati.*

KṢAPAṆAKAḤ *(sa|rom'|âñcam)*: ⌜aho arihanta! aho arihanta! Kāvāliṇīe phalasa|suhaṃ! aï, sundali! dedu, dedu dāva puṇo aṅka|pāliṃ!⌟ *(sva|gatam)* ⌜are, mahanto khu india|viālo saṃvutto! tā kiṃ ettha juttaṃ? bhodu. picchiāe ḍhakissam.⌟ *(tathā kṛtvā)*

How many big-bosomed wenches have I,
  burning with passion, hugged tight,
  both arms pressed to swelling breasts?
But I swear by the buddhas a hundred times
  that somewhere else I may find
  the joyfulness that does arise
  from squeezing Skullgirl's perky tits!

Wow! the Skullman's way is fantastic! Wow! praise be to Shaivite philosophy! This is a wonderful religion! Hey, good sir! we're entirely out of the Buddha's teaching and into the philosophy of the Supreme Lord! So, you're the master and I'm the disciple. Bestow on me the initiation in the way of the Supreme Lord!

ASCETIC: Hold on there, monklet! you've been defiled by 3.110
Skullgirl's touch. So, get out of here!

MONK: Hot damn! you'll see who's been duped by the festival of Skullgirl's embrace!

SKULLMAN: Hug the ascetic, dear.

SKULLGIRL *embraces the* ASCETIC.

ASCETIC *(delighted)*: Oh Saint! Oh Saint! The pleasure of Skullgirl's touch! Hey, beautiful! Give it to me! Give it to me! The lap-dance again! *(aside)* Yes, indeed, I've had a major transformative experience! So now what's right? So be it. I'll just have to hide myself with my peacock-fan! *(He does so.)*

⌜ayi! pīṇa|ghaṇa|tthaṇa|sohiṇi!
palitattha|kulaṅga|viloa|lloaṇe!
jaï laṃasi, Kāvāliṇi, tā kiṃ kalissadi sāvakī?⌟ [19]

⌜aho, Kāvāliaṃ jevva ekkaṃ daṃsaṇaṃ sokkha|mokkha|sāhaṇaṃ. bho, ācālia! ahaṃ tuha dāso saṃvutto. maṃ pi Mahābhailav'|âṇusāsaṇe* dikkhedu!⌟

KĀPĀLIKAḤ: upaviśyatām. *(ubhau tathā kurutaḥ.)*

KĀPĀLIKO *bhājanaṃ samādāya dhyānaṃ nāṭayati.*

ŚRADDHĀ: ⌜bhaavaṃ, palipūliaṃ sulāe bhāaṇam.⌟

KĀPĀLIKAḤ *(pītvā śeṣaṃ* BHIKṢU/KṢAPAṆAKAYOR *arpayati.)*:

idaṃ pavitram amṛtam
pīyatāṃ, bhava|bheṣajam,
paśu|pāśa|samuccheda|
kāraṇaṃ, Bhairav'|ôditam. [20]

*ubhau vimṛśataḥ.*

KṢAPAṆAKAḤ: ⌜amhāṇaṃ alihant'|âṇusāsaṇe sulā|pāṇaṃ ṇ' atthi.⌟

BHIKṢUḤ: kathaṃ Kāpālik'|ôcchiṣṭāṃ surāṃ pāsyāmi?

KĀPĀLIKAḤ *(kiñ cid vimṛśya)*: kiṃ vimṛśasi, Śraddhe? paśutvam anayor n' âdy' âpy apanīyate. ten' âsmad|vadana|saṃsarga|duṣṭāṃ pavitrāṃ surām etau manyete. tad bhavatī sva|vaktr'|āsava|pūtāṃ kṛtv" ânayor upanayatu.

Hey! Beauty with the big firm breasts! 3.115
with the eyes of a frightened doe!
If you play this way in a Skullgirl's guise,
just what can a pious Jain woman devise?

Really, Skullman's viewpoint is the one way to realize blissful freedom. Hey, Skullman! I've become your slave now. Initiate me too in the teaching of the Great Terror!

SKULLMAN: Sit down, you two. *(Both do so.)*

SKULLMAN *takes up a bowl and performs a meditation.*

FAITH: My lord, the vessel is filled with liquor.

SKULLMAN *(drinks and passes the rest to the* MONK *and the* ASCETIC.*)*: 3.120

Let this holy elixir be consumed,
the cure for being's round,
The way to release the beast from its snare,*
as the Great Terror pronounced.

*Both hesitate.*

ASCETIC: In ours, the Saint's teaching, there's no imbibing of liquor.

MONK: How could I drink down the left-overs of Skullman's liquor?

SKULLMAN *(reflective)*: What are you thinking, Faith? Today these two are still not rid of their bestiality. Hence, they imagine the holy liquor to be polluted by contact with my mouth. So, m'lady, purifying it with the wine that 3.125

yatas tairthikā api vadanti, «strī|mukhaṃ tu sadā śuci» iti.

ŚRADDHĀ: ⌜jaṃ bhaavaṃ āṇavedi!⌟ *(iti pāna|pātraṃ gṛhītvā pīta|śeṣam upanayati.)*

BHIKṢUḤ: mahān prasādaḥ! *(iti caṣakaṃ gṛhītvā pibati.)* aho! surāyāḥ saundaryam!

nipītā veśyābhiḥ
  saha na kati|vārān su|vadanā|
 mukh'|ôcchiṣṭ" âsmābhiḥ
  sa|rasa|madir" āmoda|madhurā?
Kapālinyā vaktr'|ā-
  sava|surabhim etāṃ tu madirām
 a|labdhvā jānīmaḥ
  spṛhayati sudhāyai sura|gaṇaḥ. [21]

KṢAPAṆAKAḤ: ⌜ale, bhikkhua! mā savvaṃ piba! Kāvāliṇī|vaaṇ'|ôcchiṭṭhaṃ maïlaṃ maha vi dhālaedu!⌟

3.130 BHIKṢUḤ KṢAPAṆAKĀYA *caṣakam upanayati.*

KṢAPAṆAKAḤ *(pītvā)*: ⌜aho, sulāe mahulattaṇam! aho, sādo! aho, gandho! aho, sulahittaṇam! cilaṃ khu alihant'|āṇusāsaṇe piḍido vañcido mhi edisеṇa sulā|laseṇa! ale bhikkua, gholanti me aṅgāiṃ. tā uvaviśamha.⌟

BHIKṢUḤ: evaṃ kurvaḥ. *(tathā kurutaḥ.)*

KĀPĀLIKAḤ: priye, a|mūlya|krītaṃ dāsa|dvayaṃ labdham. tan nṛtyāvas tāvat! *(ubhau nṛtyataḥ.)*

flows from your lips, serve it up to them. As even the cultists say, "a woman's mouth is always clean."*

FAITH: As my master commands! *(Taking the wine-bowl, she serves what she leaves.)*

MONK: You're most gracious! *(He takes the vessel and drinks.)* Oh-ho! The beauty of wine!

How many times have we not drunk with whores
the sweet fragrant booze
left in their pretty mouths?
But we know that even the troop of the gods,
not tasting this perfumed wine,
the liquor from Skullgirl's lips,
enjoys only ambrosia's delights.

ASCETIC: Hey, monklet! Don't swill it all! Save what's left of the liquor from Skullgirl's mouth for me!

*The* MONK *passes the wine-cup to the* ASCETIC. 3.130

ASCETIC *(after drinking)*: Wow! how sweet this wine is! Wow! what a taste! Wow! what a smell! Wow! it's perfumed! It's been a long time since I fell into the Saint's teaching, but thanks to the good taste of this wine I've been sprung free! Hey, monklet! my limbs are spinning. I'm going to sit down.

MONK: Let's both. *(Both do.)*

SKULLMAN: My dear, for no cost at all we've gotten ourselves a pair of slaves. Let's dance to it! *(They both dance.)*

KṢAPAṆAKAḤ: ⌜ale, bhikkua. eso Kāvālio—aha vā ācālio—Kāvāliṇīe saddhaṃ sohaṇaṃ ṇaccedi. tā edāe saddhaṃ amhe vi ṇaccāmha!⌟

3.135 BHIKṢUḤ: ācārya, mah"|āścaryam etad darśanaṃ! yatr' â|kleśam abhimat'|ârtha|siddhayaḥ saṃpadyante! *(mada|skhalitaṃ nṛtyataḥ.)*

KṢAPAṆAKAḤ *«ayi! pīṇa|ghaṇa|tthaṇa...» ity ādi gāyati.*

KĀPĀLIKAḤ: kiyad etad āścaryaṃ, paśya!

yatr'|ân|ujjhita|vāñchit'|ârtha|viṣay'|ā-
  saṅge 'pi sidhyanty amūḥ
pratyāsanna|mah"|ôdaya|praṇayinām
  aṣṭau mahā|siddhayaḥ,
vaśy'|âkarṣa|vimohana|pramathana|
  prakṣobhaṇ'|ôccāṭana|
prāyāḥ prākṛta|siddhayas tu viduṣāṃ
  yog'|ântarāyāḥ param. [22]

KṢAPAṆAKAḤ: ⌜ale kāpālia!⌟ *(vimṛśya)* ⌜ahava ācālia... ācālia|lāa... kul|ācālia...⌟

3.140 BHIKṢUḤ *(vihasya)*: ayam an|abhyās'|âtiśaya|pītayā madirayā dūram unmattī|kṛtas tapasvī! tat kriyatām asya mad'|âpanayanam!

KĀPĀLIKAḤ: evaṃ bhavatu. *(iti sva|mukh'|ôcchiṣṭaṃ tāmbūlaṃ* KṢAPAṆAKĀYA *dadāti.)*

ASCETIC: Hey, monklet. This Skullman—I mean, our teacher—dances real nice with Skullgirl. We should both dance with them, too!

MONK: Teacher! This philosophy is a big kick! Without 3.135
any emotional complications, whatever you wish is right there! *(They both dance, reeling drunk.)*

ASCETIC *repeats the verse "Hey! Beauty with the big firm breasts..."*

SKULLMAN: You ain't seen nothin' yet!

> Where, without renouncing attachment to
> desired objects,
> the eight major powers are attained*
> by seekers of the inmost great realizations,
> The ordinary powers—
> to hypnotize, coerce, or stupefy,
> kill, excite, expel, and more—
> are yoga-obstacles that the wise deplore.

ASCETIC: Hey, Skullman! *(hesitating)* I mean master, ... or royal master, ... or clan master ...

MONK *(laughing)*: This ascetic can't hold his liquor, drank 3.140
too much of it and has really gone off his rocker! Do something to sober him up!

SKULLMAN: So be it. *(He gives the* ASCETIC *the remains of a betel-leaf from his mouth.*)*

KṢAPAṆAKAḤ *(saṃjñāṃ labdhvā, kṣaṇaṃ svasthī/bhūya)*: ⌜ā-cāliaṃ evva edaṃ pucchissam. jādisī tuha sulāe āhalaṇa|sattī, kiṃ tādisī itthiā|pulisesu vi atthi?⌟

KĀPĀLIKAḤ: kiṃ viśeṣeṇa pṛcchyate? paśya—

vidyā|dharīṃ v", ātha sur'|âṅganāṃ vā,
  nāg'|âṅganāṃ v" âpy, atha yakṣa|kanyām,
yad yan mam' êṣṭaṃ bhuvana|traye 'pi,
  vidyā|balāt tat tad upāharāmi. [23]

3.145 KṢAPAṆAKAḤ: ⌜bho, edaṃ mae gaṇideṇa ṇṇādaṃ: jaṃ savve amhe mahā|lāa|Mahāmohassa kiṃkal" êtti.⌟

UBHAU: yathā jñātam āyuṣmatā, evam etat.

KṢAPAṆAKAḤ: ⌜tā lāa|kajjaṃ mantīyadu.⌟

KĀPĀLIKAḤ: kiṃ tat?

KṢAPAṆAKAḤ: ⌜Sattassa sudā Saddhā mahā|lāassa aṇṇāe āhalaṇī" êtti.⌟

3.150 KĀPĀLIKAḤ: kathaya, kv' âsau dāsyāḥ putrī? eṣa tām a|ciram eva vidyā|balād upāharāmi.

KṢAPAṆAKAḤ *khaṇḍinīm ādāya gaṇayati.*

ŚĀNTIḤ: sakhi, ambām uddiśy' âiva hat'|āśānām ālāpaḥ; tad avadhānena tāvad ākarṇayāvaḥ.

ASCETIC *(regaining consciousness and in a moment coming to his senses)*: I ask you this, master. As you have the power to bring in the booze, is there a similar power that acts on guys and gals?

SKULLMAN: Why do you ask me this in particular? Look—

She may be a gnostic-lady,
divine nymph, *naga*-lass, or *yaksha*-girl,
But I'll trap with gnostic power,
whichever one I desire,
if she's within this triple world.

ASCETIC: Well, here's what I managed to figure out: we're all Magnus Nescience's stooges. 3.145

BOTH*: As you, long-lived sir, now know, so it is.

ASCETIC: Then there is a task on behalf of our king that must be settled.

SKULLMAN: What's that?

ASCETIC: According to the king's command, Truth's daughter Faith should be apprehended.

SKULLMAN: Tell me, then, where is that daughter of a slave-girl? I'll bring her in before long with the power of my spells. 3.150

*The* ASCETIC *takes a piece of chalk and counts.*

PEACE: My friend, there's desperate talk that seems to be about mother; let's listen in attentively.

KARUṆĀ: ⌜sahi, evvaṃ karemha.⌟ *(ubhe tathā kurutaḥ.)*

KṢAPAṆAKAḤ *(gāthāṃ gaṇayitvā)*:

3.155 ⌜ṇ' atthi jale, ṇ' atthi vaṇe,
ṇ' atthi gili|bilesu, ṇ' atthi pāāle,
sā Viṇṇubhatti|sahidā
ṇivasadi hiae mah"|appāṇam.⌟ [24]

KARUṆĀ *(s'|ānandam)*: ⌜sahi, diṭṭhiā vaḍḍhasi. sudaṃ Viṇṇubhattīe devīe pāsa|vaṭṭiṇī Saddh" êtti.⌟

ŚĀNTIR *harṣaṃ nāṭayati.*

BHIKṢUḤ: atha Dharmasya Kāmād apakrāntasya kutra pravṛttiḥ?

KṢAPAṆAKAḤ *(punar gaṇayitvā)*:

3.160 ⌜ṇ' atthi jale, ṇ' atthi vaṇe,
ṇ' atthi gili|bilesu, ṇ' atthi pāāle,
so Viṇṇubhatti|sahido
vattaï hiae mah"|appāṇam.⌟ [25]

KĀPĀLIKAḤ *(sa|viṣādam)*: aho! mahat kaṣṭam āpatitaṃ mahā|rājasya! tathā hi—

mūlaṃ devī siddhaye Viṣṇubhaktis,
tāṃ ca Śraddh" ânuvratā Sattva|kanyā;
Kāmān muktas tatra Dharmo 'py abhūc cet,
siddhaṃ manye tad Vivekasya sādhyam. [26]

tath" âpi tāvad asu|vyayen' âpi svāminaḥ prayojanam anuṣṭheyam. tan Mahābhairavīṃ vidyāṃ Dharma|Śraddhayor āharaṇāya prasthāpayāmaḥ. *(iti niṣkrāntāḥ.)*

MERCY: We'll do that, friend. *(The two do so.)*

ASCETIC *(counting out the verse)*:

> Neither in water, nor in forest, 3.155
> not in mountain caves, nor in the abyss,
> Is she who's with Hail Vishnu,
> for she dwells in hearts magnanimous.

MERCY *(gleefully)*: You're in luck, my friend! Faith, I hear, is by the side of the goddess Hail Vishnu.

PEACE *acts joyful.*

MONK: So where would Lex, who's escaped from Lust, be about?

ASCETIC *(counting again)*:

> Neither in water, nor in forest, 3.160
> not in mountain caves, nor in the abyss,
> Is he who's with Hail Vishnu,
> for he dwells in hearts magnanimous.

SKULLMAN *(dejectedly)*: Oh-ho! Great is the trouble befallen our king! For—

> Success's source is the goddess, Hail Vishnu,
> and devoted to her is truth's girl Faith;
> If Lex has gotten free from Lust,
> then Intuition's task is, I think, vouchsafed.

Nevertheless, even though I give up my life, I shall accomplish my master's purpose. Therefore, I'll set the spell of the Great Terroress* to work to capture Faith and Lex. *(Exeunt.)*

ŚĀNTIḤ: āvām apy evaṃ hat'|āśānāṃ vyavasāyaṃ devyai Viṣṇubhaktyai nivedayāvaḥ.

3.165 *iti niṣkrāntāḥ sarve.*

*iti śrī|Kṛṣṇamiśra|yati|viracite Prabodhacandrodaye pāṣaṇḍa|viḍambano nāma tṛtīyo 'ṅkaḥ.*

PEACE: We two as well must inform goddess Hail Vishnu of this desperate plot.

*Exeunt omnes.* 3.165

*Thus concludes the Third Act, 'Charlatans' Charades,'**
*in "The Rise of Wisdom Moon,"*
*composed by the eminent Krishna·mishra·yati.*

# INTERLUDE INTRODUCING ACT FOUR

4.1 *tataḥ praviśati* MAITRĪ.

MAITRĪ: ⌜sudaṃ mae Mudiā|saāsādo, jaṃ Mahābhairavī|kaḍḍhaṇa|sambhamādo bhaavadīe Viṇṇubhattīe parittādā pia|sahī Saddh" êti. tā ukkaṇṭhieṇa hiaeṇa pia|sahīṃ pekkhissam.⌟ *(parikrāmati.)*

*tataḥ praviśati* ŚRADDHĀ.

ŚRADDHĀ *(sa|bhay'|ôtkampam)*:

4.5 ghorāṃ, nāra|kapāla|kuṇḍalavatīṃ,
vidyuc|chaṭā dṛṣṭibhir
muñcantīṃ, vikarāla|mūrtim anala|
jvālā|piśaṅgaiḥ kacaiḥ,
daṃṣṭrā|candra|kal"|âṅkur'|ântara|valaj|
jihvāṃ Mahābhairavīṃ
paśyantyā iva me manaḥ kadalik" êv'
âdy' âpy aho vepate. [1]

MAITRĪ *(sva|gatam)*: ⌜ae! esā me pia|sahī bhaa|sambhānta|hiaā, kalida|kampataralehiṃ aṅgehiṃ kiṃ vi mantaantī saṃmuh'|āadaṃ vi maṃ ṇa lakkhedi! ālavissaṃ dāva.⌟ *(prakāśam)* ⌜pia|sahi, Saddhe! kīsa tumaṃ uttāvia|hiaā maṃ vi ṇa āloesi?⌟

*Enter* LOVE. 4.1

LOVE: I've heard from Joy in person that our dear friend Faith was saved by Hail Vishnu from the fearsome clutches of the Great Terroress. So it's with my heart in my throat that I'll be seeing dear Faith. *(She walks about.)*

*Enter* FAITH.

FAITH *(trembling with fear)*:

Ferocious she was, 4.5
with earrings of human skull,*
her gaze setting loose lightning bolts,
her form made fearsome
with yellow hair all aflame.
Thus seeing the Great Terroress,
her tongue dancing
between fangs hooked
like crescent moons,
My mind quakes even today
as if it were a plantain tree.

LOVE *(aside)*: Oh no! My dear friend Faith is muttering things while her limbs are trembling violently; her heart is confounded by fear. Even though I'm right in front of her, she doesn't recognize me! So I'll just speak to her. *(aloud)* Faith, dear friend! are you so heart-sick that you can't see me?

ŚRADDHĀ *(vilokya, s'|ôcchvāsam)*: aye! me priya|sakhī Maitrī!

Kālarātri|karāl'|āsya|
dant'|ântar|gatayā mayā
dṛṣṭ" âsi, sakhi, s" âiva tvaṃ
punar atr' âiva janmani. [2]

tad ehi, pariṣvajasva mām!

4.10 MAITRĪ *(tathā kṛtvā)*: ⌜sahi, taha Viṇṇubhatti|ṇibbhatthida| ppabhāvāe Mahābhairavīe kaḍḍhaṇa|sambhamādo ajja vi vevandi de aṅgāi?⌟

ŚRADDHĀ *«ghorām» ity|ādi paṭhati.*

MAITRĪ *(sa|trāsam)*: ⌜aho! had'|āsā ghola|daṃsaṇā! adha tāe āadāe kiṃ kidaṃ?⌟

ŚRADDHĀ: śṛṇu—

śyen'|âvapātam avapatya pada|dvaye mām,
ādāya Dharmam apareṇa kareṇa, ghorā
vegena sā gaganam utpatitā nakh'|âgra|
koṭi|sphurat|piśita|piṇḍa|yug" êva gṛdhrī. [3]

4.15 MAITRĪ: ⌜haddhī! haddhī!⌟ *(iti mūrcchati.)*

ŚRADDHĀ: sakhi, samāśvasihi, samāśvasihi!

MAITRĪ *(āśvasya)*: ⌜tado tado?⌟

FAITH *(looking about and sighing)*: Oh! my dear friend Love!

> I was caught between the teeth
> of Black Night's* fierce face,
> But see that it's you, my friend,
> here in this life once again.

So come and embrace me tightly!

LOVE *(does so.)*: But, my friend, why is it that your limbs 4.10
tremble in fear of the clutches of the Great Terroress, even now that her power has been dispelled by Hail Vishnu.

FAITH *again recites "Ferocious she was..."*

LOVE *(fearfully)*: Oh! she must have been hideous and awful to behold! So what did she do when she arrived?

FAITH: Listen—

> Diving like a falcon, fierce, she fell upon us,
> seizing me in one,
> Lex in the other of two talons.
> Gaining speed, she rose in the sky,
> like a vulture with two morsels of meat
> trembling in her crooked beak.

LOVE: How awful! Really awful! *(Swoons.)* 4.15

FAITH: Pull yourself together, my friend, get a grip!

LOVE *(breathing deeply)*: And then?

ŚRADDHĀ: tataḥ param asmadīy'|ârta|nāda|sañjāta|dayayā devyā Viṣṇubhaktyā—

bhrū|bhaṅga|bhīma|paripāṭala|dṛṣṭi|pātam,
udgāḍha|kopa|kuṭilaṃ ca tathā vyaloki
sā vajra|pāta|hata|śaila|śil" êva bhūmau,
vyābhugna|jarjaratar'|âsthi yathā papāta. [4]

4.20 MAITRĪ: ⌜diṭṭhiā miī via saddūla|muhādo pabbhaṭṭā Saddhā kkhemeṇa saṃjīviā pia|sahī! tado tado?⌟

ŚRADDHĀ: tato devyā samupajāt'|âbhiniveśayā kathitam, «evaṃ asya dur|ātmano Mahāmoha|hatakasya mām avajñāya pravartamānasya sa|mūlam unmūlanaṃ kariṣyām'!» îti. ādiṣṭā c' âhaṃ devyā yathā, «gaccha, Śraddhe, brūhi Vivekam Kāma|Krodh'|ādīnāṃ nirjayāy' ôdyogaḥ kriyatām. tato Vairāgyaṃ prādur|bhaviṣyati. ahaṃ ca yathā|samayaṃ Prāṇāyām'|ādy|anuṣṭhānena yuṣmat|sainyam anugrahīṣyāmi. Ṛtaṃbhar"|ādayaś ca devyaḥ Śānty|ādi|kauśalen' Ôpaniṣad|devyā saṃgatasya bhavataḥ Prabodh'|ôdayam anuvidhāsyant'» îti. tad aham idānīṃ Viveka|niketaṃ prati prasthitā. tvaṃ punaḥ kim ācarantī divasān ativāhayasi?

MAITRĪ: ⌜amhe vi catasso baïṇīo Viṇṇubhattīe āṇāe Vivea|siddhi|kālaṇaṃ mah"|appāṇam hiae vaṭṭamha.⌟ *(saṃskṛtam āśritya)* te hi—

FAITH: After that, thanks to the goddess, with her affection aroused by our cries of lament—

She looked with brows arched,
  a fierce red-eyed gaze,
  her face distorted by anger,
And fell to earth
  like a stone split from a cliff by lightning,
  her bones like some broken thing quaking.

LOVE: Luckily my dear friend is alive and well, like a deer 4.20
that's escaped from the jaws of a wild tiger! And then?

FAITH: Then the goddess, with her mind made up, said, "So does that villain, vile Magnus Nescience, disdain me. As that's how he acts, I'll annihilate him and his clan!" And the goddess then ordered me, "Go, Faith, and tell Intuition that efforts must be made in order to defeat Lust, Anger and the others. Dispassion will thereby be manifest. And I, at the appointed hour, impelled by Breath-control and the like, will rally your troops. The goddesses, too, Verity and the others, with the skill of Peace and such, will see to it that Wisdom will be begotten from the Lord's union with Lady Úpanishad." So, I am now stationed by Intuition. And what are you doing to pass the days?

LOVE: At Hail Vishnu's order, we four sisters, too, dwell in the hearts of the magnanimous to ensure Intuition's success. *(switching to Sanskrit)* They—

dhyāyanti māṃ sukhini, duḥkhini c' Ânukampāṃ,
puṇya|kriyeṣu Muditāṃ, ku|matāv Upekṣām.
evaṃ prasādam upayāti hi rāga|lobha|
dveṣ'|ādi|doṣa|kaluṣo 'py ayam antar|ātmā. [5]

evaṃ catasro 'pi bhaginyo vayaṃ tad|abhyudaya|kāraṇen' âiva vāsarān nayāmaḥ. kutr' êdānīṃ priya|sakhī mahā|rājam avalokayiṣyati?

4.25 ŚRADDHĀ: devy" âiv' êdam uktam: «asti Rāḍh"|âbhidhāno jana|padaḥ. tatra Bhāgīrathī|parisar'|âlaṃkāra|bhūte Cakratīrthe Mīmāṃs"|ânugatayā Matyā kathañ cid dhāryamāṇa|prāṇo, vyākulen' ântar|ātmanā Viveka Upaniṣad|devyāḥ saṃgam'|ârthaṃ tapasyat'» îti.

MAITRĪ: ⌈tā gacchaü pia|sahī! ahaṃ vi taṇ|ṇioaṃ aṇuciṭṭhāmi.⌋

ŚRADDHĀ: evaṃ bhavatu.

*iti niṣkrānte.*

*viṣkambhakaḥ.*

Contemplating me for the sake of the happy,
Mercy for them who sorrow,
Joy in good works,
and Equanimity towards those of ill-will,
The inner self may reach grace,
though it be tainted
by desire, greed, or hate,
among other ills.*

Hence, we four sisters also pass our days in the interest of his success. Where, dear friend, are you going to see the King now?

FAITH: The goddess said this: "There is a land called Radha. There, at the Shrine of the Wheel,* which adorns the shores of the Ganges, Intuition somehow hangs on to life thanks to Intelligence, who follows Hermeneutics,* and distressed in his inmost self, he practices austerities for the sake of union with Lady Úpanishad." 4.25

LOVE: So go there, dear friend! I am going to set about my own task as well.

FAITH: So be it.

*Exeunt ambo.*

*Thus the interlude.*

# ACT FOUR

# INTUITION'S ENDEAVOR

4.30 *tataḥ praviśati* RĀJĀ PRATĪHĀRĪ *ca.*

RĀJĀ: āḥ! pāpa Mahāmoha|hataka! sarvathā hatas tvay"|âyaṃ mahā|janaḥ. tathā hi—

śānte 'n|anta|mahimni nirmala|cid|ā-
nande taraṅg'|āvalī|
nirmukte 'mṛta|sāgar'|âmbhasi manāṅ
magno 'pi n' ācāmati,
niḥsāre mṛga|tṛṣṇik"|ârṇava|jale
śrānto 'pi mūḍhaḥ pibaty,
ācāmaty, avagāhate, 'bhiramate,
majjaty, ath' ônmajjati. [6]

atha vā saṃsāra|cakra|vāhakasya Mahāmohasy' â|bodho mūlam. tasya ca tattv'|âvabodhād eva nivṛttiḥ. yataḥ—

amuṣya saṃsāra|taror a|bodha|
mūlasya n' ônmūla|vināśanāya
Viśveśvar'|ārādhana|bīja|jātāt
tattv'|âvabodhād aparo 'bhyupāyaḥ. [7]

4.35 «prāyaḥ su|kṛtinām arthe
devā yānti sahāyatām,
a|panthānaṃ tu gacchantaṃ
s'|ôdaro 'pi vimuñcati.» [8]

iti tattva|vido vyāharanti. tathā ca devyā Viṣṇubhaktyā samādiṣṭam, «udyogaḥ kriyatām Kām'|ādi|vijaye. tad aham api bhavad|arthe gṛhīta|pakṣ" âiv'» êti. tatra Kāmas tā-

*Enter the* KING *and a female* GATEKEEPER. 4.30

KING: Oh! damn vile Magnus Nescience! You've oppressed the great folk in every respect. Thus—

Though immersed in waters of immortal elixir,
peaceful, of limitless power,
taintless spirit's bliss,
free from incessant waves,
the fools gulp not a drop of it,
But worn out though they be
in a vain mirage of the sea,
they drink, choke it down,
dive, swim, sink, and drown.

And the root is the unenlightenment of Magnus Nescience, the very motor of the wheel of *sansára*. It is from awakening to reality that he may be turned back. Hence—

To uproot once and forever *sansára*'s tree,
which in unknowing takes root,
But for awakening to reality,
seeded by faith in the Lord of the World,
there is no other way.

"The gods usually offer assistance 4.35
to aid those doing good,
But even a brother abandons
one who gets lost in the woods."*

So say those who know the reality of things. And hence the goddess Hail Vishnu ordained that "an effort must be made to gain victory over Lust and the others. I, too, for your sake have taken sides." Given this, then, the first of vat prathamo vīro Vastuvicāreṇ' âiva jīyate. tad bhavatu. tam eva tāvat tan|nirvijayāy' ādiśāmi. Vedavati! āhūyatāṃ Vastuvicāraḥ!

PRATĪHĀRĪ: ⌜jaṃ devo āṇavedi.⌟ *(iti niṣkramya* VASTUVICĀREṆA *saha praviśati.)*

VASTUVICĀRAḤ: aho! nirvicāra|saundary'|âbhimāna|vardhiṣṇunā Kāma|hatakena vañcitaṃ jagat. atha vā dur|ātmanā Mahāmohen' âiva! tathā hi—

«kānt"» êty, «utpala|locan"» êti, «vipula|
śroṇī|bhar"» êty, «unnamat|
pīn'|ôttuṅga|payodhar"» êti, «su|mukh'|â-
mbhoj"» êti, «su|bhrūr» iti—
dṛṣṭvā mādyati modate 'bhiramate
prastauti vidvān api
pratyakṣ'|â|śuci|putrikāṃ striyam. aho
Mohasya duś|ceṣṭitam! [9]

4.40 api ca yathā|vastu vicārayatām a|manda|matīnām api piśita|piṇḍ'|âvanaddh'|âsthi|pañjara|mayī svabhāva|durgandha|bībhatsa|veṣā nār" îti n' âsti vimatiḥ. tatra vispaṣṭa eva tāvad itara|guṇ'|âdhyāsaḥ. tathā hi—

muktā|hāra|latā, raṇan|maṇimayā
haimās tulā|koṭayo,
rāgaḥ kuṅkuma|saṃbhavaḥ, surabhayaḥ
pauṣpā vicitrāḥ srajaḥ,

their heros, Lust may be vanquished by Analyst. So be it. I'll order him to gain that victory. Veda-lady!* call the Analyst!

GATEKEEPER: As my lord commands. *(Exits, then enters with* ANALYST.*)*

ANALYST: Oh my! the world is deceived by that vile Lord Lust, who promotes beauty's thoughtless conceits. Or else by the nefarious Magnus Nescience himself! So—

"She's pretty," "eyes lotuses," "big booty,"
  "her breasts plump and perky,"
  "a lotus-face," "fine brows"—
All Nescience's evil designs!
For even the wise, beholding woman, visibly
    most impure,
  nonetheless go and lose their heads,
  delight and then frolic and purr.

And even among those who are not dimwits, who investi- 4.40
gate things as they are, there are still some who are not yet turned off by women, who are but frames of bone wrapped up in a mass of flesh, their very nature clothed in a loathsome stench.* In that case, it is evident that there has been a superimposition upon them of their apparent qualities. Just so—

Feeble-minded men regard women,
  through strings of pearls,
  jangling gems, golden anklets,
  saffronated rouge,
  perfumed flower wreaths,

vāsaś citra|dukūlam alpa|matibhir
nāryām aho kalpitam—
bāhy'|ântaḥ paripaśyatāṃ tu nirayaṃ
«nār"» îti nāmnā kṛtaṃ. [10]

*(ākāśe)* āḥ! pāpa Kāma|caṇḍāla! kim evam an|ālambanam ev' āvir|bhavatā bhavatā vyākulī|kriyate mahā|janaḥ? tathā hy ayam evaṃ manyate—

«bālā mām iyam icchat' îndu|vadanā,
s'|ānandam udvīkṣate,
nīl'|êndīvara|locanā mama parī-
rambhaṃ bhṛśaṃ vāñchati.» [11*ab*]

are mūḍha!

4.45 kā tvām icchati? kā ca paśyati? paśo!
māṃs'|âsthibhir nirmitā
nārī veda na kiṃ cid atra, sa punaḥ
paśyaty a|mūrtaḥ Pumān. [11*cd*]

PRATĪHĀRĪ: ⌈ido ido edu mahā|bhāo!⌋ *(ity ubhau parikrāmataḥ.)* ⌈eso mahā|rāo ciṭṭhadi. tā uvasappadu bhavam.⌋

VASTUVICĀRAḤ *(upasṛtya)*: jayatu, jayatu devaḥ! eṣa Vastuvicāraḥ praṇamati.

RĀJĀ: ih' ôpaviśyatām.

VASTUVICĀRAḤ *(upaviśya)*: deva, eṣa te kiṅkaraḥ saṃprāptaḥ. tad ājñay" ânugṛhyatām!

4.50 RĀJĀ: Mahāmohena sah' âsmākaṃ saṃpravṛttaḥ saṅgrāmaḥ. tad atra Kāmas tasya prathamo vīraḥ. tasya ca prativīratay" âsmābhir bhavān eva nirūpitaḥ.

and patterned linen robes—
But for those who see what's outside and in,
it's only hell that is compelled
by the one called "woman."

*(to the heavens)* Oh! you damn outcaste Lust! For just what objective do you manifestly disturb everyone? This is the sort of thing they get into their heads—

"This girl wants me,
her moon-face joyful as she looks me over,
Her eyes blue lotuses,
her desire intense to embrace me."

But look here, stupid!

Just who wants you? Who sees you? 4.45
Idiot! She's made up of flesh and bone.
Woman here knows nothing at all,
for who sees is the incorporeal Man alone.*

GATEKEEPER: Come this way, good sir! *(The two walk about.)* The King is here seated. You may approach, sir.

ANALYST *(approaching)*: Victory, victory, lord! This Analyst salutes you.

KING: Sit down over here.

ANALYST *(sitting)*: Lord, I am here as your factotum. Favor me with your command!

KING: We have gone to war with Magnus Nescience. Their first hero is Lust. We thought of you, sir, as a suitable opponent to him. 4.50

VASTUVICĀRAḤ: dhanyo 'smi, yena svāmin" âham evaṃ saṃbhāvitaḥ.

RĀJĀ: atha kayā śāstra|vidyayā bhavān Kāmaṃ jeṣyati?

VASTUVICĀRAḤ: āḥ! pañca|śaraḥ kusuma|dhanvā jetavya, ity atr' âpi śāstra|grahaṇ'|âpekṣā. paśya—

dṛḍhataram apidhāya
dvāram ārāt kathaṅ cit,
smaraṇa|viparivṛttau
darśane yoṣitām vā,
pariṇati|virasatvaṃ
deha|bībhatsatāṃ vā
pratipadam anucinty' ônmūlayiṣyāmi Kāmam. [12]

4.55 RĀJĀ: sādhu, sādhu.

VASTUVICĀRAḤ: api ca—

vipula|pulināḥ kallolinyo,
nirantara|nirjharī|
masṛṇita|śilāḥ śailāḥ, sāndra|
drumā vana|rājayaḥ,
yadi śama|giro Vaiyāsikyo,
budhaiś ca samāgamaḥ—
kva piśita|vasā|mayyo nāryas?
tadā kva ca Manmathaḥ? [13]

ANALYST: I am fortunate that my master has regarded me so.

KING: And by what martial art will you, sir, vanquish Lust?

ANALYST: Ah! the five arrowed one with the flower bow* is to be defeated, and this depends on the choice of weapons. Look—

When you're scoping the ladies,
and memories of them breed fancies,
somehow, firmly and quickly,
having shut that door,
You must reflect at each step
that changes end in satiation,
their bodies bring trepidation;
Thus I'll uproot Cupidon!

KING: So far, so good. 4.55

ANALYST: And—

Densely forested mountains,
stones smoothed by ceaseless cascades,
rivers with broad, sandy shores,
The calming words of sage Vyasa,*
the assembly of the wise—
Where's there a place among them for women,
formed of flesh and blood?
And where is there a place here
for mind-maddening Lord Lust?

«nār"» îti nāma prathamam astraṃ Kāmasya. tena tasyāṃ jitāyāṃ tat|sahāyāḥ sarva eva viphal'|ārambhā bhaṅgam āsādayiṣyanti. tathā hi—

candraś, candanam, indu|dhāma|dhavalā
rātryo, dvi|reph'|āvalī|
jhaṅkār'|ônmukharā vilāsa|vipin'|ô-
pāntā, vasant'|ôdayaḥ,
mandra|dhvāna|ghan'|ôdayāś ca divasā,
mandāḥ kadamb'|ânilāḥ—
śṛṅgāra|pramukhāś ca Kāma|suhṛdo
nāryāṃ jitāyāṃ jitāḥ. [14]

4.60 tad alam ativilambena. ādiśatu svāmī.

so 'haṃ prakīrṇaiḥ parito vicāraiḥ
śarair iv' ônmathya balaṃ pareṣām,
sainyaṃ Kurūṇām iva Sindhu|rājaṃ
Gāṇḍīva|dhanv" êva nihanmi Kāmam. [15]

RĀJĀ: tat sajjī|bhavatu bhavāñ śatru|vijayāya!

What's called "woman" is Lust's first weapon. So when she is conquered, all his allies, their undertakings fruitless, find only defeat. Hence—

The moon, sandal perfume,
a night beautified by moonlight,
echoing with the hum
of swarms of bees,
Playful wooded precincts
in early spring,
Languid days,
clouds starting to tremble with thunder,
in the *kadam*-grove a fresh breeze—
When one defeats woman,
these, Lust's friends,
leaders in romance,
all fall as well in defeat.

But enough of my running on. Tell me your order, master. 4.60

I, who by reasoned arguments all around,
have overturned others' forces,
as if with volleys of arrows,
So too do slay Lord Lust,
as once was done to the Kurus' army
and to the Sindhu-king
by the master of the Gandíva bow.*

KING: Then ready yourself, sir, to vanquish the enemy!

VASTUVICĀRAḤ: yad ādiśati devaḥ. *(iti niṣkrāntaḥ.)*

RĀJĀ: Vedavati! Krodhasya vijayāya Kṣam" āhūyatām!

4.65 PRATĪHĀRĪ: ⌜jaṃ devo āṇavedi.⌟ *(iti niṣkramya* KṢAMAYĀ *saha praviśati.)*

KṢAMĀ:

krodh'|ândhakāra|vikaṭa|bhru|kuṭī|taraṅga|
bhīmasya sāndhya|kiraṇ'|âruṇa|ghora|dṛṣṭeḥ
niṣkampa|nirmala|gabhīra|payodhi|dhīrā
dhīrāḥ parasya parivāda|giraḥ kṣamante. [16]

*(sa|ślāgham ātmānaṃ nirvarṇya)* aho! aham...

klamo na vācāṃ, śiraso na śūlaṃ,
na citta|tāpo, na tanor vimardaḥ,
na cāpi Hiṃs"|ādir an|artha|yogaḥ—
ślāghyā paraṃ Krodha|jaye 'ham ekā. [17]

*ity ubhe parikrāmataḥ.*

4.70 PRATĪHĀRĪ: ⌜eso devo. uvasappatu pia|sahī.⌟

ANALYST: As my lord commands. *(Exits.)*

KING: Veda-lady! Call Patience for the conquest of Anger!

GATEKEEPER: As my lord commands. *(Exits and then enters with* PATIENCE.*)* 4.65

PATIENCE:

The wise forbear hateful words from their foes—
  fierce gaze, sunset red,
  pure terror;
  brows bent in anger,
  waves in the darkness—
As if they were tranquil oceans,
  unmoving, clear, fathomless.

*(describing herself proudly)* Oh! and I...

I alone am to be praised
  for conquering Anger,
  without wasted efforts:
  no strain to the voice,
  no ache to the head,
  no distress to the mind,
  no bodily combat,
  no Harm and all that.

*The two walk about.*

GATEKEEPER: Here is our lord. Do approach him, dear friend. 4.70

KṢAMĀ *(upasṛtya)*: jayatu, jayatu devaḥ! eṣā devasya dāsī Kṣamā s'|âṣṭ'|âṅgaṃ praṇamati.

RĀJĀ: Kṣame, atr' ôpaviśyatām.

KṢAMĀ *(upaviśya)*: ājñāpayatu devaḥ. kim|artham āhūto dāsa|janaḥ?

RĀJĀ: Kṣame, asmin saṅgrāme dur|ātmā Krodhas tvayā jetavyaḥ.

4.75 KṢAMĀ: devasy' ânugrahān Mahāmoham api jetuṃ paryāpt" âsmi; kiṃ punaḥ Krodhaṃ tanu|cara|mātram? tad aham a|cirād eva ...

taṃ pāpa|kāriṇam a|kāraṇa|bādhitāraṃ
svādhyāya|deva|pitṛ|yajña|tapaḥ|kriyāṇām,
Krodhaṃ sphuliṅgam iva dṛṣṭibhir udvamantaṃ
Kātyāyan" îva mahiṣaṃ vinivārya hanmi. [18]

RĀJĀ: Kṣame, śṛṇumas tāvat Krodha|vijay'|ôpāyam.

KṢAMĀ: deva, vijñāpayāmi.

«kruddhe—smera|mukh'|âvadhīraṇam,
ath' āviṣṭe—prasāda|kramo,
vyākrośe—kuśal'|ôktir, ātma|durit'|ôc-
ched'|ôtsavas—tāḍane.
dhig! jantor a|jit'|ātmano 'sya mahatī
daivād upetā vipad

PATIENCE *(approaching)*: Victory, victory, lord! I, my lord's slave Patience, salute you with eight points prostrate.

KING: Patience, sit over here.

PATIENCE *(sitting)*: As my lord commands. For what reason have you summoned this slave?

KING: In this combat, Patience, it is you who must defeat that scoundrel Anger.

PATIENCE: Given the order of my lord, I am up to vanquishing even Magnus Nescience; how much more his toady Anger? So before long I ... 4.75

Anger, that sinner,
who gratuitously destroys
holy tradition, gods, ancestors,
sacrifice, ascesis and rites,
and spits out sparks with his glances—
As Durga did the buffalo-demon,*
so will I slaughter him.

KING: Patience, let us hear, then, the means by which Anger is conquered.

PATIENCE: I shall explain, my lord.

"Before vexation—disregard with a bright smile,
Before fury—a gracious aspect,
Before rage—soothing speech,
Before violence—I delight in my own evil's end.
For, alas! the creature whose self is out of control
is fated to great and certain ruin."

durvār"» êti dayā|ras'|ârdra|manasaḥ,
Krodhasya kutr' ôdayaḥ? [19]

4.80 RĀJĀ: sādhu, sādhu.

KṢAMĀ: deva, Krodhasya vijayād eva tad|anuyāyino 'pi Hiṃsā|Pāruṣya|Māna|Mātsary'|ādayo vijitā eva bhaviṣyanti.

RĀJĀ: tat pratiṣṭhatāṃ bhavatī vijayāya.

KṢAMĀ: yad ājñāpayati devaḥ. *(iti niṣkrāntā.)*

RĀJĀ *(*PRATĪHĀRĪṂ *prati)*: Vedavati! āhūyatāṃ Lobhasya jetā Santoṣaḥ!

4.85 PRATĪHĀRĪ: ⌜jaṃ devo āṇavedi⌟ *(iti niṣkramya* SANTOṢEṆA *saha praviśati.)*

SANTOṢAḤ *(vicintya, s'|ânukrośam)*:

phalaṃ sv'|êcchā|labhyaṃ
prativanam a|khedaṃ kṣiti|ruhāṃ,
payaḥ sthāne sthāne
śiśira|madhuraṃ puṇya|saritām,
mṛdu|sparśā śayyā
su|lalita|latā|pallava|mayī,
sahante santāpaṃ
tad api dhaninām dvāri kṛpaṇāḥ. [20]

With such a thought, made moist by love,
Where can Anger come to live?

KING: Excellent, excellent.

PATIENCE: My lord, from the conquest of Anger, too, his camp-followers Harm, Abuse, Pride, Envy and more will be conquered.

KING: So, honored lady, set upon their conquest.

PATIENCE: As my lord commands. *(Exits.)*

KING *(to the* GATEKEEPER*)*: Veda-lady! Call in Greed's conqueror Contentment!

GATEKEEPER: As my lord commands. *(Exits, then enters with* CONTENTMENT.*)*

CONTENTMENT *(thinking, compassionately)*:

Fruits are there for the taking
from trees in every grove
effortlessly,
Water cool and sweet
from sacred streams flows
everywhere,
Soft are the beds
made from tender shoots
of pleasing vines,
And all the while the poor
afflictions endure
at rich men's doors.

*(ākāśe)* are mūrkha! dur|ucchedaḥ khalv ayaṃ bhavato vyā-mohaḥ. tathā hi—

samārambhā bhagnāḥ
kati kati na vārāṃs tava paśoḥ,
pipāsos tucche 'smin
draviṇa|mṛga|tṛṣṇ"|ârṇava|jale?
tath" âpi pratyāśā
viramati na te? n' âpi śatadhā
vidīrṇaṃ yac ceto,
niyatam aśani|grāva|ghaṭitam? [21]

4.90 idaṃ ca te lobh'|ândhasya ceṣṭitaṃ cetasi camat|kāram ātan-oti! yataḥ—

«lapsye, labdham idaṃ ca, labhyam adhikaṃ;
tan|mūla|labhyaṃ, tato
labhyaṃ c' âparam.» ity an|āratam aho
labhyaṃ dhanaṃ dhyāyasi,
n' âitad vetsi: punar bhavantam a|cirād
Āśā|piśācī balāt
sarva|grāsam iyaṃ grasiṣyati mahā|
lobh'|ândhakāra|vṛtam. [22]

api ca—

*(facing heaven)* O you fool! Your muddle is really hard to stop. So—

How many times have not your plans been
shattered, beast,
as you seek to drink
wealth's wretched waters
from a mirage?
Have not your hopes yet come to an end?
Is not your heart,
thus broken a hundredfold,
truly made of stone?

The effect that you have on the mind of one blind with 4.90
greed is truly astounding! For—

"I will get, this is gotten,
and that's to be gotten as well;
then capital must be gotten
so that something more can be had."
Though thus you think ceaselessly
on riches to be acquired,
here's what you do not know:
this demon Hope will soon by force
devour all her mouth can hold,
including you, who lie within
great greed's darkest folds.

Moreover—

dhanaṃ tāval labdhaṃ,
katham api tath" âpy asya niyato
vyayo vā nāśo vā;
tava sati viyogo 'sty ubhayathā.
an|utpādaḥ śreyān
kim u, kathaya, pathyo 'tha vilayo?
vināśo labdhasya
vyathayatitarāṃ; na tv an|udayaḥ. [23]

kiñ ca—

4.95 mṛtyur nṛtyati mūrdhni, śaśvad uragī
ghorā jarā|rūpiṇī
tvām eṣā grasate, parigrahamayair
gṛdhrair jagad grasyate.
dhūtvā bodha|jalair a|bodha|bahulaṃ
tal|lobha|janyaṃ rajaḥ,
santoṣ'|âmṛta|sāgar'|âmbhasi punar
magnaḥ sukhaṃ jīvati. [24]

PRATĪHĀRĪ: ⌜eso sāmi. tā uvasappatu mahā|bhāo!⌟

SANTOṢAḤ *(tathā kṛtvā)*: jayatu, jayatu svāmī! eṣa Santoṣaḥ praṇamati!

RĀJĀ: ih' ôpaviśyatām. *(iti sva|sannidhāv upaveśayati.)*

SANTOṢAḤ *(sa|vinayam upaviśya)*: eṣa preṣya|janaḥ. ājñāpyatāṃ devena.

4.100 RĀJĀ: vidita|prabhāvo bhavān, tad alam ativilambena. Lobhaṃ jetuṃ Vārāṇasīṃ prati pratiṣṭhatām.

The wealth that you've somehow obtained
will be lost, for sure,
whether by decline or by destruction;
either way, what's yours is gone.
Say! were it better that it never arose,
or more beneficial that it goes?
The loss of what's gained
brings much pain;
not so what one never knows.

And—

Death ever dances on your head, 4.95
the horrid snake old-age swallows you whole,
while that vulture, family, gobbles the world.
Having washed with wisdom's spring
dust born of greed, packed in unknowing,
One lives in joy if immersed anew
in Contentment's ambrosia sea.

GATEKEEPER: This is the master. You may approach him, good sir!

CONTENTMENT *(does so.)*: Victory, victory, master! I, Contentment, salute you!

KING: Sit down here. *(Offering a seat next to himself.)*

CONTENTMENT *(politely taking his seat)*: I am at your disposal. May my lord issue his command.

KING: Your power, sir, is known, so we need not tarry with 4.100
formalities. Position yourself in Varánasi for the defeat of Greed.

SANTOṢAḤ: yad ājñāpayati devaḥ. so 'ham—

nānā|mukhaṃ vijayinaṃ jagatāṃ trayāṇāṃ
deva|dvi|jāti|vadha|bandhana|labdha|vṛddhim,
rakṣo|'dhinātham iva Dāśarathiḥ prasahya
nirjitya Lobham a|vaśaṃ tarasā pinaṣmi. [25]

*iti niṣkrāntaḥ.*

*tataḥ praviśati vinīta|veṣaḥ* PURUṢAḤ.

4.105 PURUSAḤ: deva, saṃbhṛtāni vijaya|prayāṇa|maṅgalāni, pratyāsannaś ca mauhūrtikā|veditaḥ prasthāna|samayaḥ.

RĀJĀ: yady evaṃ, senā|prasthāpanāy' ādiśyantāṃ senā|patayaḥ.

PURUSAḤ: yad ājñāpayati devaḥ. *(iti niṣkrāntaḥ.)*

NEPATHYE: bho, bhoḥ! sainikāḥ!

sajjyantāṃ kumbha|bhitti|
cyuta|mada|madirā|matta|bhṛṅgāḥ kar'|îndrā!
yujyantāṃ syandaneṣu
prasabha|jita|maruc|caṇḍa|vegās turaṅgāḥ!
kuntair nīl'|ôtpalānāṃ
vanam iva kakubhām antarāle sṛjantaḥ
pādātāḥ saṃcarantu,
prasabham asi|lasat|pāṇayo 'py aśva|vārāḥ. [26]

CONTENTMENT: As my lord commands. As for me—

Hard and fast will I defeat
powerless Greed, pulverize him,
As Ten Chariot's son did the demons' lord,*
the many-faced conqueror of the three worlds,
who obtained success by the murder and capture
of the gods as well as the brahmins.

*Exit.*

*Enters a* PERSON *in plain dress.*

PERSON: My lord, the auspices conducing to victory are in place, and the hour of action, as forecast by the astrologers, approaches. 4.105

KING: If it be so, then issue the order to the generals that the army set out.

PERSON: As my lord commands. *(Exit.)*

OFFSTAGE: Hey, hey! Soldiers!

Harness the royal elephants—
the spirits spilt from their brows
are liquor that maddens the bees!
Let chariots be joined to their steeds,
quite tame but fast as a fierce cyclone!
And may the infantry march in formation,
lances poised in all directions,
like a garden of lotuses,
While the men of the cavalry
brandish swords glinting in their hands.

4.110 RĀJĀ: bhavatu! kṛta|maṅgalāḥ pratiṣṭhāmahe. *(*PĀRIPĀRŚVAKAṂ *prati)* sārathir ādiśyatām, «sāṅgrāmikaṃ rathaṃ sajjī|kṛty' ôpanay'» êti.

PĀRIPĀRŚVAKAḤ: yad ājñāpayati devaḥ. *(iti niṣkrāntaḥ.)*

*tataḥ praviśati yath"|ôktaṃ ratham ādāya* SĀRATHIḤ.

SĀRATHIḤ: deva! sajjī|kṛto rathaḥ. tad ārohatv āyuṣmān.

RĀJĀ *kṛta|maṅgala|vidhir ārohaṇaṃ nāṭayati.*

4.115 SĀRATHIḤ *(ratha|vegaṃ nirūpayan)*: āyuṣman, paśya, paśya—

uddhūta|pāṃsu|paṭal'|ânumita|prabandha|
 dhāvat|khur'|âgra|caya|cumbita|bhūmi|bhāgāḥ,
nirmathyamāna|jaladhi|dhvani|ghora|heṣam
 ete rathaṃ gagana|sīmni vahanti vāhāḥ. [27]

iyaṃ ca n' âtidūre darśana|patham avatīrṇā tri|bhuvana|pāvanī Vārāṇasī nagarī.

amī dhārā|yantra|
 skhalita|jala|jhaṅkāra|mukharā,
vibhāvyante bhūyaḥ
 śaśi|kara|rucaḥ saudha|śikharāḥ,
vicitrā yatr' ôccaiḥ
 śarad|amala|megh'|ânta|vilasat|
taḍil|lekhā|lakṣmīṃ
 vitarati patāk'|āvalir iyam. [28]

KING: So be it! We set out having performed the auspicious rites. *(to his* ATTENDANT*)* Tell the charioteer to ready a battle-car and bring it here. 4.110

ATTENDANT: As my lord commands. *(Exit.)*

*Enters the* CHARIOTEER *with the car as described.*

CHARIOTEER: My lord! this chariot has been readied. You may mount, long-living master.

*The* KING, *having performed an auspicious rite, acts as if mounting the chariot.*

CHARIOTEER *(demonstrating the speed of the car)*: Look, long-living master, look— 4.115

These horses—
earth stroked by their stampeding hooves,
coursing continuously,
as from the dust-clouds we infer—
Guide our chariot to the ends of space;
neighing fearsomely,
resounding like the ocean's boiling waves.

And this, not too far off, just coming into view, is the city of Varánasi, purifying the three worlds:

Numbers of palace spires may be seen,
brightened by moonbeams and humming,
fountain-sprayed waters murmuring.
A row of flags is unfurled high upon them,
splendid like streaks of lightning
dancing at the edges
of autumn's white clouds.

etāś ca prati|mukula|lagna|madhup'|āvalī|raṇita|mukharā, jṛmbh'|ārambha|vigalan|makaranda|bindu|durdināḥ, kusuma|surabhayo n' âtidūre śyāmāyamāna|ghana|cchada|cchāyā|taravo nagara|paryant'|âraṇya|bhūmayaḥ. yatr' âite maruto 'pi gṛhīta|Pāśupata|vratā dhūlim uddhūlayantas tāpasā iva lakṣyante. tathā hi—

4.120 toy'|ārdrāḥ sura|saritaḥ, sitāḥ parāgair,
arcantaś cyuta|kusumair iv' êndu|maulim,
prodgītāṃ madhupa|rutaiḥ stutiṃ paṭhanto—
nṛtyanti pracala|latā|bhujaiḥ samīrāḥ. [29]

RĀJĀ *(s'|ānandam ālokya)*:

eṣ" ântar|dadhatī tamo|vighaṭanād
ānandam Ātma|prabhaṃ,
cetaḥ karṣati candra|cūḍa|vasatir
Vidy" êva mukteḥ padam.
bhūmeḥ kaṇṭha|vilambin" îva kuṭilā
mukt'|āvalir Jāhnavī,
yatr' âivaṃ hasat' îva phena|paṭalair
vakrāṃ kalām aindavīm. [30]

And here, not far, are forest lands surrounding the city, where each bud vibrates with the hum of the bees attached to it and a shower of pollen-nectar falls from the abundance of fresh blossoms, there are floral perfumes and the shade-trees are so thick with leaves that they blacken the earth. There, even the winds have assumed the vows of the Páshupatas, for, you'll observe, they scatter the dust as do the ascetics.* Thus—

Moistened by the waters of the river divine, 4.120
whitened with pollen-grains,
lauding the moon-crested god with flowers
that fall,
chanting melodious hymns through the drone
of the bees—
Thus do the winds dance,
waving the vines
as if they were arms.

KING *(looking joyfully)*:

Igniting the Self's blissful light within,
after the darkness is vanquished,
This dwelling of the moon-crested god,
like Scientia,*
draws the mind right up to the point of freedom.
The Ganges winds like a string of pearls
hanging on the neck of the earth,
bent like the lunar crescent,
laughing with billows of froth.

SŪTAḤ *(parikramya)*: āyuṣman, paśya, paśya! tad idaṃ sura|sarit|parisar'|âlaṃkāra|bhūtaṃ bhagavataḥ pāvanam an|āder ādi|Keśavasya Viṣṇor āyatanam.

RĀJĀ *(sa|harṣam)*: are!

4.125 eṣa devaḥ purā|vidbhiḥ
  kṣetrasy' ātm" êti gīyate,
atra dehaṃ samutsṛjya
  puṇya|bhājo viśanti yam. [31]

SŪTAḤ: āyuṣman, paśya, paśya! ete tāvat Kāma|Krodha|Lobh'|ādayo 'smad|darśana|mātrād ev' êto deśād dūram atikrāmanti!

RĀJĀ: evam etat! tad bhavatu. sv'|âbhīṣṭa|siddhaye bhagavantaṃ namasyāmaḥ. *(rathād avatīrya, praviśy', âvalokya ca)* jaya, jaya, bhagavan!

amara|caya|camū|cakra|cūḍā|maṇi|śreṇi|nīrājit'|ôpānta|pāda|dvay'|âmbhoja! rājan|nakha|dyota|kirmīrita|svarṇa|pīṭha! sphurad|dvaita|vibhrānti|santāna|santāpa|santapta|vandāru|saṃsāra|nidr"|âpahār'|âika|dakṣa! kṣamā|maṇḍal'|ôddhāra|saṃhāra|saṃghaṭṭa|saṃghṛṣṭa|daṃṣṭr'|âgra|koṭi|sphurac|chaila|cakra! kram'|ākrānta|loka|traya!

CHARIOTEER *(walking about)*: Look, my long-living lord, look! Over here, adorning the banks of the sacred river, is the shrine of the Blessed Lord Vishnu as the beginningless Primordial Késhava.*

KING *(joyfully)*: Oh indeed!

This divinity was praised by past seers 4.125
as the very soul of this realm;
Sloughing off the body here,
the meritorious are united with him.

CHARIOTEER: Look, my long-living lord, look! There they are—Lust, Anger, Greed and the others—at just the sight of us they're fleeing this land!

KING: So it is! So be it. We'll salute the Blessed Lord for the accomplishment of our wish! *(Descending from the chariot, he makes an entrance, looking about.)* Victory, victory, O Blessed Lord!

Your two lotus feet are suffused with the radiance of the array of gems crowning the immortals' assembled martial host! your golden footrest sparkles with the sunlight of your shining nails! you alone have the skill to awaken from *sansára*'s slumbers your praise-singers who are continually afflicted with the fever of dualism's manifest confusions! your tusk-tips* shine like mountain ranges pressed tightly together as supports upholding the round earth! your steps have traversed the three realms!*

prabala|bhuja|bal'|ôddhūta|Govardhana|cchatra|nirvārit'|Ākhaṇḍal'|ôdyojit'|âkāṇḍa|caṇḍ'|âmbu|vāh'|âtivarṣa|trasad|gokula|trāṇa|vismāpit'|âśeṣa|viśva|prabho!

vibudha|ripu|vadhū|varga|sīmanta|sindūra|sandhyā|mayūkha|cchaṭ'|ônmārjan'|ôddāma|dhām'|âdhipa! trasta|daity'|êndra|vakṣas|taṭī|pāṭan'|âkuṇṭha|bhāsvan|nakha|śreṇi|pāṇi|dvaya|srasta|vistāri|rakt'|ârṇav'|āmagna|loka|traya!

tri|bhuvana|ripu|Kaiṭabh'|ôddaṇḍa|kaṇṭh'|âsthi|kūṭa|sphuṭ'|ônmārjit'|ôdātta|cakra|sphuraj|jyotir|ulkā|śat'|ôḍḍāmar'|ôddaṇḍa! khaṇḍ'|êndu|cūḍa|priya! prauḍha|dor|daṇḍa|vibhrānta|Manthācala|kṣubdha|dugdh'|âmbudhi|protthita|Śrī|bhujā|vallarī|saṃśleṣa|saṃkrānta|pīna|stan'|ābhoga|patr'|āvalī|lāñchit'|ôraḥ|sthala! sthūla|muktā|phal'|ôttāra|hāra|prabhā|maṇḍala|prasphurat|kaṇṭha! Vaikuṇṭha! bhaktasya lokasya saṃsāra|moha|cchidaṃ dehi bodh'|ôdayaṃ deva! tubhyaṃ namaḥ! [32]

You are the lord of the whole world that you amazed by protecting the cowherds, terrified as they were by torrential rains falling from unseasonal, ominous clouds conjured up by mountain-splitting Indra, for you sheltered them by raising aloft with the force of your powerful arms the Go·várdhana mountain as an umbrella!*

You are the sovereign whose majestic luster eclipses twilight's rays, vermilion like the parted hair of the wives of the gods' rivals!* you submerged the three realms in the ocean of blood dripping plentifully from your two hands, the rows of glowing nails still sharp after tearing through the chest of the terrified lord of the demons!*

Your mighty arms were as splendid as a meteor shower reflecting the light glinting off your great discus after it was wiped clean by the piled vertebrae in the stout neck of Káitabha, enemy of the three realms!* O you who are beloved of the crescent-moon-crowned!* your chest is marked with red lines where pressed by swelling eager breasts, tightly embraced as you were in the tendril arms of goddess Glory after she emerged from the ocean of milk churned by the stout staffs of your arms shaking Mount Mándara!* and your throat gleams with a halo of light from magnificent necklaces of fat pearls! O Vaikúntha!* grant to all your devotees dawning awareness, cutting through *sansára*'s nescience! O god! Salutation to you!*

*(nirgamanaṃ nāṭayitvā vilokya ca)* sādhur ayam ev' âsmākaṃ nivās'|ôcito deśaḥ. tad atr' âiva skandh'|āvāraṃ niveśayāmaḥ.

4.130 *iti niṣkrāntau.*

*iti śrī|Kṛṣṇamiśra|viracite Prabodhacandrodaya|nāmni nāṭake Vivek'|ôdyogo nāma caturtho 'ṅkaḥ.*

*(Acts out his departure while looking about.)* 'Tis good, this land is fit for our dwelling. We shall establish our royal capital right here.

*Exeunt ambo.* 4.130

*Thus concludes Act Four, entitled 'Intuition's Endeavor,'**
*in "The Rise of Wisdom Moon," composed by*
*the eminent Krishna·mishra·yati.*

# PROLOGUE TO ACT FIVE

5.1 *tataḥ praviśati* ŚRADDHĀ.

ŚRADDHĀ *(vicintya)*: prasiddhaḥ khalv ayaṃ panthāḥ. yataḥ—

nirdahati kulam a|śeṣaṃ
jñātīnāṃ vaira|saṃbhavaḥ krodhaḥ,
vanam iva ghana|pavan'|āhata|
taru|vara|saṅghaṭṭa|saṃbhavo dahanaḥ. [1]

*(s'|âsram)* aho! dur|vāro dāruṇaḥ s'|ôdara|vyasana|janmā śok'|ânalaḥ, yo Viveka|jala|dhārā|śatair api na mandī|kriyate! tathā hi—

5.5 dhruvaṃ dhvaṃso bhāvī
jala|nidhi|mahī|śaila|saritām;
ato mṛtyoḥ śīryat|
tṛṇa|laghuṣu kā jantuṣu kathā?
tath" âpy uccair bandhu|
vyasana|janitaḥ ko 'pi viṣamo,
Viveka|pronmāthī
dahati hṛdayaṃ śoka|dahanaḥ. [2]

yena tathā krūra|prakṛtiṣv api bhrātṛṣu Kāma|Krodh'|ādiṣu, kathā|śeṣatāṃ gateṣu

nikṛntat' îva marmāṇi,
dehaṃ śoṣayat' îva me,
dahat' îv'|ântar|ātmānaṃ
krūraḥ śok'|âgnir ucchikhaḥ. [3]

*Enter* FAITH. 5.1

FAITH *(thoughtfully)*: This path is well known. For,

> By anger born of rivalry
> scorched is our entire consanguine clan,
> Like a forest by a blaze
> set by friction of the trees
> swayed by a stormy breeze.

*(crying)* Oh! the terrible fire of grief born from sibling-troubles is hard to control; not even a hundred rain-clouds of Intuition can assuage it! Just so—

> Oceans, earth, hills and streams 5.5
> will certainly disappear;
> What's left to say now of death
> among creatures light as wilting hay?
> Too much, then, this assault on Intuition,
> trouble sprung from crimes among relations,
> This conflagration of sorrow
> that burns my heart.

For even brothers such as Lust and Anger, though they were by nature cruel, have vanished but for the memory.

> The cruel flames of sorrow's blaze
> seem to cut my intestines;
> They desiccate my body
> and scorch my inner soul.

*(vicintya)* ādiṣṭ" âsmi devyā Viṣṇubhaktyā, yathā: «vatse Śraddhe! aham atra Hiṃsā|prāya|samara|darśana|parāṅ-mukhī. tena Vārāṇasīm utsṛjya, Śālagrām'|âbhidhāne bhagavataḥ kṣetre kañ cit kālam ativāhayāmi. tvaṃ tu yathā|vṛttam samara|vṛttāntam āgatya me nivedayiṣyas'» îti. tad ahaṃ devyāḥ sakāśaṃ gatvā sarvam etat samara|vṛttāntam āvedayāmi. *(parikramy' âvalokya ca)* etac Cakratīrtham, yatr' âsau saṃsāra|sāgar'|ôttāra|taraṇi|karṇa|dhāro bhagavān Hariḥ svayaṃ prativasati. *(praṇamya)* iyaṃ ca mahā|munibhir upāsyamānā bhagavatī Viṣṇu-bhaktiḥ Śāntyā saha kim api mantrayate. yāvad upasar-pāmi. *(iti parikrāmati.)*

*tataḥ praviśati* VIṢṆUBHAKTIḤ ŚĀNTIŚ *ca.*

5.10 ŚĀNTIḤ: devi! prabala|cint"|ākula|hṛdayām iva bhavatīm ālokayāmi.

VIṢṆUBHAKTIḤ: vatse, etasmin vīra|vara|kṣaye mahati sām-parāye jāte na jānāmi balavatā Mahāmohen' âbhiyukta-sya vatsa|Vivekasya kīdṛśo vṛttānta iti. tena duḥ|sthitam iva me hṛdayam.

ŚĀNTIḤ: kim atra vicintyate? nanu bhagavatī cet kṛt'|ânu-grahā, tan niyatam eva rājño Vivekasya vijaya. iti jānāmi!

*(thoughtfully)* I have been given this order by goddess Hail Vishnu: "Faith, my child! I am here numbed by the sight of the battle with Lady Harm, above all. So, having relinquished Varánasi, I'll bide my time for a while at a place called Saltreetown* in the fields of the Lord. You, then, will come and inform me of the news of the battle just as it transpired." Therefore, I am going to the goddess, to tell her of all that has happened in the battle. *(walking about, looking around)* This is the Shrine of the Wheel,* where Lord Vishnu, the helmsman* of the craft plying over *sansára*'s ocean, himself dwells. *(bowing)* And here is the blessed lady Hail Vishnu, attended by the great sages, and taking some counsel with Peace. I'll just approach. *(She walks about.)*

*Then* HAIL VISHNU *enters with* PEACE.

PEACE: Goddess! It appears to me that your heart, my lady, is distraught with grave concerns. 5.10

HAIL VISHNU: My child, in this great battle that has become a holocaust of real heroes I do not know the tidings of my darling Intuition, engaged in combat with the mighty Magnus Nescience. Hence, my heart is ill at ease.

PEACE: What's there to worry about? If you, blessed lady, have extended your grace, then the victory of King Intuition is certain. I just know it!

VIṢṆUBHAKTIḤ: vatse—

yady apy abhyudayaḥ prāyaḥ
  pramāṇād avadhāryate,
kāmaṃ tath" âpi suhṛdām
  an|iṣṭ'|āśaṅki mānasam. [4]

viśeṣataś ca, Śraddhāyāś ciram an|āgamanaṃ manasi saṃdehaṃ āpādayati.

ŚRADDHĀ *(upasṛtya)*: bhagavati, praṇamāmi!

VIṢṆUBHAKTIḤ: Śraddhe, sv|āgatam!

ŚRADDHĀ: devyāḥ prasādena!

ŚĀNTIḤ: amba! praṇamāmi!

ŚRADDHĀ: putri, māṃ pariṣvajasva!

ŚĀNTIḤ *tathā karoti.*

ŚRADDHĀ: vatse, devyā Viṣṇubhakteḥ prasādān muni|jana|cetaḥ|padaṃ prāpnuhi!

VIṢṆUBHAKTIḤ: atha tatra kiṃ vṛttam?

ŚRADDHĀ: yad devyāḥ prātikūlyam ācaratām ucitam!

HAIL VISHNU: My child—

> Though one may be sure of success
> through reasoned inference,
> Still, for one's loves, the heart does fear
> an adverse consequence.

Above all, as Faith's arrival has taken so long, it puts doubts in my mind. 5.15

FAITH *(approaching)*: I salute you, blessed lady!

HAIL VISHNU: Welcome, Faith!

FAITH: By the goddess's grace!

PEACE: I salute you, mother!

FAITH: Embrace me, daughter! 5.20

PEACE *does so.*

FAITH: My child, by the grace of goddess Hail Vishnu, may you win a place in the hearts of the sages!

HAIL VISHNU: So what's the news?

FAITH: Just what's fitting for those who act contrary to you, goddess!

5.25 VIṢṆUBHAKTIḤ: tad vistareṇ' āvedaya.

ŚRADDHĀ: ākarṇayatu bhavatī. devyām ādi|Keśav'|āyatanād apakrāntāyām eva, kiṅ cid utsṛṣṭa|pāṭalimni bhagavati bhāsvati, vijaya|ghoṣaṇ'|āhūyamān'|âneka|vara|vīra|bahulatara|siṃha|nāda|badhirita|dig|ante, saṃtata|ratha|turaṅga|khura|khaṇḍita|bhū|maṇḍal'|ôcchalad|vipula|rajaḥ|paṭal'|ântarita|kiraṇa|mālini, prabalatara|karṇa|tāl'|āsphālan'|ôccalat|samada|kari|kumbha|sindūra|sandhyāyamāna|daśa|diśi, pralaya|jala|dhara|dhvāna|bhīṣana|rave, teṣām asmākaṃ ca saṃnaddhe sainya|sāgare mahā|rāja|Vivekena Naiyāyikaṃ darśanaṃ dautye prahitam. gatvā ca ten' ôkto Mahāmohaḥ:

«Viṣṇor āyatanāny apāsya, saritāṃ
kūlāny, araṇya|sthalīḥ
puṇyāḥ, puṇya|kṛtāṃ manāṃsi ca, bhavān
mlecchān vrajet s'|ânugaḥ.
no cet, santu kṛpāṇa|dārita|bhavat|
pratyaṅga|dhārā|kṣarad|
rakta|sphīta|vidīrṇa|vaktra|visarat|
pheṭ|kāriṇaḥ pheravāḥ.» [5]

HAIL VISHNU: Do tell in detail. 5.25

FAITH: Please listen, my lady. When you, goddess, retreated from the shrine of the Primordial Késhava, and Lord Sun had released somewhat his reddish hue, then, in the sea of their and our armies locked in combat, where to the ends of space one was deafened by the lion's roar of the multitude of supreme heroes calling out cries of victory, the solar circle of rays was eclipsed by the great mass of dust raised from an earth continuously trodden by the hooves of the chariots' steeds, while the ten directions were as if in a twilight tinged by the vermillion that appeared on the heads of maddened elephants owing to their ears' forceful fanning motion, and there was a roar of terrifying thunder from epoch-ending clouds. It was then that our great king Intuition dispatched the Philosophy of Logic* as a messenger. Going forth, he said this to Magnus Nescience:

"You and your rabble must quit Vishnu's shrines,
merit-makers' minds,
riverbanks and holy forest groves,
and depart to barbarous abodes.
If not, let jackals barking,
with their snouts wide-open, gaping,
lap up streams of blood flowing
from your every limb
cut by my blade."

VIṢṆUBHAKTIḤ: tatas tataḥ?

ŚRADDHĀ: tato, devi, vikaṭa | lalāṭa | taṭa | tāṇḍavita | bhru | kuṭinā kruddhena Mahāmohena «anubhavatv asya dur|naya|paripākasya phalaṃ Viveka|hataka!» ity abhidhāya, svayaṃ pāṣaṇḍ' | āgamāḥ pāṣaṇḍa | tarka | śāstraiḥ samaṃ samarāya prathamaṃ samudyojitāḥ. atr' ântare 'smākam api sainya|śirasi—

5.30 ved'|ôpaved'|âṅga|purāṇa|dharma|
śāstr'|êtihās'|ādibhir ucchrita|śrīḥ,
Sarasvatī padma|karā śaśāṅka|
saṅkāśa|kāntiḥ sahas" āvir|āsīt. [6]

VIṢṆUBHAKTIḤ: tatas tataḥ?

ŚRADDHĀ: tato, devi, Vaiṣṇava | Śaiva | Saur' | ādayo devyāḥ sakāśam āgatāḥ.

VIṢṆUBHAKTIḤ: tatas tataḥ?

ŚRADDHĀ: tad|anantaraṃ ca—

5.35 Sāṃkhya|Nyāya|Kaṇāda|bhāṣita|mahā|
bhāṣy'|ādi|śāstrair vṛtā,
sphūrjan|nyāya|sahasra|bāhu|nivahair
uddyotayantī diśaḥ,
Mīmāṃsā samar'|ôtsuk" āvir|abhavad
Dharm'|êndu|kānt'|ānanā,
vāg|devyāḥ puratas trayī|tri|ṇayanā,
Kātyāyan" îv' âparā. [7]

HAIL VISHNU: And then?

FAITH: Then, goddess, Magnus Nescience, furious, with his brow curled as if dancing upon his hideous forehead, said: "Let that wretch Intuition taste the fruit ripened from his misdeeds!" And so saying, he first sent into battle the heretical doctrines, accompanied by their sophistries.* At that moment, at the head of our army—

At once Sarásvati was present, 5.30
holding a lotus and pretty as the moon,
She whose glory is exalted by the Vedas,
their addenda, traditions, lawbooks,
epics and other texts.*

HAIL VISHNU: What then?

FAITH: Then, goddess, the teachings of Vishnu, Shiva, the Solar Divinity,* among others, arrived in that goddess's presence.

HAIL VISHNU: Then?

FAITH: Right after than—

Lady Hermeneutics, delighting in combat, 5.35
appeared, her face the moonlight of Law,
While in her train were Number and Logic,
Atomism, Linguistics—science galore!
With a thousand arms of splendid reason
throughout the quarters did she shine,
Like a second Durga, before the speech-goddess,
with the three Vedas for eyes.*

ŚĀNTIḤ: aye! kathaṃ punaḥ svabhāva|pratidvandvinām āgamānāṃ tarkāṇāṃ ca samavāyaḥ saṃpannaḥ?

ŚRADDHĀ: putri—

samān'|ânvaya|jātānāṃ,
  paraspara|virodhinām,
paraiḥ pratyabhibhūtānāṃ
  prasūte saṅgatiḥ śriyam. [8]

tena veda|prasūtānāṃ teṣām avāntara|virodhe 'pi veda|saṃrakṣaṇāya, nāstika|pakṣa|pratikṣepaṇāya śāstrāṇāṃ sāhityam eva. āgamānāṃ tu tattvaṃ vicārayatām a|virodha eva. tathā hi—

5.40 jyotiḥ śāntam, an|antam, a|dvayam, a|jaṃ
  tat|tad|guṇ'|ônmīlanād
«Brahm'» êty, «»Acyuta ity, «Umā|patir» iti,
  prastūyate n' âikadhā.
tais tair eva sad|āgamaiḥ, śruti|sakhair,
  nānā|patha|prasthitair
gamyo 'sau Jagadīśvaro, jala|nidhir
  vārāṃ pravāhair iva. [9]

VIṢṆUBHAKTIḤ: tatas tataḥ?

PEACE: Goodness! how were these doctrines and philosophies, by nature at odds with one another, ever brought into accord?

FAITH: My daughter—

Those born to a common line,
but in mutual enmity,
When overpowered by a foe
had best renew their harmony.

For, though there are inner conflicts among those born from the Veda, when it comes to protecting the Veda and dispensing with nihilistic factions,* there is a concordance among their teachings. Indeed, they are without discrepancy in their doctrines' analyses of reality.* Thus—

The Light, at peace and limitless, 5.40
without duality, unborn,
By the admixture of qualities varies,
and is praised as "Brahma,"
"Vishnu," or "Uma's Lord."
It is through the true traditions,
set upon diverse paths,
accompanied by aural revelations,*
That the Lord of the World is found,
as currents in a single ocean bound.

HAIL VISHNU: And then?

ŚRADDHĀ: tato, devi, parasparaṃ kari|turaga|ratha|padātīnāṃ nirantara|śara|nikara|dhārā|sampāt'|ôpadarśita|durdinānāṃ teṣāṃ asmākaṃ ca yodhānāṃ tumulaḥ samprahāraḥ prāvartata. tathā hi—

bahula|rudhira|toyās
tatra tatra sravantyo,
nibiḍa|piśita|paṅkāḥ
kaṅka|raṅk'|âvakīrṇāḥ,
śara|dalita|viśīrṇ'|ôt-
tuṅga|mātaṅga|śaila|
skhalita|raya|viśīrṇa|
cchatra|haṃs'|âvataṃsāḥ. [10]

evam ati|mahati dāruṇe saṅgrāme para|pakṣa|virodhitayā pāṣaṇḍ'|āgamair agresarī|kṛtaṃ lokāyataṃ tantram anyonya|sainya|vimardair vinaṣṭam. anantaraṃ pāṣaṇḍ'|āgamā nirmūlatayā sad|āgam'|ârṇava|pravāheṇa paryastāḥ. Saugatās tāvat Sindhu | Gāndhāra | Pārasika | Māgadh' | Āndhra | Hūṇa | Vaṅga | Kaliṅg' | ādīn mleccha | prāyān pradeśān praviṣṭāḥ. pāṣaṇḍa|digambara|kāpālik'|ādayas tu pāmara|bahuleṣu Pāñcāla|Mālav'|Âbhīr'|Ānarta|sāgar'|ânūpeṣu nigūḍhaṃ sañcaranti. Nyāy'|ânugatayā Mīmāṃsayā pragāḍha|prahāra|jarjarī|kṛtā nāstika|tarkās teṣām ev' āgamānām anupathaṃ prayātāḥ.

FAITH: Then, goddess, the mutual combat among their and our warriors—including the elephants, cavalry, chariots, and infantry who made the day seem stormy on account of the continuously falling shower of multitudinous missiles—became a tumultuous brawl. And so—

The rivers there had waters thick with blood,
Their flesh-filled marshes haunted by
haggard herons,*
And scattered with parasols, like flocks of geese,
carried by currents that flowed
from mountainous elephants
split asunder by raining arrows.

And in that very great and terrible combat, the materialist system, which had been pushed out in front by the heretical traditions owing to its conflict with others' factions, perished while being mauled by one army after another.* Right after that the heretical traditions, being torn up from the roots, were swept away by the flood of the true doctrines. Thus the Buddhists installed themselves mostly among the barbarians in Sind, Gandhára, Persia, Mágadha, Andhra, among the Huns, and in Bengal and Orissa. The heretic Jains, Skullmen and others, as well, are roaming in hiding among the plentiful outcastes in maritime regions such as Panchála, Malva, Abhíra and Anárta.* The nihilistic sophistries of their received traditions, punctured by the deep blows of Hermeneutics allied with Logic, then took to the road.

5.45 VIṢṆUBHAKTIḤ: tatas tataḥ?

ŚRADDHĀ: tato Vastuvicāreṇa Kāmo hataḥ; Kṣamayā Krodha|Pāruṣya|Hiṃs"|ādayo nipātitāḥ; Santoṣeṇa Lobha|Tṛṣṇā|Dainy'|Ânṛta|Paiśunyavāk|Stey'|Âsatpratigrah'|ādayo nigṛhītāḥ; Anasūyayā Mātsaryaṃ jitam; Parotkarṣabhāvanayā Mado niṣūditaḥ; Paraguṇādhikyena Mānaḥ khaṇḍitaḥ.

VIṢṆUBHAKTIḤ *(sa|harṣam)*: sādhu, sādhu! sampannam! atha Mahāmohasya ko vṛttāntaḥ?

ŚRADDHĀ: devi, Mahāmoho 'pi yog'|ôpasargaiḥ saha na jñāyate kva nilīnas tiṣṭhat' îti.

VIṢṆUBHAKTIḤ: asti tarhi mahān an|artha|śeṣaḥ. pariharaṇīyaś c' âsau. yataḥ—

5.50 an|ādara|paro vidvān
īhamānaḥ sthirāṃ śriyam
agneḥ śeṣam, ṛṇāc cheṣam,
śatroḥ śeṣaṃ na śeṣayet. [11]

atha Manasaḥ ko vṛttāntaḥ?

ŚRADDHĀ: devi, ten' âpi putra|pautr'|ādi|vyasana|janita|śok'|āvegena jīv'|ôtsargāy' âdhyavasitam.

HAIL VISHNU: What next? 5.45

FAITH: Then Analyst killed off Lust; Patience brought down Anger, Coarseness, Harm and their kind; Contentment defeated Greed, Craving, Self-Pity, Untruth, Slander, Theft, Fraud and more; Generosity conquered Envy; Altruism demolished Self-Intoxication;* while Admiration-for-others destroyed Pride.

HAIL VISHNU *(joyfully)*: Good, good! It's done! But what news of Magnus Nescience?

FAITH: My goddess, Magnus Nescience, together with the deviations from yoga,* remains hidden I-don't-know-where.

HAIL VISHNU: Then there is a great, outstanding debility. And it's to be done away with. For—

> The wise-man who desires lasting success, 5.50
> but for his rivals lacks proper respect,
> Should recall that one ought not let thrive
> fire's embers, unpaid debts,
> or foes who survive.

And what news of Thought?

FAITH: He, goddess, has resolved to commit suicide, so does he despair due to grief born from the loss of his sons, grandsons, and the rest.

VIṢṆUBHAKTIḤ *(smitaṃ kṛtvā)*: yady evaṃ syāt, sarva eva vayam kṛta|kṛtyā bhavāmaḥ! Puruṣaś ca parāṃ nirvṛtim āpadyeta. kin tu kutas tasya dur|ātmano jīva|tyāgaḥ?

ŚRADDHĀ: evaṃ devyāṃ Prabodh'|ôdayāya gṛhīta|saṅkalpāyām a|cirād eva śarīreṇ' âiva saha na bhaviṣyati.

5.55 VIṢṆUBHAKTIḤ: tad bhavatu! asya vairāgy'|ôtpattaye Vaiyāsikīṃ Sarasvatīṃ preṣayāmaḥ.

*iti niṣkrānte.*

*praveśakaḥ.*

HAIL VISHNU *(breaking into a smile)*: If that's how it is, then all of us are done with our tasks. The Inner Man, now, will attain supreme beatitude. But how is that mischief-maker about to abandon his life?*

FAITH: When the goddess has turned her intentions to Wisdom's rise, then it won't be long before, together with the body, he is no more.

HAIL VISHNU: So be then! We'll send Vyasa's Speech-goddess* to inspire him to dispassion. 5.55

*Exeunt ambo.*

*Thus the prologue.*

# ACT FIVE

# THE DAWN OF DISPASSION

*tataḥ praviśati* MANAḤ SAṄKALPAŚ *ca.*

MANAḤ *(s'|âsram)*: hā! putrakāḥ! kva gatāḥ stha? datta me prativacanam! bhoḥ! kumārakāḥ! Rāga | Dveṣa | Mada | Mātsary' | ādayaḥ, pariṣvajadhvaṃ māṃ! sīdanti mam' âṅgāni. hā! na kaś cid vṛddhaṃ mām a|nāthaṃ saṃbhāvayati. kva gatā Asūy" | ādayaḥ kanyakāḥ? Āśā | Tṛṣṇā | Hiṃs" | ādayo vā snuṣāḥ? atha tā api manda|bhāgyasya me sama|kālam eva daiva|hataken' âpahṛtāḥ. *(sa|vaiklavyam)*

5.60 visarpati viṣ'|âgnivad,
dahati sarva|marm'|āvidhas,
tanoti bhṛśa|vedanāḥ,
kaṣati sarva|kāṣaṃ vapuḥ,
vilumpati vivekitām,
hṛdi ca moham unmīlayaty,
aho, grasati jīvitaṃ
prasabham eṣa śoka|jvaraḥ. [12]

*iti mūrcchitaṃ patati.*

SAṄKALPAḤ: rājan, samāśvasihi! samāśvasihi!

MANAḤ *(samāśvasya)*: kathaṃ devī Pravṛttir api na māṃ evam|avasthaṃ samāśvāsayati?

SAṄKALPAḤ *(s'|âsram)*: deva, kuto 'dy' âpi Pravṛttiḥ? yataḥ śruta|kuṭumba|vyasana|sañjāta|śok'|ânala|dagdha|hṛdayā, hṛday'|āsphoṭaṃ vinaṣṭā.

*Then enter* THOUGHT *with* INTENTION.

THOUGHT *(crying)*: Alas! my sons! where have you gone? Give me your response! Oh! my lads!—Attachment, Aversion, Drunkard, Envy, and the others—embrace me! My limbs grow weak. Oh! No one thinks of me, old and vulnerable. Where have Jealousy and the other girls got to? or my daughters-in-law Hope, Craving, Harm and the rest? They, too, by cursed fate, are all at once lost to me, unlucky that I am. *(distraught)*

It spreads like the fire of poison, 5.60
gut-piercing, burning all pleasure,
Profusing sharp pain,
afflicting this whole broken frame.
Intelligence it destroys,
and brings foolishness to my heart.
Truly, it gnaws at my life,
this fever of sorrowful strife.

*He falls unconscious.*

INTENTION: Get a grip, my king! Get a grip!

THOUGHT *(regaining composure)*: How is it that even my lady Eva Lucienne does not console me when I am in such a state?

INTENTION *(crying)*: My lord, where on this day is Eva Lucienne? For she has perished, broken hearted, her heart scorched by the flames of grief ignited on hearing of her family's destruction.

5.65 MANAḤ: hā! priye! kv' âsi? dehi me prativacanam! nanu, devi—

svapne 'pi, devi, ramase na vinā mayā tvaṃ,
svāpe tvayā virahito mṛtavad bhavāmi.
dūrī|kṛt" âsi vidhi|dur|lalitais, tath" âpi
jīvaty aho! tu Mana, ity asavo dur|antāḥ. [13]

*punar mūrcchati.*

SAṄKALPAḤ: rājan, samāśvasihi! samāśvasihi!

MANAḤ *(samāśvasya)*: alam asmākam ataḥ paraṃ jīvitena. Saṃkalpa! citāṃ āracaya, yāvad anala|praveśena śok'|ânalaṃ nirvāpayāmi.

5.70 *tataḥ praviśati* SARASVATĪ.

SARASVATĪ: preṣit" âsmi bhagavatyā Viṣṇubhaktyā, yathā «sakhi, Sarasvati. gacch' âpatya|vyasana|khinnasya Manasaḥ prabodhanāya. yathā ca tasya vairāgy'|ôtpattir bhavati, tathā yatasv'» êti. tad bhavatu! tat|sannidhim ev' ôpasarpāmi. *(upasṛtya)* vatsa, kim evam ativiklavo 'si? nanu vidita|pūrv" âiva bhavatā bhāvānām a|nityatā, adhītāni ca tvay" āitihāsikāny upākhyānāni. tathā hi—

THOUGHT: Oh! my dear! where are you? let me hear your 5.65
answer! Indeed, my lady—

> Even in a dream, my goddess,
> you'll find no delight without me,
> While without you, even in sleep,
> a lifeless corpse will I be.
> But though by fate's evil game,
> you've been taken far away,
> Know that Thought, oh! still lives,
> his vital force hard to allay.

*He swoons again.*

INTENTION: Get a grip, my king! Get a grip!

THOUGHT *(regaining composure)*: It's useless for me to live any longer. Intention! Prepare the pyre, so that by entering the flames the fire of grief will be extinguished.

*Then enter* SARÁSVATI. 5.70

SARÁSVATI: I've been sent by the blessed lady Hail Vishnu, who said, "Sarásvati, my friend. Go to enlighten Thought, who is distraught because of the loss of his children. Endeavor that he may realize dispassion." So be it! I'll just approach him. *(approaching)* My child, how is it that you are so distressed? For certainly you have already seen the impermanence of things and learned the tales from the histories. Thus—

bhūtvā kalpa|śat'|āyuṣo 'mbuja|bhuvaḥ,
s'|Êndrāś ca dev'|âsurā,
Manv|ādyā munayo, mahī jaladhayo
naṣṭāḥ parāḥ koṭayaḥ.
mohaḥ ko 'yam aho mahān udayate,
lokasya śok'|āvahaḥ,
sindhoḥ phena|same gate vapuṣi yat
pañc'|ātmake pañcatām? [14]

tad bhāvaya bhāvānām a|nityatām. nity'|ânitya|vastu|darśinaṃ na spṛṣati śok'|āvegaḥ. yataḥ—

ekam eva sadā Brahma
satyam, anyad vikalpitam;
ko mohaḥ kas tadā śoka
ekātmyam anupaśyataḥ? [15]

5.75 MANAḤ: bhagavati! śok'|āvega|dūṣite Manasi Viveka eva me n' âvakāśaṃ labhate.

SARASVATĪ: vatsa, sneha|doṣa eṣaḥ. prasiddha ev' âyam arthaḥ, snehaḥ sarv'|ânartha|prabhava iti. tathā hi—

upyante viṣa|valli|bīja|viṣamāḥ
kleśāḥ priy'|ākhyā narais;
tebhyaḥ snehamayā bhavanti na|cirād,
vajr'|âgni|garbh'|âṅkurāḥ,
yebhyo 'mī śataśaḥ kukūla|hutabhug|
dāhaṃ dahantaḥ śanair

Living for a hundred eons,
  Brahmas, gods, titans, and Indra, too,
Sages such as Manu,
  earths and oceans, in their millions,
  come to an end, it's true.
What's this great nescience that arrives,
  carrying the world to grief,
When the fifth state is reached
  by this five-natured body,*
  that's no more than foam in the sea?

So do reflect upon the impermanence of things. For one who always has the vision of impermanence feels not the agitation of grief. Just so—

Ever one and true is Brahman,
  but imagined otherwise;
What ignorance or grief can there be,
  when oneness rests before the eyes?

THOUGHT: Blessed lady! when Thought is afflicted by grief's 5.75
agitations, I find no place even for Intuition.

SARÁSVATI: This, my child, is the trouble with affection. For it is well known that affection is the source of all that is vain. Hence—

Afflictions called "dear ones" are sown by men
  like the hazardous seeds of poisonous vines;
Before long they grow into our loves,
  shoots shot through with lightning fire.
And from these spring the trees of grief
  topped with a thousand blazing flames,

deham dīpta|śikhā|sahasra|śikharā
rohanti śoka|drumāḥ. [16]

MANAḤ: devi! yady apy evaṃ, tath" âpi na śaknomi śok'|ânala|dagdhaḥ prāṇān dhārayitum. sādhu saṃpannaṃ, yad anta|kāle tvaṃ tāvad dṛṣṭ" âsi.

SARASVATĪ: idaṃ c' âparam a|kṛtyaṃ, yad ātma|haty"|âdhyavasāya iti. api ca, amīṣām apakāriṇām arthe ko 'yam atyāveśo bhavataḥ? paśya tāvat—

5.80 kva cid upakṛtiḥ kart" âmībhiḥ?
kṛtā? kriyate 'tha vā?
tava na ca bhavanty ete puṃsāṃ
sukhāya parigrahāḥ.
dadhati virahe marma|cchedaṃ,
tad|artham apārthakaṃ;
tad api vipul'|āyasāiḥ sīdanty,
aho bata! jantavaḥ. [17]

api ca—

tīrṇāḥ pūrṇāḥ kati na sarito?
laṅghitāḥ ke na śailā?
n' ākrāntā vā kati vana|bhuvaḥ
krūra|sañcāra|ghorāḥ?
pāpair etaiḥ kim iva dur|itaṃ
kārito n' âsi kaṣṭaṃ,
yad dṛṣṭās te dhana|mada|maṣī|
mlāna|vaktrā durīśāḥ? [18]

Slow-roasting the body in a hundred ways,
  like a fire devouring hay.

THOUGHT: Goddess! although that's indeed how things are, scorched as I am by the flames of grief, I cannot bear to live. It is enough for me that I see you in my final hours.

SARÁSVATI: To set upon suicide is the greatest crime. Just why is it, anyway, that you are so possessed on account of these ne'er-do-wells? Look—

Do these in any way aid you? 5.80
  or did they? or will they still?
Relations are not there for your pleasure,
  or for that of any man.
In parting gut-ache's all they'll give you,
  what's done for them is vain;
But, alas! people sink into ruin
  increasing their own level of pain.

What's more—

How many full rivers have you not forded?
  which mountains did you not traverse?
How many jungles have you not crossed,
  terrifying with dangers roaming there?
What hardship did you not endure for
    these wretches,
  hard to see for the taskmasters they are,
  faces ink-stained with their lust for treasure?

MANAḤ: devi, evam etat. tath" âpi—

lālitānāṃ svajātānāṃ
   hṛdi sañcaratāṃ ciram,
prāṇānām iva vicchedo,
   marma|cchedād arun|tudaḥ. [19]

5.85 SARASVATĪ: vatsa, mamatā|vāsanā|nibandhano 'yaṃ vyāmohaḥ. uktaṃ ca—

mārjāra|bhakṣite duḥkhaṃ yādṛśaṃ gṛha|kukkuṭe,
na tādṛṅ mamatā|śūnye kalaviṅke 'tha mūṣake. [20]

tat sarvathā sarv'|ânartha|bījasya mamatvasy' ôcchede yatnaḥ kartavyaḥ. paśya—

prādur|bhavanti vapuṣah kati vā na kīṭā
   yān yatnataḥ khalu tanor apasārayanti?
mohaḥ ka eṣa jagato, yad apatya|saṃjñāṃ
   teṣāṃ vidhāya pariśoṣayati sva|deham? [21]

MANAḤ: bhagavati! evam tath" āpi dur|ucchedyas tu mamatva|granthiḥ. tathā hi—

5.90 nirantar'|âbhyāsa|dṛdhī|kṛtasya
   na sneha|sūtra|grathitasya jantoḥ
jānāmi kiñ cid, bhagavaty, upāyaṃ,
   mamatva|pāśasya yato vimokṣaḥ. [22]

THOUGHT: So it is, goddess. But at the same time—

Beloved blood-relations,
who've long dwelt in the heart,
Like life itself when lost,
bring pain piercing one's vital parts.

SARÁSVATI: This foolishness, my child, stems from the inclination to selfishness. As it's said— 5.85

As much as you do suffer,
for the house-hen consumed by a cat,
Not so for a mouse or a sparrow,
for you're without attachment to that.

So you should strive to eliminate selfishness, which is seed of all that is vain. Look—

How many worms have not appeared in the body
that one takes trouble to purge from that frame?
But what in the world is this nescience
that parches one's body,
while calling them "kin" in name?

THOUGHT: So be it, goddess! The knot of selfishness is indeed hard to cut. Surely—

I, blessed lady! know no means 5.90
for creatures to attain liberation;
For they're ensnared by selfishness,
tied up in strings of love,
tightened by continuous habituation.

SARASVATĪ: vatsa! bhāvānām a|nityatā|bhāvanam eva tāvan mamatv'|ôcchedasya pratham'|ôpāyaḥ. tath" âpi—

na kati pitaro,
dārāḥ, putrāḥ, pitṛvya|pitāmahā
mahati vitate
saṃsāre 'smin gatās tava koṭayaḥ?
tad iha suhṛdāṃ
vidyut|pāt'|ôjjvalān kṣaṇa|saṃgamān
sapadi hṛdaye
bhūyo bhūyo niveśya sukhī bhava. [23]

MANAḤ: bhagavati, tava prasādād apāsta eva vyāmohaḥ. kin tu—

tava mukha|śaśadhara|dīdhiti|
galitair vimal'|ôpadeśa|pīyūṣaiḥ,
kṣālitam api me hṛdayaṃ
malinaṃ śok'|ōrmibhiḥ kriyate. [24]

5.95 tad ārdrasya śoka|prahārasya bheṣajam prajñāpayatu bhagavatī.

SARASVATĪ: vatsa, nan' ûpadiṣṭam eva munibhiḥ—

«a|kāṇḍa|pāta|jātānām
ārdrāṇāṃ marma|bhedinām.
gāḍha|śoka|prahārāṇām
a|cint" âiva mah"|âuṣadham» iti. [25]

SARÁSVATI: My child! the contemplation of the impermanence of things is the primary means to cut through selfishness. Just so—

In this great and broad *sansára*,
how many millions have not passed,
Of your fathers, wives, and sons,
uncles and grandparents?
The moment's gathering of friends here
is but a lightning flash;
Grasp this now in your heart, and again!
and with this knowledge be glad.

THOUGHT: Thanks to your grace, blessed lady, my foolishness is dispelled. What's more—

The taintless nectar of advice,
that pours from your moon-like mouth as light,
Washes the soil from my heart
that was left there by waves of grief.

So please teach me, blessed lady, the cure for the fresh 5.95
bruises of grief.

SARÁSVATI: That, my child, has been taught by the sages—

"For the lances of profound affliction
tearing through your innards,
Fresh wounds that no arrow could inflict,
impassivity is panacea."

MANAḤ: bhagavati! evam etat. dur|vāraṃ tu cetaḥ, yataḥ—

apy etad vāritaṃ, cintā|
santānair abhibhūyate,
muhur|vāt'|āhatair bimbam
abhra|cchedair iv' āindavam. [26]

5.100 SARASVATĪ: vatsa, śrūyatām. cetaso 'yaṃ vikāraḥ. tataḥ kva cic chānte viṣaye ceto niveśyatām.

MANAḤ: tat prasīdatu bhagavatī! ko 'sau śānto viṣayaḥ?

SARASVATĪ: vatsa, guhyam etat. tath" āpy ārtānām upadeśe na doṣaḥ—

nityaṃ smarañ jalada|nīlam udāra|hāra|
keyūra|kuṇḍala|kirīṭa|dharaṃ Hariṃ vā,
grīṣme su|śītam iva vāri, nirasta|śokaṃ
Brahma prapadya, bhaja nirvṛtim ātmanīnām. [27]

MANAḤ *(vicintya s'|ôcchvāsam)*: sarvathā trāto 'smi bhagavatyā. *(iti pādayoḥ patati.)*

5.105 SARASVATĪ: vatsa, samprati upadeśa|sahiṣṇu te hṛdayaṃ jātam. ata etad aparam ucyate—

THOUGHT: Blessed lady! So it is. But the mind is hard to restrain, for—

> Though restrained, it is overpowered
> by care's incessant stream,
> As the moon's reflection in that instant
> when cloud-cover arrives with the breeze.

SARÁSVATI: Listen, my child. This is but a modification of 5.100
mind. Rather, let the mind come to rest upon some tranquil object.

THOUGHT: By your grace, blessed lady! Just what is this tranquil object?

SARÁSVATI: It is secret,* my child. Nonetheless, there's no fault in teaching it to those who are afflicted—

> Always mindful of Vishnu,
> cloud-blue, with fine pearls,
> bracelets, earrings and crown,
> Or by attaining Brahman,
> a cool pond in summer,
> where your sorrows are drowned,
> May you cleave to the self's highest end.

THOUGHT *(sighing thoughtfully)*: You have in every way protected me, lady. *(He falls at her feet.)*

SARÁSVATI: Your heart, my child, has now grown receptive 5.105
to these teachings. This, then, too is said—

vaśaṃ prāpte mṛtyoḥ
pitari, tanaye vā, suhṛdi vā,
śucā santapyante
bhṛśam udara|tāḍaṃ jaḍa|dhiyaḥ.
a|sāre saṃsāre
virasa|pariṇāme tu viduṣāṃ
viyogo vairāgyaṃ
draḍhayati vitanvañ śama|sukham. [28]

*tataḥ praviśati* VAIRĀGYAM.

VAIRĀGYAM *(vicintya)*:

asrākṣīn nava|nīla|nīraja|dal'|ô-
pānt'|âtisūkṣm'|āyata|
tvaṅ|mātr'|ântarit'|āmiṣam yadi vapur
n' âitat prajānāṃ patiḥ,
pratyagra|kṣarad|asra|visra|piśita|
grāsa|grahaṃ gṛhṇato
gṛdhra|dhvāṅkṣa|vṛkāṃs tanau nipatataḥ
ko vā kathaṃ vārayet? [29]

5.110 api ca—

sadā lolā lakṣmīr:
viṣaya|ja|rasāḥ prānta|virasā;
vipad|gehaṃ deho;
mahad api dhanaṃ, bhūri nidhanam;
guruḥ śoko lokaḥ;
satatam abal" ânartha|bahulā—
tath" âpy asmin ghore
pathi, bata! ratā n' Ātmani ratāḥ. [30]

When death overcomes a father, son, or friend,
dull wits are struck hard by sorrow,
guts wrenched.
But for the wise, in worthless *sansára*,
insipid change,
separation strengthens dispassion and the joy
of peace brings.

*Enter* DISPASSION.

DISPASSION *(thoughtfully)*:

If the Lord of Creatures had not created
this body of flesh,
Within only skin stretched fine as the tip
of the petal of a blue lotus fresh,
What would ward off the vultures, crows and wolves
when they pounce on this corpse, and how?
As they rip out mouthfuls of stinking meat
from which warm blood spills down?

Similarly— 5.110

Fortune is forever fickle:
relish for objects, in the end tasteless;
this mortal body, home to calamity;
great the wealth, more so the death;
mundane society, sorrow a-plenty;
the weaker sex, frivolity ever to excess—
So it is then, alas!
that pleased with this fearsome path,
one cherishes the Self not a whit.

SARASVATĪ: vatsa, etad Vairāgyaṃ tvām upasthitam. tad etat saṃbhāvaya.

MANAḤ: kv' âsi putraka?

VAIRĀGYAM *(upasṛtya)*: ahaṃ, bho, abhivādaye.

5.115 MANAḤ: vatsa, jāta|mātreṇa tvayā tyakto 'smi. pariṣvajasva mām!

VAIRĀGYAM *tathā karoti.*

MANAḤ: vatsa, tvad|darśanāt praśānto me śok'|āvegaḥ.

VAIRĀGYAM: tāta, ko 'tra śok'|āveśaḥ? yataḥ—

pānthānām iva vartmani, kṣiti|ruhāṃ
nadyām iva bhraśyatāṃ,
meghānām iva puṣkare, jala|nidhau
sāṃyātrikāṇām iva
saṃyogaḥ pitṛ|mātṛ|bandhu|tanaya|
bhrātṛ|priyāṇāṃ yadā
siddho dūra|viyoga eva, viduṣāṃ
śok'|ôdayaḥ kas tadā? [31]

5.120 MANAḤ *(s'|ānandam)*: devi, evam etat, yad āha vatsaḥ. saṃprati hi—

nāryas tā nava|yauvanā. madhu|kara|
vyāhāriṇas te drumāḥ.
pronmīlan|nava|mallikā|surabhayo
mandās ta ev' ânilāḥ.
ady' ôdātta|viveka|mārjita|tamaḥ|
stoma|vyalīkaṃ punas

SARÁSVATI: This, my child, is Dispassion who comes before you. Do consider him.

THOUGHT: Where are you, son?

DISPASSION *(approaching)*: It is I, who salute you.

THOUGHT: My child, I abandoned you right at birth. Em- 5.115
brace me!

DISPASSION *does so.*

THOUGHT: Seeing you, child, the grief that distressed me is calmed.

DISPASSION: Father, who can be grief-stricken here? For—

As travelers on the highway,
trees fallen in a stream,
Clouds within the atmosphere,
or voyagers on the sea,
Just so when this conjunction,
of parents, children, siblings dear
Is revealed as long separation,
for the wise what grief is near?

THOUGHT *(joyfully)*: So it is, goddess, as this child says. Now 5.120
indeed—

The women—they were young and fresh.
The trees—they were buzzing with bees.
The breezes—they were gentle,
perfumed by fresh-bloomed jasmine.
But today Thought sees them as lies,
water filling the mirage of a sea,

tān etān mṛga|tṛṣṇik"|ârṇava|payaḥ|
prāyān Manaḥ paśyati [32]

SARASVATĪ: vatsa, yady apy evaṃ, tath" âpi gṛhiṇā muhūrtam apy an|āśrama|dharmiṇā na bhavitavyam. tad adya| prabhṛti Nivṛttir eva te saha|dharma|cāriṇī.

MANAḤ *(sa|lajjam)*: yad ādiśati devī.

SARASVATĪ: Śama|Dama|Santoṣ'|ādayaś ca putrās tvām anucarantu! Yama | Niyam' | ādayaś c' āmātyāḥ! Viveko 'pi tvad|anugrahād Upaniṣad|devyā saha yauvarājyam anubhavatu. etāś ca Maitry|ādayaś catasro bhaginyo bhagavatyā Viṣṇubhaktyā tava prasādanāya prahitās. tāḥ sa| prasādam anumānaya!

5.125 MANAḤ: yad ādiśati devī. mūrdhni niveśitāḥ sarvā ev' ājñāḥ. *(iti sa|harṣaṃ pādayoḥ patati.)*

SARASVATĪ: Yama|Niyam'|ādayaś c' āmātyāḥ s'|ādaram āyuṣmatā draṣṭavyāḥ. etair eva sah' āyuṣmān sāmrājyam anutiṣṭhatu. tvayi ca svāsthyam āpanne Kṣetra|jño 'pi svāṃ prakṛtim āpatsyate. yataḥ—

tvat|saṅgāc chāśvato 'pi
prabhava|laya|jar"|ôpapluto, buddhi|vṛttiṣv
eko nān" êva devo,
ravir iva jaladher vīciṣu vyasta|mūrtiḥ.
tūṣṇīm ālambase cet,
katham api vitatā, vatsa, saṃhṛtya vṛttīr,

For the false darkness that gathered
has been well-cleansed intuitively.

SARÁSVATI: Although it is so, my child, a householder must not be for even a moment exempt from the regulation of life's stages. Hence, from this day forward, Diva Lucienne is your lawful wife.

THOUGHT *(embarrassed)*: As the goddess instructs.

SARÁSVATI: May Tranquility, Self-Discipline, Contentment and other such sons accompany you! And may Restraint, Regulation and so on be your ministers! As for Intuition, by your favor may he be installed as crown prince together with goddess Úpanishad. The four sisters, Love and the others, have been sent by the blessed lady Hail Vishnu for your pleasure. Look after them with kindness!

THOUGHT: As the goddess instructs. All your commands 5.125
are borne atop my crown. *(He joyfully falls at her feet.)*

SARÁSVATI: Restraint, Regulation and so on—these ministers you must regard with respect. For together with them you, long-lived, must govern your realm. In your achieving integrity, the Field-commander,* too, will attain to his proper nature. For—

It's through contact with you that the god,
though eternal, is plunged into birth, death
and age,
One, though varied in thought's modulations,
like the sun's broken forms in the ocean's waves.
When somehow, my child, you come to restrain
manifold modulations and in silence do dwell,

bhāty ādarśe prasanne
ravir iva sahaj'|ānanda|sāndras tad|ātmā. [33]

tad bhavatu. jñātīnām udaka|kṛtyāya nadīm avatarāmaḥ.

MANAḤ: yad ājñāpayati devī.

5.130 *iti niṣkrāntāḥ sarve.*

*iti śrī|Kṛṣṇamiśra|viracite Prabodhacandrodaya|nāmni nāṭake Vairāgya|prādur|bhāvo nāma pancamo 'ṅkaḥ.*

Then as the sun in a clear mirror shines brightly
so the Self in innate bliss will swell.

So be it. Let us go down to the river to perform the water-offering for our kin.*

THOUGHT: As the goddess commands.

*Exeunt omnes.* 5.130

*Thus concludes Act Five, entitled "The Dawn of Dispassion,"* in "The Rise of Wisdom Moon," composed by the eminent Krishna·mishra·yati.*

# PROLOGUE TO ACT SIX

6.1 *tataḥ praviśati* ŚĀNTIḤ.

ŚĀNTIḤ: ādiṣṭ" āsmi mahā|rāja|Vivekena, yathā: «vatse, viditam eva bhavatyā kila—

astaṃ gateṣu tanayeṣu, vilīna|Mohe,
Vairāgya|bhāji Manasi praśamaṃ prapanne,
kleśeṣu pañcasu gateṣu samaṃ samīhāṃ,
tattv'|âvabodham abhitaḥ Puruṣas tanoti. [1]

tad bhavatī tvaritataraṃ devīm Upaniṣadam anunīya mat|sakāśam ānayatv» iti. *(vilokya sa|harṣam)* mam' âmbā sa|harṣam kim api mantrayant" îta ev' âbhivartate.

6.5 *tataḥ praviśati* ŚRADDHĀ.

ŚRADDHĀ: aye! adya khalu cireṇa rāja|kulam avalokya me pīyūṣeṇ' êva locane pūrṇe!

a|satāṃ nigraho yatra, santaḥ pūjyā Śam'|ādayaḥ.
ārādhyate Jagat|svāmī vaśyair dev'|ânujīvibhiḥ. [2]

ŚĀNTIḤ *(upasṛtya)*: amba, kiṃ mantrayantī kva prasthit" âsi?

ŚRADDHĀ *«aye, ady'» êty|ādi paṭhati.*

6.10 ŚĀNTIḤ: atha Manasi kīdṛśī svāminaḥ Puruṣasya pravṛttiḥ?

*Enter* PEACE. 6.1

PEACE: I have been ordered by our sovereign Intuition, thus: "You have seen, my child, that—

With the demise of Nescience,
  and the decline of his sons,
Thought, enjoying Dispassion, knows peace.
The five afflictions now departed,
  the Inner Man at once, thoroughly
Extends his desire to know
  the true nature of reality.

Therefore, lady, you must quickly entreat goddess Úpanishad and bring her to me." *(looking about)* My mother is approaching joyfully with something to convey.

*Enter* FAITH. 6.5

FAITH: My, my! Seeing today the royal family at last fills my eyes with ambrosia!

Where the wicked have been chastised,
  the righteous, Restraint first, are extolled.
The Lord of the World is worshipped
  by his subjects who the divine life uphold.

PEACE *(approaching)*: Mother, what is it that you've come to say?

FAITH *repeats "My, my! Seeing today..."*

PEACE: So how does the Master, the Inner Man, now act upon Thought? 6.10

ŚRADDHĀ: yādṛśī vadhye nigrāhye ca bhavati.

ŚĀNTIḤ: tat kiṃ svāmy eva sāmrājyam alaṃ|kariṣyati?

ŚRADDHĀ: evam etat, yady ātmānam pratisaṃdhatte, tato devaḥ svarāṭ samrāḍ vā bhavati.

ŚĀNTIḤ: atha devasya Māyāyāṃ kīdṛśo 'nugrahaḥ?

6.15 ŚRADDHĀ: nanu «nigraha» iti vaktavye katham «anugrahaḥ» śakyate vaktum? devo 'pi hi «sarv'|ânartha|bījam iyaṃ Māyā, sarvathā nigrāhy"» êti manyate.

ŚĀNTIḤ: yady evaṃ, kutas tarh' îdanīṃ rāja|kulasya sthitiḥ?

ŚRADDHĀ: śṛṇu, vatse—

nity'|ânitya|Vicāraṇā praṇayinī,
Vairāgyam ekaṃ su|hṛt,
san|mitrāṇi Yam'|ādayaḥ, Śama|Dama|
prāyāḥ sakhāyo matāḥ,
Maitry|ādyāḥ paricārikāḥ, saha|carī
nityaṃ Mumukṣā, balād
ucchedyā ripavaś ca Moha|Mamatā|
Saṃkalpa|Saṅg'|ādayaḥ. [3]

ŚĀNTIḤ: atha Dharme svāminaḥ kīdṛśaḥ praṇayaḥ?

FAITH: As towards one to be executed or imprisoned.*

PEACE: So is it the Master himself who adorns his sovereign realm?

FAITH: Just so. If he recollects himself, the god becomes indeed both self-luminous and sovereign.*

PEACE: Then what favor does the god show to Illusion?

FAITH: In this case, one should speak of "captivity," so how 6.15
can one talk of "favor?" For the god thinks that this Illusion is the seed of all that is meaningless, and so must in every respect be restrained.

PEACE: If that's how things are, then what is the state of the royal family just now?

FAITH: Listen, my child—

> Discernment of eternal and ephemeral his beloved,
> Dispassion his best friend,
> Restraint is first among boon-companions,
> with Tranquility, Discipline and more thought
> to help,
> Love and her sisters are servant-girls,
> Desire-for-freedom an ever-present attendant—
> Thus with force might they eliminate their foes:
> Nescience, Selfishness, Willfulness,* Attachment,
> and all the rest.

PEACE: And how does the Master's regard Lex?

6.20 ŚRADDHĀ: putri, Vairāgya|saṃnikarṣāt prabhṛti nitāntam ih'|âmutra|phala|bhoga|virasa eva svāmi. tena—

sa narakād iva pāpa|phalād bhayaṃ
bhajati puṇya|phalād api nāśinaḥ;
iti samujjhita|kāma|samanvayaṃ
sukṛta|karma kathañ cana manyate. [4]

kin tv asau pratyak|pravaṇatāṃ svāmino vicintya, kṛtaṃ kartavyam iv' ātmānaṃ matvā, svayam eva Dharmaḥ ślatha|vyāpāro 'bhūt.

ŚĀNTIḤ: atha yān upasargān gṛhītvā Mahāmoho nilīya sthitas, teṣāṃ ko vṛttāntaḥ?

ŚRADDHĀ: putri, tathā dur|avasthāṃ gaten' âpi Mahāmoha|hatakena svāminaḥ prarocanāya Madhumatyā vidyayā sah' ôpasargāḥ preṣitāḥ. ayam abhiprāyaḥ, yady eteṣv āsaktaḥ svāmī, Viveka Upaniṣac|cintām api na kariṣyat' îti.

6.25 ŚĀNTIḤ: tatas tataḥ?

ŚRADDHĀ: tatas tayā saha tair gatvā k" âpi svāmina aindrajālikī vidy" ôpadarśitā. tathā hi—

FAITH: My daughter, from the moment he came into contact with Dispassion, the Master has quite lost his taste for the enjoyment of fruits, whether in this life or the next. Therefore— 6.20

> Just as he fears hell, evil's reward,
> so too merit's fruits that disappear;
> Thus does he think on deeds well done,
> abandoning desire's every connection.

But Lex, too, in considering the Master's innermost propensity, and so thinking his own tasks to be accomplished, has relaxed his efforts.

PEACE: Then, since Magnus Nescience has gone into hiding, having taken the deviations* with him, what news is there of them?

FAITH: Daughter, in order to entice the Master, that vile Magnus Nescience, despite his falling on hard times, dispatched the deviations together with the spell of the "Honeyed One."* His intention was that, should the Master become preoccupied with them, then Intuition would have no thought for Úpanishad.

PEACE: And then? 6.25

FAITH: Then they went there with it and revealed the spell, with its magical conjurations, to the Master. Whereupon—

śabdān eṣa śṛṇoti yojana|śatād,
āvir|bhavanti svatas
tās tā veda|purāṇa|bhārata|kathās,
tark'|ādayo vāṅmayāḥ.
grathnāti svayam icchayā śuci|padaiḥ
śāstrāṇi kāvyāni vā.
lokān bhrāmyati, paśyati sphuṭa|ruco
ratna|sthalīr Mairavīḥ. [5]

Madhumatīṃ ca bhūmim āpannaḥ, sthān'|âbhimāninībhir devatābhir upacchandyate: «bho! ih' ôpaviśyatām! n' âtra janma|mṛtyū. an|upādhi|ramaṇīyo deśaḥ. eṣa tvām upasthito vividha|vilāsa|lāvaṇya|puṇya|mayo, maṅgal'|ârtha|vyagra|pāṇiḥ, praṇaya|peśalo vidyādharī|janaḥ. tad ehi! yato 'tra—

kanaka|sikatila|sthalāḥ sravantīḥ,
pṛthu|jaghanāḥ kamal'|ānanā varorūḥ,
marakata|dala|komalā van'|ālīr
bhaja, nija|puṇya|jitāṃś ca sarva|bhogān.» [6]

6.30 ŚĀNTIḤ: tatas tataḥ?

He hears sounds a hundred leagues' distant,
and to him speech's works—
Vedas, *puránas*, epics and tales,
dialectics and more besides,
make themselves manifest.
In pure language, at will he composes
poetry or scientific texts.
Traveling through the worlds, he beholds
the Meru worlds, blazing with their grounds
of gems.*

Arriving then in the land of the Honeyed One, he is greeted there by godlings who are proud of that station: "Oh! do take your seat! Here there are neither birth nor death. It's a place to be enjoyed without limitation. There are spell-binding damsels, variously playful, charming and refined, hands outstretched with auspicious offerings, and tender with their affection there to attend you. So do come! For here—

Rivers with sandy, golden shores,
girls with plump thighs and lotus mien,
Wooded lanes with soft, emerald leaves—
Enjoy you these!
For all of them are pleasures sprung
from your virtuous deeds."

PEACE: What then? 6.30

ŚRADDHĀ: putri, tad ākarṇya Māyayā «ślāghyam etad» ity uktam. Manasā c' ânumoditam. Saṅkalpena protsāhitam. svāmī samprati san|mitra|patham iv' āpannaḥ.

ŚĀNTIḤ *(sa|khedam)*: hā dhik! hā dhik! punar api tām eva saṃsāra|vāgurām api patitaḥ svāmī!

ŚRADDHĀ: na khalu, na khalu.

ŚĀNTIḤ: tatas tataḥ?

6.35 ŚRADDHĀ: tataḥ pārśva|vartinā Tarkeṇa tān sarvān krodh'|āveśa|kaṣāyita|nayanam āloky' âbhihitaḥ svāmī, «svāmin! kim evam ebhir viṣay'|āmiṣa|grāsa|gṛdhnubhir āsthānī|dhūrta|bakaiḥ punar api teṣv eva viṣama|viṣay'|âṅgāreṣu nipātyamānam ātmānaṃ n' âvabudhyase? nanu bhoḥ—

> bhava|sāgara|tāraṇāya yā*
> su|cirād yoga|tarīs tvay' āśritā,
> adhunā parimucya tāṃ madāt,
> katham aṅgāra|nadīṃ vigāhase?» [7]

ŚĀNTIḤ: tatas tataḥ?

ŚRADDHĀ: tatas tad vacanam ākarṇya, «svasti viṣayebhya!» ity abhidhāy' âvadhīritā Madhumatī.

ŚĀNTIḤ: sādhu! sādhu! idānīṃ kva prasthitā bhavatī?

6.40 ŚRADDHĀ: ādiṣṭ" āhaṃ svāminā yathā, «Vivekaṃ draṣṭum icchām'» îti.

FAITH: My daughter, having heard that, Illusion declared it just fine. Thought, too, was delighted. Intention got all excited. It even seemed that the Master had found a congenial modus vivendi.

PEACE *(troubled)*: Alas! alas! the Master has fallen once again into *sansára*'s snare!

FAITH: Not so, not at all.

PEACE: So then?

FAITH: Reason, who was standing nearby, then looked at 6.35
them all, his eyes blood-shot with anger, and to the Master said, "Master! Don't you understand that you've been dragged down once again into the brimstone of base objects by this rogues' gallery of gluttons consuming carnal objects? For indeed—

> To sail o'er the sea of this world,
> yoga's boat is your enduring resort.
> Having set it adrift in folly now,
> why drown in a river of blazing coals?"

PEACE: And then?

FAITH: Then, after hearing those words, the Master said, "peace be upon those objects!" and thus repudiated the Honeyed One.

PEACE: Good! good! Now where are you staying, lady?

FAITH: I have been given an order by our Master, who says, 6.40
"I wish to see Intuition."

ŚĀNTIḤ: tat tvaratāṃ bhavatī.

ŚRADDHĀ: tad ahaṃ rāja|sannidhiṃ prasthitā.

ŚĀNTIḤ: aham api mahā|rājen' Ôpaniṣadam ānetum ādiṣṭā. tad bhavatu! sva|niyogaṃ saṃpādayāvaḥ.

*iti niṣkrānte.*

6.45 *praveśakaḥ.*

PEACE: So make haste, blessed lady.

FAITH: Then I'll be staying beside the king.

PEACE: I, too, have been instructed by the king to bring Úpanishad. So be it! Let's both fulfill our appointed tasks.

*Exeunt ambo.*

*Thus the prologue.* 6.45

# ACT SIX

# LIVING LIBERATION

*tataḥ praviśati* PURUṢAḤ.

PURUṢAḤ *(vicintya sa|harṣam)*: aho! māhātmyaṃ devyā Viṣṇubhakteḥ! yat|prasādān mayā—

tīrṇāḥ kleśa|mah"|ōrmayaḥ, parihṛtā
bhīmā mamatva|bhramāḥ.
śāntā mitra|kalatra|bandhu|makara|
grāha|graha|granthayaḥ.
krodh'|āurv'|âgnir apākṛto, vighaṭitās
tṛṣṇā|latā|vistarāḥ.
pāre tīram avāpta|kalpam adhunā
saṃsāra|vārām nidheḥ. [8]

*tataḥ praviśaty* UPANIṢAC CHĀNTIŚ *ca.*

6.50 UPANIṢAT: sakhi! kathaṃ tathā niranukrośasya svāmino mukham ālokayiṣyāmi, yen' âham itara|jana|yoṣ" êva suciram ekākinī parityaktā?

ŚĀNTIḤ: devi, kathaṃ tathā|vidha|vipat|patito deva upālabhyate?

UPANIṢAT: sakhi, na dṛṣṭā tvayā me tādṛśy avasthā, yen' âivaṃ bravīsi. śṛṇu—

bāhvor bhagnā dalita|maṇayaḥ
śreṇayaḥ kaṅkaṇānāṃ,
cūḍā|ratna|graha|nikṛtibhir
dūṣitaḥ keśa|pāśaḥ.
kaiḥ kair n' âhaṃ hata|vidhi|balād
īhitā dur|vidagdhair
dāsī|kartuṃ sapadi duritair
dūra|saṃsthe Viveke. [9]

*Enter the* INNER MAN.

INNER MAN *(thinking joyfully)*: Ha! magnanimous indeed is the goddess Hail Vishnu! For I, owing to her grace—

I've traversed the great flood of affliction,
the fearsome confusions of "mine" dispelled.
The knots that bound me in the crocodile jaws
of friends, wife and family are quelled.
The submarine fire of anger extinguished,
from craving's spreading vines I am free.
The other shore of *sansára*'s ocean
is where I have landed today.

*Enter* ÚPANISHAD *with* PEACE.

ÚPANISHAD: My friend! how can I look upon the loveless face of the Master? After all, for a long time he rejected me, all alone, as if I were someone else's woman. 6.50

PEACE: Why is it, goddess, that you so blame our lord, who had fallen into such difficulty?

ÚPANISHAD: You didn't see, my friend, just what state I was in, which is why you're speaking like this. Listen—

My golden arm-bracelets were broken,
their jewels were scattered about,
And the locks of my hair were sullied,
when my crown-gem was seized with abuse.
While Intuition was away,
I was at once to be made a slave
By small-minded knaves,
for my rites then were powerless,
and who among them desired me not?

ŚĀNTIḤ: sarvam etan Mahāmohasya dur|vilasitam. n' âtra devasy' âparādhaḥ. tena hi tathā Manaḥ Kām'|ādi|dvāreṇa prabodhayatā tvatto dūrī|kṛto Vivekaḥ. etad eva kula|strīṇāṃ naisargikaṃ śīlaṃ, yad vipan|magnasya svāminaḥ samaya|pratīkṣaṇam iti. tad ehi, darśanena priy'|ālāpena sambhāvaya devam. saṃpraty apahatā vidviṣaḥ. saṃpūrṇās te mano|rathāḥ.

6.55 UPANIṢAT: sakhi, saṃpraty āgacchantī vatsayā Gītay" âhaṃ rahasy uktā, yathā «bhartā, svāmī ca Puruṣas tvayā yathā|praśnam uttareṇa saṃbhāvayitavyaḥ, yathā Prabodh'|ôtpattir bhaviṣyat'» îti. tat kathaṃ gurūṇām adhyakṣaṃ dhārṣṭyam avalambiṣye?

ŚĀNTIḤ: devi, a|vicāraṇīyam etad vākyam bhagavatyā Gītāyāḥ. ayam eva c' ârtho devyā bhagavatyā Viṣṇubhaktyā Viveka|svāmino niruktaḥ. tad ehi. sambhāvaya darśanena bhartāram ādi|Puruṣaṃ ca.

UPANIṢAT: yathā vadati priya|sakhī. *(iti parikrāmati.)*

*tataḥ praviśati* RĀJĀ ŚRADDHĀ *ca.*

RĀJĀ: ayi vatse! api drakṣyati Śāntiḥ priyām Upaniṣadam?

6.60 ŚRADDHĀ: deva! gṛhīt'|ôddeś" âiva Śāntir gatā, kathaṃ tām na drakṣyati?

RĀJĀ: katham iva?

PEACE: All of this is Magnus Nescience's evil game. There's no fault of the lord here. It was he who, through Lust and the others, gave ideas to Thought, so that Intuition was alienated from you. And it is the normal rule among the women of our clan to await the right moment when their Master has fallen on hard times. So do come, and honor our lord with your sight and sweet words. Our enemies have been vanquished now. Your wishes are fulfilled.

ÚPANISHAD: My friend, now, as I was arriving, my child 6.55
Gita said to me in secret that "your husband and the Master, the Inner Man, should be honored by your responding in accord with their questions, whereby Wisdom's rise will occur." But how can I dare to be so bold in the presence of these elders?*

PEACE: My lady, you must not doubt the words of blessed Gita. For this was the meaning also disclosed to master Intuition by the holy Hail Vishnu. So come. Honor with your sight your husband and the Inner Man.

ÚPANISHAD: As my dear friend says. *(Walks around.)*

*Then enter the* KING *with* FAITH.

KING: Oh child! will Peace be seeing dear Úpanishad?

FAITH: My lord! as Peace received your assignment and 6.60
went off, how could she fail to see her?

KING: How indeed?

ŚRADDHĀ: deva, prāg eva kathitam etad devyā Viṣṇubhakty" āsīt, yathā Mandar'|âbhidhāne śaile Viṣṇor āyatane devyā Gītāyā saha tarka|vidyā|bhayād anupraviṣṭ" êti.

RĀJĀ: kathaṃ punas tarka|vidyā|bhayam?

ŚRADDHĀ: deva, tam etam arthaṃ s" âiva prastoṣyati. tad āgacchatu devaḥ. eṣa svāmī tvad|āgamanam eva dhyāyan vivikte vartate.

6.65 RĀJĀ *(upasṛtya)*: svāmin, abhivādaye!

PURUṢAḤ: vatsa, krama|viruddho 'yaṃ samudācāraḥ. yato jñāna|vṛddhatayā bhavān ev' âsmākam upadeśa|dānena pitṛ|bhāvam āpannaḥ. kutaḥ—

purā hi dharm'|âdhvani naṣṭa|saṃjñā,
devās tam arthaṃ tanayān apṛcchan.
jñānena samyak parigṛhya te vai,
«he putrakāḥ! saṃśṛṇut'» êty avocan. [10]

tad bhavān pitṛtven' âsmāsu vartatām, ity eṣa eva dharmaḥ.

ŚĀNTIḤ: eṣa, devi, devena saha svāmī vivikte vartate. tad upasarpatu devī.

FAITH: My lord, goddess Hail Vishnu related earlier that, owing to her fear of the science of reason, she has taken refuge with goddess Gita in the shrine of Vishnu on the Mándara mountain.*

KING: How is it that she's frightened of the science of reason?

FAITH: My lord, she'll explain the meaning of that. So come, my lord. The Master is sequestered in expectation of your arrival.

KING *(approaching)*: I salute you, Master! 6.65

INNER MAN: My child, these courtesies reverse the right order of things! For you, owing to seniority in knowledge, by granting instruction to us have attained the station of our father. Wherefore—

> In the past, when knowledge was lost
> in the way of the law,
> The gods asked their sons what it meant.
> Having then well embraced them
> with knowledge, did they respond,
> "Listen most carefully, O sons!"*

Therefore you must be fatherly toward us; for this indeed is the law.

PEACE: Goddess, the Master is sequestered with our lord. You may approach, goddess.

UPANIṢAD *upasarpati.*

ŚĀNTIḤ: svāmin! eṣ" Ôpaniṣad|devī pāda|vandanāy' āgatā.

PURUṢAḤ: na khalu! na khalu! yato māt" êyam asmākaṃ tattv'|âvabodh'|ôdayena. tad eṣ" âiv' âsmākaṃ namasyā! atha vā—

> anugraha|vidhau devyā
> mātuś ca mahad antaram;
> mātā gāḍhaṃ nibadhnāti,
> bandhaṃ devī nikṛntati. [11]

UPANIṢAT *Vivekam avalokya, namas|kṛtya dūre samupaviśati.*

PURUṢAḤ: amba, kathyatām, kva bhavatyā nītā ete divasāḥ?

UPANIṢAT: svāmin—

> nītāny amūni maṭha|catvara|śūnya|dev'|ā-
> gāreṣu mūrkha|mukharaiḥ saha vāsarāṇi. [12*ab*]

PURUṢAḤ: atha te jānanti kim api bhavatyās tattvam?

UPANIṢAT: na khalu, na khalu! kiṃ tu—

> te sv'|êcchayā mama girāṃ Draviḍ'|âṅgan"|ôkta|
> vācām iv' ârtham a|vicārya vikalpayanti. [12*cd*]

ÚPANISHAD *approaches.* 6.70

PEACE: Master! This is goddess Úpanishad, who has come to do homage to your feet.

INNER MAN: By no means! Not at all! For in terms of awakening to reality, she is our mother. Rather that we should be saluting her! To put it otherwise—

> Great is the difference in nurture's way,
> Between the mother and the goddess;
> For the mother binds one tightly,
> While the goddess cuts through the bonds.

ÚPANISHAD *looking at* INTUITION, *then saluting and sitting off to the side.*

INNER MAN: Tell me, mother, where have you spent all these days? 6.75

ÚPANISHAD: Master—

> These times have passed with fools who talk
> In vacant temples, cloisters, courts.

INNER MAN: But do they know anything of your real nature?

ÚPANISHAD: By no means, not at all! But—

> Fancifully, disregarding the sense, 6.80
> have they imagined my words,
> As though the phrases were the prattle
> of Dravidian girls.*

tena kevalaṃ teṣāṃ par'|ârtha|haraṇa|prayojanam eva mad|vicāraṇam.

PURUṢAḤ: tatas tataḥ?

UPANIṢAT: tataḥ, kadā cit—

> kṛṣṇ'|âjin'|âgni|samid|ājya|juhū|sruv'|ādi|
> pātrais, tath" êṣṭi|paśu|soma|mukhair makhaiś ca
> dṛṣṭā mayā parivṛt'|âkhila|karma|kāṇḍa|
> vyādiṣṭa|paddhatir ath' âdhvani Yajñavidyā. [13]

6.85 PURUṢAḤ: tatas tataḥ?

UPANIṢAT: tato mayā cintitam, «api nām' âiṣā pustaka|bhāra|vāhinī me jñāsyati tattvam» iti, ata ev' âsyāḥ sannidhau kāni cid vāsarāṇi nayāmi.

PURUṢAḤ: tatas tataḥ?

UPANIṢAT: tatas, tām aham upasthitā, tayā c' âham ukt" âsmi: «bhadre, kiṃ te samīhitam?» iti. tato may" ôktam, «ārye! a|nāth" âsmi. tvayi nivastum icchām'» îti.

PURUṢAḤ: tatas tataḥ?

6.90 UPANIṢAT: tatas tay" ôktaṃ, «bhadre! kiṃ te karm'?» êti. tato may" ôktam—

My thought, for them, is only a means to plunder other people's money.

INNER MAN: What then?

ÚPANISHAD: Then, at some point—

> Along the way have I beheld—
> Among black antelope hides, fires, kindling, ghee,
> pots, ladles and other utensils,
> Oblations, animal victims, burnt offerings as well—
> The ceremonial preparations
> That swirl about the Sacrificial Science,
> its methods taught in the Ritual Section.*

INNER MAN: And then? 6.85

ÚPANISHAD: Well then I thought, "Perhaps this pile of book-learning will come to know my true nature," and so I passed some time in her vicinity.

INNER MAN: What followed?

ÚPANISHAD: Then, when I approached her, she addressed me: "What is it you wish, good lady?" And I responded, "Venerable one! I am unprotected. I want to stay with you."

INNER MAN: Then?

ÚPANISHAD: Then she asked me, "Good lady! What kind of work do you do?" To this I said— 6.90

«yasmād viśvam udeti, yatra ramate,
yasmin punar līyate,
bhāṣā yasya jagad vibhāti, sahaj'|ā-
nand'|ôjjvalaṃ yan|mahaḥ,
śāntaṃ, śāśvatam, a|kriyaṃ, yam a|punar|
bhāvāya bhūt'|ēśvaraṃ
dvaita|dhvāntam apāsya yānti kṛtinaḥ—
prastaumi taṃ pūruṣam» iti. [14]

Yajñavidyā vicintya—

«Pumān a|kartā katham īśvaro bhavet?
kriyā bhav'|ôccheda|karī na vastu|dhīḥ.
kurvan kriyā eva naro bhava|cchidaḥ
śataṃ samāḥ śānta|manā jijīviṣet. [15]

tan manye n' âtiprayojanaṃ bhavatyāḥ parigraheṇa. tath" âpi yadi kartāraṃ bhoktāraṃ Puruṣaṃ stuvantī kiyantaṃ kālam atra vastum icchasi, ko doṣaḥ?»

6.95 RĀJĀ *(s'|ôpahāsam)*: aho! dhūm'|ândhakāra|śyāmalita|dṛśo duṣ|prajñatvaṃ Yajñavidyāyāḥ, yen' âivaṃ ku|tark'|ôpahatā! yataḥ—

"Whence the universe arises,
 where it halts,
 and where it ends;
Whose light illuminates the world,
 and which as radiance
 blazes with innate bliss;
Peaceful, eternal, inactive,
 to which, as the Lord of Beings,
The blessed, dispelling dualism's darkness,
 take recourse so as not to become again—
 to that Inner Man I bend."

Sacrificial Science thought about it—

"How might the Man, who is no creator,
  be our lord?
 For rites delimit the world,
 but not so the knowledge of reality.
The man performing rites,
 the world delimiting,
 might wish with peace of mind
 to live a century.*

Therefore, I don't think I have much in the way of means to support you. Still, if you wish to stay here for a while praising the Inner Man as agent and enjoyer,* there's no harm."

KING *(with mocking laughter)*: Uh-oh! The silliness of Sacrificial Science, her eyes blurred with the smoke's blinding soot, has overwhelmed her with bad logic! Hence— 6.95

ayaḥ svabhāvād a|calaṃ balāc calaty
a|cetanaṃ cumbaka|sannidhāv iva,
tanoti viśv'|ēkṣitur īkṣit'|ēritā
jaganti Māy" ēśvarat" êyam Īśituḥ. [16]

tasmāt tamo|'ndhānām ev' êyam an|īśvara|dṛṣṭiḥ. a|bodha|prabhavaṃ ca saṃsāraṃ karmabhiḥ śamayantī Yajñavidyā nūnam andha|tamasam andha|kāreṇ' âpaninīṣati!

svabhāva|līnāni, tamo|mayāni,
prakāśayed yo bhuvanāni sapta,
tam eva vidvān atimṛtyum eti,
n' ânyo 'sti panthā bhava|mukti|hetuḥ. [17]

PURUṢAḤ: tatas tataḥ?

6.100 UPANIṢAT: tato Yajñavidyayā vimṛśy' ôktam, «sakhi! tvat|saṃnikarṣād dur|vāsan"|ôpahatair asmad|antevāsibhiḥ karmasu ślath'|ādarair bhavitavyam. tat prasīdatu bhavatī sv'|âbhilaṣita|deśa|gamanāya.»

PURUṢAḤ: tatas tataḥ?

UPANIṢAT: tato 'haṃ tām atikramya prasthitā.

As iron, by nature immobile, insentient,
indeed moves when loadstone is near,
It is Illusion, the Lord's sovereign power,
who arranges the worlds,
impelled as she is by the sight
of the Seer of all.*

So this is the atheism of those blinded by the dark. Sacrificial Science, by trying to subdue with rites this *sansára* that's powered by ignorance, is just trying to remove darkness with a blinding fog!

Who illuminates the seven spheres,*
that by nature tend to dissolution,
and are of darkness formed,
In him the wise surpass mortality,
for there is no other way
to reach freedom from the world.

INNER MAN: What followed?

6.100 ÚPANISHAD: Then Sacrificial Science became reflective and said, "My friend! owing to your presence our adherents are overcome by bad habits and so will be lax in their respect for the rites. So, if you please, lady, go to some other country as you wish."

INNER MAN: What then?

ÚPANISHAD: Then I set off, having left her.

PURUṢAḤ: tatas tataḥ?

UPANIṢAT: tataḥ karma|kāṇḍa|vicāriṇī saha|carī Mīmāṃsā mayā dṛṣṭā—

6.105 vibhidya karmāṇy adhikāra|bhāñji,
śruty|ādibhiś c' ânugatā pramāṇaiḥ,
aṅgair vicitrair abhiyojayantī
prāpt'|ôpadeśair atideśakaiś ca. [18]

PURUṢAḤ: tatas tataḥ?

UPANIṢAT: tato 'haṃ tām api tath" âiv' āśrayam abhyarthitavatī. atha tay" âpy ukt" âsmi «bhadre, kiṃ|karm' âs'?» îti. tato mayā tad eva «yasmād viśvam» ity|ādi paṭhitam.

PURUṢAḤ: tatas tataḥ?

UPANIṢAT: tato Mīmāṃsayā pārśva|vartināṃ mukham ālokya' âbhihitam, «asty ev' âsmākaṃ lok'|ântara|phal'|ôpabhoga|yogya|Puruṣ'|ôpanayanen' ôpayogaḥ. tad dhriyatām karm'|ôpayukt"!» êti. tatra teṣām madhye ken' âpy antevāsin" âitad anumoditam eva. apareṇa tu prasiddha|pratiṣṭhena Mīmāṃsā|hṛday'|âdhidaivatena kumārila|svāmin" ôktaṃ: «devi! n' êyaṃ karm'|ôpayuktaṃ Puruṣam upanayati. kin tv a|kartāram, a|bhoktāram īśvaram, na c' âsāv īśvaraḥ karmas' ûpayujyate.» ath' âpareṇ' ôktam, «atha kiṃ laukikāt puruṣād anya īśvaro nām' âsti?» tatas tena vihasya punar uktam, «asti. tathā hi—

INNER MAN: And next?

ÚPANISHAD: Then I spied her companion, Lady Hermeneutics, who is concerned with the Ritual Section,*—

Dividing up the rites, allotting their functions, 6.105
conforming to valid reasons,
among them traditions,
She fits herself out with the varied parts
of received instructions
and their extensions.*

INNER MAN: Then?

ÚPANISHAD: Then I also sought a refuge with her. And she also addressed me, asking, "What work do you do, good lady?" And I recited again "Whence the universe..."

INNER MAN: What happened next?

ÚPANISHAD: Then Lady Hermeneutics faced her adherents and said, "By her demonstration of an Inner Man fit to enjoy rewards in the world to come, this indeed is useful to us. So let her be held to ritual work!" At that, among them, there were some of her followers who rejoiced about it. But another, the master Kumárila,* who is famed as a high authority, the chief divine at the heart of Hermeneutics, spoke up: "The Inner Man she adduces is of no use for the rites, goddess! But he's a lord who's neither agent, nor enjoyer, and such a lord has no application in the rites." Then someone else said, "Besides the empirical person, what other lord is there?" But the former mocked him and spoke again: "There is. For—

6.110 ekaḥ paśyati ceṣṭitāni jagatām,
anyas tu moh'|ândha|dhīr.
ekaḥ karma|phalāni vāñchati, dadāty
anyas tu tāny arthine.
ekaḥ karmasu śiṣyate, tanu|bhṛtāṃ
śāst" âiva devo 'paro.
niḥsaṅgaḥ Puruṣaḥ kriyāsu sa kathaṃ
‹kart"› êti saṃbhāvyate?» [19]

RĀJĀ *(sa|harṣam)*: sādhu, Kumārila|svāmin, sādhu! prājño 'sy, āyuṣmān bhava!

«dvau tau suparṇau sa|yujau, sakhāyau
samāna|vṛkṣaṃ pariṣasvajāte.
ekas tayoḥ pippalam atti pakvam,
anyas tv an|aśnann abhicākaśīti.» [20]

PURUṢAḤ: tatas tataḥ?

UPANIṢAT: tato 'haṃ Mīmāṃsām abhimantrya prasthitā.

6.115 PURUṢAḤ: tatas tataḥ?

UPANIṢAT: tato mayā bahubhiḥ śiṣyair upāsyamānās tarka|vidyā avalokitāḥ.

kā cid dvi|tri|viśeṣa|kalpana|parā,
nyāyaiḥ parā tanvatī
vādaṃ sa|cchala|jāti|nigraha|mayair
jalpaṃ vitaṇḍām api.

One sees the world's actions, 6.110
while the other's mind is clouded by unknowing.
One desires work's rewards,
while the other dispenses them to the seeker.
One trains himself in rites,
while the other, that god,
is corporeal beings' trainer.
How can you imagine the Inner Man,
unattached to deeds,
to be a so-called 'Creator?'"

KING *(joyfully)*: Good, master Kumárila, bravo! You're a sage, and you should live long!

"There are two friends, birds, joined as one,
clinging to the same tree.
One of them eats the ripened figs,
while the other, not eating, just sees."*

INNER MAN: What then?

ÚPANISHAD: Then, having spoken to Lady Hermeneutics, I moved on.

INNER MAN: And next? 6.115

ÚPANISHAD: Then, I looked into the sciences of reason, which were being practiced by many disciples.

There are some whose supreme idea is two or three distinctions;
others elaborate the rules—
made up of double-talk, fallacies, foregone conclusions—
for their doctrines, hot air, and abuses.

anyā tu prakṛter vibhajya puruṣasy'
ôdāharantī bhidāṃ
tattvānāṃ gaṇan'|âparā mahad|ahaṃ|
kār'|ādi|sarga|kramaiḥ. [21]

PURUṢAḤ: tatas tataḥ?

UPANIṢAT: tath" âiv' âham tāḥ samupasthitā. tābhiś c' ânuyuktayā mayā tad eva karm' ôpāhṛtam, «yasmād viśvam» ity|ādi. tatra tābhiḥ sa|prakāś'|ôpahāsam uktam, «āḥ vācāle! param'|âṇubhyo viśvam utpadyate. nimitta|kāraṇam īśvaraḥ.» anyayā tu sa|krodham uktam, «āḥ pāpe! katham īśvaram eva vikāriṇam kṛtvā vināśa|dharmiṇam upapādayasi? nanu re pradhānād viśv'|ôtpattiḥ.»

6.120 RĀJĀ: aho! dur|matayas tarka|vidyā etad api na jānanti! sarvaṃ prameya|jātam ghaṭ'|ādivat kāryam iti, param'|âṇu|pradhān'|ôpādāna|kāraṇam apy upekṣaṇīyam ev' êti. api ca—

ambhaḥ|śīta|kar'|ântarikṣa|nagara|
svapn'|êndrajāl'|ādivat
kāryaṃ meyam a|satyam etad, udaya|
dhvaṃs'|ādi|yuktaṃ jagat;
śuktau rūpyam iva, sraj' îva bhujagaḥ,
sv'|ātm'|âvabodhe Harāv
a|jñāte prabhavaty, ath' âstam ayate
tattv'|âvabodh'|ôdayāt. [22]

Still others, dividing person from primal nature
proclaim the enumerations they cherish
of phenomena in evolving progression,
starting with the great one, then egoism.*

INNER MAN: What occurred next?

ÚPANISHAD: As it happened, I joined them. And when they asked me, I explained my work to them, reciting, "Whence the universe arises..." as before. At that, clearly mocking me, they said, "You babbler! The universe arises from atoms. The Lord serves as an organizing cause." And others then spoke in anger: "Damn you! How is it that, by making the Lord to be just a cause of modifications, you just prove that he is subject to annihilation? Rather, it is from the prime matter that the universe originates."*

KING: Oh dear! the base-minded sciences of reason don't 6.120
even know this! They say that all that occurs as an object of knowledge is a causal result, as is a pot, but in that case the material cause, whether atoms or prime matter, must also be rejected.* And thus—

Like a reflected moon, a fairy-town, a dream, or
a conjuration,
this world in knowledge and act is unreal,
subject to generation and corruption;
Like silver in a shell, or a snake in a garland,
it appears when God—awareness of one's
true self—is unknown,
but vanishes just when awareness of reality dawns.*

vikāra|śaṅkā tu mugdha|vadhūnāṃ vilasitam iva. tathā hi—

śāntaṃ jyotiḥ katham an|udit'|ân|
asta|nitya|prakāśaṃ
viśv'|ôtpattau vrajati vikṛtiṃ
niṣkalaṃ nirmalaṃ ca?
śaśvan nīl'|ôtpala|dala|rucām
ambu|vāh'|āvalīnāṃ
prādur|bhāve bhavati viyataḥ
kīdṛśo vā vikāraḥ? [23]

PURUṢAḤ: sādhu! sādhu! prīṇayati mānasaṃ mam' âyaṃ prajñāvato vimarśaḥ. (UPANIṢADAṂ *prati*) tatas tataḥ?

6.125 UPANIṢAT: tatas tābhiḥ sarvābhir eva kruddhābhir uktam, «aho! viśva|vilayena muktim eṣā vadantī, nāstika|pathaṃ prasthitā, nigṛhyatām!» iti. tataḥ sa|saṃrambhaṃ māṃ nigrahītuṃ pradhāvitāḥ sarvāḥ.

PURUṢAḤ (*sa|trāsam*): tatas tataḥ?

UPANIṢAT: tato 'haṃ satvarataraṃ parikramya Daṇḍak'|âraṇyaṃ praviṣṭā. tato Mandara|śail'|ôpakalpitasya Madhusūdan'|āyatanasya n' âtidure—

bāhvor bhagnā dalita|maṇayah
śreṇayaḥ kaṅkaṇānāṃ,
cūḍā|ratna|graha|nikṛtibhir
dūṣitaḥ keśa|pāśaḥ.
chinnā mukt'|āvalir, apahṛtam,
srastam aṅgād dukūlam,

And the worry that this might be subject to modification is no more than the playful fancy of foolish girls. For—

How might the peaceful light—
unborn, unsubsiding, ever aglow,
unblemished and untainted—be modified
when the universe does arise?
For what change is there of eternal sky
when in it are manifest
Multitudes of rain-bearing clouds,
colored like blue-petaled lotuses?

INNER MAN: Excellent! Excellent! These sage considerations are pleasing to my mind. *(to* ÚPANISHAD*)* And then?

ÚPANISHAD: Then all of them spoke in anger: "Ah-ha! She 6.125
says that freedom is due to the universe subsiding! She should be restrained from wandering down the path of nihilism!" And then in a flurry they all ran to take hold of me.

INNER MAN *(frightened)*: What next?

ÚPANISHAD: Then I quickly moved on and entered the Dándaka forest.* And then, when the shrine of the Slayer of Madhu* on the Mándara mountain was not far away—

My golden arm-bracelets were broken,
their jewels were scattered about,
And the locks of my hair were sullied,
when my crown-gem was seized with abuse.
With my pearl-necklace broken,
garments fallen, from my body torn,

bhītā Gīt"|āśramam atha galan|
nūpur" âhaṃ praviṣṭā. [24]

PURUṢAḤ: tatas tataḥ?

6.130 UPANIṢAT: tato dev'|āyatanān nirgatya daṇḍa|pāṇibhiḥ puruṣair atinirdayam tāḍyamānās tā dig|antam atikrāntāḥ sarvāḥ.

RĀJĀ *(sa|harṣam)*: na khalu bhavatīm atikrāmato bhagavān viśva|sākṣī kṣamate.

PURUṢAḤ: tatas tataḥ?

UPANIṢAT: tatra ca vatsayā Gītayā māṃ tatr' āgatām avalokya sa|saṃbhramaṃ «mātar! mātar!» iti parirabhy' ôpaveśit" âsmi. vidita|vṛttāntayā tayā c' ôktam, «amba, n' âtra khedayitavyaṃ Manaḥ. ye khalu tvām a|pramāṇī|kṛtya yath"|êṣṭam asura|sattvāḥ pracariṣyanti, teṣām Īśvara eva śāstā. uktaṃ ca tena bhagavatā tān adhikṛtya—

‹tān ahaṃ dviṣataḥ, krūrān,
saṃsāreṣu nar'|âdhamān
kṣipāmy ajasram a|śubhān
āsurīṣv eva yoniṣu› iti.» [25]

6.135 PURUṢAḤ *(sa|kautukam)*: devi, tvat|prasādāj jñātum icchāmi ko 'yam «īśvaro» nām' êti?

UPANIṢAT *(sa|smitam)*: ko nām' ātmānam a|jānantam pratyuttaraṃ dāsyati?

My anklets shaking, terrified
I entered Gita's ashram.

INNER MAN: Then what?

ÚPANISHAD: Then, having fled the divinity's shrine, they were mercilessly pummeled by persons with cudgels, until they all departed to the ends of the earth.* 6.130

KING *(joyfully)*: The all-seeing Lord, indeed, cannot bear to see you assaulted, my lady.

INNER MAN: What next?

ÚPANISHAD: Once there, my child Gita took a look at me as I arrived, and crying, "Mother! mother!" hurried to embrace me and usher me in. Once she knew what had taken place, she said, "Mother, there's no reason here to trouble Thought. For those who have treated you with disparagement, demonic creatures who will do as they please, the Lord will be their instructor. And it was with reference to them that the blessed lord said—

'Hateful, cruel and wretched men,
in *sansára* I ever hurl,
Unholy that they are,
into demonic wombs.'"*

INNER MAN *(inquisitively)*: Goddess, by your grace I wish to know who is this one you call the "Lord?" 6.135

ÚPANISHAD *(smiling*)*: Who indeed is going to answer your question in ignorance of the self?

PURUṢAḤ *(sa|harṣam)*: katham? mam' ātmā param'|ēśvaraḥ?

UPANIṢAT: evam etat. tathā hi—

asau tvad|anyo na sanātanaḥ Pumān,
bhavān na devāt Puruṣottamāt paraḥ.
sa eva bhinnas tad|anādi|māyayā,
dvidh" êva bimbaṃ salile vivasvataḥ [26]

6.140 PURUṢAḤ *(*VIVEKAṂ *prati)*: bhagavan, uktam apy arthaṃ bhagavatyā na samyag avadhārayāmi.

avachinnasyav bhinnasya,
jarā|maraṇa|dharmiṇaḥ
mama bravīti dev" îyaṃ
nity'|ānanda|cid|ātmatām. [27]

VIVEKAḤ: pad'|ârth'|âparijñānād ayaṃ vāky'|ârth'|ân|avabodhas.

PURUṢAḤ: tad|avabodhāya bhagavān upāyam ājñāpayatu.

VIVEKAḤ: ayam ucyate—

6.145 «eṣo 'sm'» îti vivicya «n'|êti»|padataś
cittena sārdhaṃ kṛte,
tattvānāṃ vilaye cid|ātmani pari-
jñāte tvam|arthe punaḥ,

INNER MAN *(joyfully)*: How's that? Is it then my self that is the supreme lord?

ÚPANISHAD: So it is. Thus—

> This eternal Man is no different from you,
> You are not other than the Supreme Person divine.
> Due to beginningless illusion this one differs from you,
> Like the sun's reflection in water, there seem to be two.

INNER MAN *(to* INTUITION*)*: Blessed lord, I can't quite seem to get the meaning of what the blessed lady has said. 6.140

> This goddess speaks of my ever blissful, conscious state of self,
> Though I'm delimited and divided, subject to aging and death.

INTUITION: This failure to understand the meaning of the utterance is due to the lack of recognition of that to which it refers.

INNER MAN: Instruct me, blessed lord, so that I may comprehend.

INTUITION: This is said—

> Having distinguished, "I am this," 6.145
> with a thought provoked by the word "not,"
> Phenomena then come to rest as you comprehend
> the conscious self as the meaning of "thou,"

śrutvā «tat tvam as'» îti, bādhita|bhava|
dhvāntaṃ tad ātma|prabhaṃ,
śāntaṃ jyotir an|antam antar|udit'|ā-
nandaṃ samuddyotate. [28]

PURUṢAḤ *s'|ānandaṃ śrutam arthaṃ paribhāvayati.*

*tataḥ praviśati* NIDIDHYĀSANAM.

NIDIDHYĀSANAM: ādiṣṭo 'smi bhagavatyā Viṣṇubhaktyā, yathā, «nigūḍham asmad|abhiprāyam Upaniṣad Vivekena saha bodhayitavyā. tvayā ca Puruṣeṇa vastavyam» iti. *(vilokya)* eṣā devī Viveka|Puruṣābhyāṃ n' âtidūre vartate. yāvad upasarpāmi. *(upasṛtya, Upaniṣadaṃ prati jan'|ântikam)* devyā Viṣṇubhaktyā samādiṣṭaṃ, yathā: «saṃkalpa|yonayo devatā bhavanti. mayā ca samādhānena viditaṃ, tath" āpannasattvā bhavat" îti. tatra ca krūra|sattvā Vidyā nāma kanyā tvad|udare vartate, Prabodha|candraś ca. tatra Vidyāṃ saṅkarṣaṇa|vidyayā Manasi saṅkrāmayiṣyasi. Prabodha|candraṃ Puruṣe samarpya vatsa|Vivekena saha mat|samīpam āgamiṣyas'» îti.

UPANIṢAT: yad ādiśati mahā|devī. *(iti* VIVEKAM *ādāya niṣkrāntā.)*

When hearing "thou art that;"
the world's darkness then erased,
for "that" is the self's radiance,
The peaceful limitless light
shines as blissfulness dawning within.*

INNER MAN *joyfully reflects upon the meaning of what he has heard.*

*Enter* CONTEMPLATION.

CONTEMPLATION: I have been commanded by the blessed lady Hail Vishnu, saying, "It is our hidden intention that Úpanishad is to be fulfilled together with Intuition. You must stay by the Inner Man." *(looking around)* The goddess is not far from Intuition and the Inner Man. I'll just approach. *(approaching, and whispering to* ÚPANISHAD *alone)* The goddess Hail Vishnu has dispatched me with this message: "The divinities are born from conception.* Just as I have realized through absorption, so it is that you are pregnant. Within your womb there is a fierce being, a girl named Scientia, as well as Wisdom Moon. Of them, having attracted Scientia with a spell, you will cause her to take possession of Thought. Wisdom Moon, on being restored to the Inner Man will come beside me, together with dear Intuition."

ÚPANISHAD: As the great goddess commands. *(Taking* INTUITION, *she departs.)*

NIDIDHYĀSANAṂ PURUṢAṂ *praviśati.*

PURUṢAḤ *dhyānaṃ nāṭayati.*

NEPATHYE: āścaryam! āścaryam!

uddāma|dyuti|dāmabhis taḍid iva
pradyotayantī diśaḥ,
pratyagra|sphuṭad|utkaṭ'|âsthi Manaso
nirbhidya vakṣaḥ|sthalam,
kany" êyaṃ sahasā samaṃ parikarair
Mohaṃ grasantī, bhajaty
antar|dhānam, upaiti c' âika|Puruṣaṃ
śrīmān Prabodh'|ôdayaḥ. [29]

*tataḥ praviśati* PRABODHACANDRAḤ.

PRABODHACANDRAḤ:

kiṃ v" āptaṃ? kim apohitaṃ? kim uditaṃ?
kiṃ vā samutsāritaṃ?
syūtaṃ kiṃ nu? vilāyitaṃ nu? kim idaṃ?
kiñ cin, na vā kiñ cana?
yasminn abhyudite vitarka|padavīṃ
n' âivaṃ samārohati
trailokyaṃ sahaja|prakāśa|dalitaṃ,
so 'haṃ Prabodh'|ôdayaḥ. [30]

*(parikramya)* eṣa Puruṣaḥ. yāvad upasarpāmi. *(upasṛtya)* bhagavan, Prabodha|candro 'ham abhivādaye!

CONTEMPLATION *disappears into the* INNER MAN. 6.150

INNER MAN *acts as in meditation.*

BACKSTAGE: Wonderful! Wonderful!

Like lightning illumining the directions,
with chains of brilliance unrestrained,
Breaking through Thought's breastplate,
the thick bone just now burst asunder,
This girl all at once devours Nescience,
with his minions too,
Then disappears herself,
while glorious Wisdom's rise
approaches the sole Inner Man.

*Then enter* WISDOM MOON.

WISDOM MOON:

What is obtained? What removed? 6.155
What arisen?What expelled?
What's been sewn up? What put to rest?
What is this? Is it something, or nothing at all?
This triple world finds not reason's course,
for it is dispelled by the innate light,
When that emerges, namely I
who am Wisdom's rise.

*(walking around)* Here's the Inner Man. I'll just approach him. *(Approaches.)* Blessed sir! I, Wisdom Moon, salute you!

PURUṢAḤ *(s'|āhlādam)*: ehi, putra! pariṣvajasva mām!

PRABODHACANDRAS *tathā karoti.*

PURUṢAḤ *(āliṅgya s'|ānandam)*: aho! vighaṭita|timira|paṭalaṃ saṃjātam! tathā hi—

6.160 Moh'|ândha|kāram avadhūya, vikalpa|nidrām
unmathya, ko 'py ajani bodha|tuṣāra|raśmiḥ.
Śraddhā|Viveka|Mati|Śānti|Yam'|ādi yena
viśv'|ātmakaḥ sphurati: Viṣṇur ahaṃ sa eṣaḥ. [31]

sarvathā kṛta|kṛtyo 'smi bhagavatyā Viṣṇubhakteḥ prasādāt. so 'ham idānīm—

saṅge na kena cid upetya, kam apy a|pṛcchan,
gacchann a|tarkita|phalaṃ vidiśaṃ diśaṃ vā,
śānto vyapeta|bhaya|śoka|kaṣāya|mohaḥ,
sāyaṃ gṛhe munir ahaṃ bhavit" âsmi sadyaḥ. [32]

*tataḥ praviśati* VIṢṆUBHAKTIḤ.

VIṢṆUBHAKTIḤ *(sa|harṣam upasṛtya)*: cireṇa khalv asmākaṃ saṃpannāḥ sarve mano|rathāḥ, yena praśānt'|ârātiṃ bhavantam avalokayāmi.

INNER MAN *(delightedly)*: Come, son! Embrace me!

WISDOM MOON *does so.*

INNER MAN *(hugs him joyfully.)*: Oh! The blindfold of ignorance has been removed! Just so—

Having dispelled Nescience's darkness, 6.160
shaken off the sleep of conceptual activity,
The moon of awakening
has somehow become manifest.
With Faith, Intuition, Intelligence,
Peace, Restraint and the rest,
The universal Self bursts into view:
I am he, this very one, Vishnu.

My every task is fulfilled by the grace of the blessed Hail Vishnu. It is I, now who am—

Unattached in all respects, nothing left to ask,
wandering in all quarters and directions
without destination fixed,
At peace and free
from fear, grief, ignorance, and impropriety,
a sage at home in evening's calm,*
purified instantly.

*Enter* HAIL VISHNU.

HAIL VISHNU *(approaching joyfully)*: All of our wishes at long last are accomplished, so that I see you as one whose enemies are no more.

6.165 PURUṢAḤ: devyā Viṣṇubhakteḥ prasādāt kiṃ nāma duṣkaram? *(iti pādayoḥ patati.)*

VIṢṆUBHAKTIḤ (PURUṢAM *utthāpayati.)*: uttiṣṭha, vatsa. kiṃ te bhūyaḥ priyam upaharāmi?

PURUṢAḤ: kiṃ ataḥ param api priyam asti? yataḥ—

pūrvaṃ tāvad Viveka|
pramukha|nija|balair nirjite s'|ânubandhe
Mohe 'smākaṃ kul'|ârau,
tadanu samudite, hanta, Vairāgya|yoge,
Śānti|Śraddh"|ādi|yatnāt
punar Upaniṣadā sādhitāt samprayogād,
asmābhis tvat|prasādād
dhruvam ayam adhunā labdha eva Prabodhaḥ.
[33]

saṃsār'|âpāra|sindhu|
plava|kuśala|mahā|karṇa|dhāre Mur'|ârau
bhaktir mukteḥ parā sā
prasaratu jananī sārvakālaṃ janasya!
kiñ c' ânyat sva|prakāśaṃ
paratarам amala|jyotir ānanda|sāndraṃ
śānt'|ātmāno mun'|îndrāḥ
pramudita|manasaḥ santataṃ bhāvayantu! [34]

INNER MAN: With goddess Hail Vishnu's grace, what could be hard to accomplish? *(He falls before her feet.)* 6.165

HAIL VISHNU *(bidding the* INNER MAN *to stand)*: Stand, my child. What further favor might I grant you?

INNER MAN: What favor is there beyond this? For—

At first the enemy of our clan,
Nescience with his hangers-on,
Was defeated by the native strength
of Intuition, above all;
then, indeed, union with Dispassion arose.
Now we've attained forever Wisdom,
by your grace in tandem
with what Úpanishad has done
Through exertions that were by Peace,
Faith and others begun.

May our mother, lofty devotion to Mura's Foe,*
the great helmsman at ease in the boat
o'er *sansára*'s shoreless sea,
Guide the folk to freedom eternally!
What's more, ever higher,
may the sages supreme,
peaceful souls with joyful minds,
forever contemplate
the rich bliss of taintless light
that self-illuminates!*

6.170 praśānt'|ârātir agamad Vivekaḥ kṛta|kṛtyatām,
nīrajaske sad|ānande pade c' âhaṃ niveśitaḥ. [35]

tath" âp' îdam astu…

BHARATA|VĀKYAM:

parjanyo 'smin jagati mahatīṃ
vṛṣṭim iṣṭāṃ vidhattāṃ.
rājānaḥ kṣmāṃ galita|vividh'|ô-
paplavāṃ pālayantu.
tattv'|ônmeṣ'|âpahata|tamasas
tvat|prasādān mahāntaḥ
saṃsār'|âbdhiṃ viṣaya|mamat"|ā-
taṅka|paṅkaṃ tarantu. [36]

*iti niṣkrāntāḥ sarve.*

*iti śrī|Kṛṣṇamiśra|viracite Prabodhacandrodaya|nāmni nāṭake jīvan|muktir nāma ṣaṣṭho 'ṅkaḥ.*

Intuition, freed from enemies, 6.170
his task was done,
Making me to dwell within
bliss eternal's taintless station.

So may this come to pass...

THE VOICES OF THE CHORUS:

May the clouds release on the world
the great rain for which we've prayed.
May our kings, diverse woes subdued,
stand guard upon the earth.
And by your grace, may persons great,
darkness dispelled by dawning truth,
Traverse *sansára*'s sea,
a mire wherein dangers stem
from taking objects as the self's properties.

*Exeunt omnes.*

*Thus concludes Act Six, entitled 'Living Liberation,'**
*in "The Rise of Wisdom Moon," composed by*
*the eminent Krishna·mishra·yati.*

# CHĀYĀ

*The following is a Sanskrit paraphrase* (chāyā) *of the Prakrit passages (marked with* ⌜corner brackets⌟ *in the play). References are to act and paragraph.*

1.9 eṣ" âsmi. ājñāpayatv ārya|putraḥ, ko niyogo 'nuṣṭhīyatām iti.

1.15 āścaryam, āścaryam! yena tathā nija|bhuja|bala|vikram'|âika|nirbhartsita|sakala|rāja|maṇḍalen' ākarṇ'|ākṛṣṭa|kaṭhina|kodaṇḍa|daṇḍa|bahala|ghana|varṣat|santata|śara|dhārā|nikara|jarjarat|turaṅga|taraṅga|mālam, nirantara|nipatat|tīkṣṇa|khadga|vikṣipta|sva|hasta|śastra|paryast'|ôttuṅga|mātaṅga|mahā|mahīdhara|sahasram, bhramad|bhuja|daṇḍa|Mandar'|âbhighāta|ghūrṇamāna|sakala|patti|salila|saṃghātaṃ karṇa|sainya|sāgaraṃ nirmathya, Madhumathanen' êva kṣīra|samudram, āsāditā samara|vijaya|lakṣmīḥ. tasya sāmpratam sakala|muni|jana|ślāghanīyaḥ katham īdṛśa upaśamaḥ saṃvṛttaḥ?

1.34 ārya|putra! garīyān khalu mahā|rāja|Mahāmohasya pratipakṣo Viveka, iti tarkayāmi.

1.39 ārya|putra, evaṃ etat. tath" âpi mahā|sahāya|saṃpannaḥ śaṅkitavyo 'rātiḥ. yato 'sya Yama|Niyama|pramukhā amātyā mahā|balāḥ śrūyante.

1.45 śrutaṃ mayā, yuṣmākaṃ Śama|Dama|Viveka|prabhṛtīnāṃ c' âikam utpatti|sthānam iti.

1.49 ārya|putra, yady evaṃ, tat kin|nimittaṃ yuṣmākaṃ s'|ôdarāṇām ap' īdṛśaṃ vairam?

1.53 śāntaṃ pāpaṃ, śāntaṃ pāpam! ārya|putra, kiṃ etat pāpaṃ vidveṣa|mātreṇa tair ārabdham? atha vā upāyo 'pi ko 'py atra mantritaḥ?

1.55 ārya|putra, tat kiṃ n' ôdghāṭyate?

1.57 ārya|putra, kīdṛśaṃ tat?

1.59 hā dhik! katham punar asmākaṃ kule rākṣas"—îti vepate me hṛdayam!

1.61 atha tayā rākṣasyā kiṃ kartavyam?

1.64 ārya|putra! paritrāyasva, paritrāyasva!

1.68 ārya|putra, kiṃ tasyā rākṣasyā utpattir asmākaṃ pratipakṣāṇāṃ sammatā?

1.70 katham punar ātmano vināśa|kāriṇyā Vidyāyā utpattis tair dur|vinītaiḥ ślāghyate?

1.83 ārya|putra, kim ātmano doṣaṃ loko vijānāti?

1.87 ārya|putra, yato 'sau sahaj'|ānanda|sundara|svabhāvo nitya|prakāśa|sphurat|sakala|tribhuvana|pracāraḥ Parameśvaraḥ śrūyate. tasmāt katham etair dur|vidagdhair bandhitvā mahāmoha|sāgare nikṣiptaḥ?

1.90 ārya|putra, nanu andhakāra|lekhayā sahasra|raśmes tiras|kāro yan Māyayā tathā prasphuran|mahā|prakāśa|sāgarasya devasy' âpy abhibhavaḥ.

1.93 ārya|putra, kiṃ punaḥ kāraṇaṃ, yena sā tath" ôdāra|caritaṃ dur|vidagdhā pratārayati?

1.97 ārya|putra, kiṃ nāma tat kāraṇam?

1.100 yādṛśī mātā, putro 'pi tādṛśa eva jātaḥ.

1.103 ārya|putra, evaṃ dīrgha|dīrghatara|nidrā|vidrāvita|prabodhe Parameśvare kathaṃ Prabodh'|ôtpattir bhaviṣyati?

1.105 kim iti gurutara|lajjā|bhara|namita|śekharas tūṣṇīṃ|bhūto 'si?

1.107 anyās tāḥ striyo, yāḥ svarasa|pravṛttasya vā dharma|patha|vyāpāra|pravṛttasya vā bhartur hṛday'|ēpsitaṃ vighnanti.

1.110 ārya|putra, yady evaṃ kula|prabhor dṛḍha|granthi|niṣṭhāpita bandha|mokṣo bhavati, tatas tayā nity'|ânubaddha ev' ārya|putro bhavatu! suṣṭhu me priyam.

2.76 ācārya, yady eṣa eva puruṣ'|ârtho yat khādyate pīyate ca, tat kim ity etais tairthikaiḥ saṃsāra|saukhyaṃ parihṛty' ātmā ghora|ghoraiḥ parāka|sāntapana|ṣaṣṭha|kāl'|âśana|prabhṛtibhir duḥkhaiḥ kṣapyate?

2.79 ācārya, evaṃ khalu tairthikā ālapanti, duḥkha|miśritaṃ saṃsāra|saukhyaṃ pariharaṇīyam iti.

2.107 aham Utkala|deśād āgato 'smi. tatra sāgara|tīra|sanniveśe Puruṣottama|śabditaṃ devat"|āyatanam. tasmin Mada|Mānābhyāṃ bhaṭṭārakābhyāṃ mahā|rāja|sakāśaṃ preṣito 'smi.

2.107 eṣā Vārāṇasī. etad rāja|kulam. yāvat praviśāmi.

2.107 eṣa bhaṭṭārakaś Cārvākeṇa sārdhaṃ kim api mantrayaṃs tiṣṭhati. bhavat', ûpasarpāmy enam.

2.107 jayatu, jayatu bhaṭṭārakaḥ. idaṃ patraṃ nirūpayatu bhaṭṭārakaḥ.

2.109 bhaṭṭāraka! Puruṣottamād.

2.116 yad deva ājñāpayati.

2.133 ārya|putra ājñāpayatu.

2.136 ārya|putra, svayam eva tāvad aham etasminn arthe nityam abhiyuktā. sāmpratam ārya|putrasy' ājñayā brahm'|âṇḍa|koṭibhir api na me udaraṃ pūrayiṣyate.

2.139 eṣ" âsmi! ājñāpayatv ārya|putraḥ!

2.149 yad deva ājñāpayati.

2.150 sakhi, cira|dṛṣṭasya mahā|rājasya kathaṃ mukhaṃ prekṣiṣye? nanu mahā|rājo māṃ upālambhiṣyate.

2.151 sakhi, tvad|darśane ātmānam api mahā|rājo na cetayiṣyati, tataḥ kathaṃ upālambhiṣyate?

2.152 kasmān māṃ alīka|saubhāgyāṃ saṃbhāvya viḍambayasi?

2.153 sakhi, sāmpratam eva prekṣiṣye 'līkatvaṃ saubhāgyasya! anyac ca ghūrṇamāna|nidr"|ākulaṃ iva priya|sakhyā locanaṃ prekṣye. tat kiṃ khalu priya|sakhyā vinidratāyāḥ kāraṇam?

2.154 sakhi, eka|vallabh" âpi yā strī bhavati, tasyā api nidrā dur|labhā nāma. kiṃ punar asmākaṃ sakala|vallabhānām?

2.155 ke punaḥ priya|sakhyā vallabhāḥ?

2.156 mahā|rājaḥ, tata upari Kāmaḥ, Krodho, Lobhaś ca. atha v" âlaṃ viśeṣeṇa! atra kule yo jāto hṛdaya|nihitayā rātri|divasāny abhiramate mayā na vinā—bālaḥ, sthaviro, yuvā ca.

2.157 nanu Kāmasya Ratiḥ, Krodhasya Hiṃsā, Lobhasya Tṛṣṇā priy" êti śrūyate. tāsāṃ kathaṃ priya|janaṃ nityaṃ ramayant" īrṣyāṃ na janayasi?

2.158 īrṣy" êti kiṃ bhaṇyate? tā api mayā vinā muhūrtam api na tuṣyanti!

2.159 ata eva bhaṇāmi, tava sadṛśī subhagā iha pṛthivyāṃ n' âst' îti, yasyāḥ saubhāgya|vairāgya|vijvarita|hṛdayāḥ sa|patnyo 'pi saṃprasādaṃ pratīcchanti. sakhi, anyad api bhaṇāmi. evaṃ nidr"|ākula|hṛdayā visaṃsthula|skhalac|caraṇa|nūpura|jhaṅkāra|mukharayā gatyā mahā|rājaṃ saṃbhāvayantī śaṅkita|hṛdayaṃ kariṣyati priya|sakh", îti tarkayāmi.

2.160 kim atra śaṅkitavyam? nv asmākaṃ mahā|rāja|niyuktānām ev' âiṣo '|vinayaḥ. api ca, darśana|mātra|prasādita|puruṣāṇāṃ yuvatīnāṃ kīdṛśaṃ bhayam.

2.163 eṣa mahā|rājaḥ. upasarpatu priya|sakhī.

2.164 jayatu, jayatu mahā|rājaḥ!

2.170 mahā|rāja, aham api sāṃprataṃ nava|yauvanā saṃvṛttā. na khalu bhāv'|ânubandhaḥ premā kālen' âpi vighaṭate. ājñāpayatu bhartā, kin|nimittaṃ bhartrā smṛt" âsmi?

2.173 mahān prasādaḥ!

2.176 etāvan|mātre viṣaye alaṃ bhartur abhiniveśena! vacana|mātreṇ' âiva bhartur dāsa iva sarva ājñāṃ kariṣyati. sā khalu mayā mithyā dharmo, mithyā mokṣo, mithyā veda|mārgo, mithyā sukha|vighna|karāṇi, mithyā śāstra|pralapitāni, mithyā svarga|phalam iti bhaṇyamānā veda|mārgam eva parihariṣyati, kiṃ punar Upaniṣadam. api ca—

2.177 viṣay'|ānanda|vimukte mokṣe doṣān darśayantyā / Upaniṣadā hi viraktā jhaṭiti kriyate mayā Śraddhā.

2.179 hanta! prakāśa evaṃ pravṛttena bhartrā lajje.

3.7 sakhi, evaṃ viṣama|jvalana|jvāl”|āvalī|tīkṣṇāny akṣarāṇi jalpantī sarvathā vilupta|jīvitāṃ māṃ karoṣi. tasmāt prasīda muhūrtaṃ, dhārayatu jīvitaṃ priya|sakhī. yāvad itas tataḥ puṇyeṣv āśrameṣu muni|jana|samākuleṣu Bhāgīrathī|tīreṣu su|nipuṇaṃ nirūpayāvaḥ. sā kadā cid api Mahāmoha|bhītā katham api pracchannaṃ nivasati.

3.10 sakhi, evaṃ bhaṇāmi. yadi sāttvikī Śraddhā, tato na tasyā īdṛśīṃ durgatiṃ saṃbhāvayāmi. na khalu tādṛśyaḥ puṇyamayyaḥ tādṛśīṃ a|saṃbhāvanīyāṃ vipattim anubhavanti.

3.14 sakhy, evaṃ bhavatu.

3.16 sakhi, rākṣaso, rākṣasaḥ!

3.18 paśya, paśya! ya eṣa galan|mala|paṅka|picchila|bībhatsa|duḥprekṣya|deha|cchavir, ulluñchita|cikura|bharo, mukta|vasana|veṣa|durdarśanaḥ, śikhi|śikhaṇḍa|picchikā|hasta ita ev’ âbhivartate.

3.20 tarhi ka eṣa bhaviṣyati?

3.22 sakhi, evaṃ prasphuran|mayūkha|māl”|ôdbhāsita|bhuvan’|ântarāle jvalat|pracaṇḍa|mārtāṇḍa|maṇḍale divasa|mukhe kathaṃ piśācānām avakāśaḥ?

3.24 sakhi, muhūrtaṃ tiṣṭha, yāvad itaḥ Śraddhām anveṣayāmi.

3.26 namo ’rhadbhyo, ’rhadbhyaḥ! nava|dvāra|gṛha|madhye ātmā dīpa iva pradīptaḥ. eṣa jina|vara|bhāṣitaḥ param’|ârtho dharmo mokṣa|saukhya|daḥ!

3.26 re re śrāvakāḥ! śṛṇuta, śṛṇuta!

3.27 mala|maya|pudgala|piṇḍe sakala|jalair api kīdṛśī śuddhiḥ? / ātmā vimala|svabhāva ṛṣi|paricaraṇair jñātavyaḥ.

3.28 kiṃ bhaṇatha, kīdṛśam ṛṣiparicaraṇam iti? tac chṛṇuta!

3.29 dūre caraṇa|praṇāmaḥ, kṛta|satkāraṃ ca, bhojanaṃ mṛṣṭam, / īrṣyā|malaṃ na kāryam ṛṣīṇāṃ dārān ramamāṇānām.

3.30 Śraddhe! itas tāvat!

3.32 kim ājñāpayati rāja|kulam?

3.33 śrāvakāṇāṃ kuṭumbaṃ muhūrtam api mā parityaja.

3.34 yad ājñāpayati rāja|kulam.

3.35 samāśvasitu priya|sakhī. na khalu nāma|mātreṇa priya|sakhyā bhetavyam. yataḥ śrutaṃ mayā Ahiṃsāyāḥ sakāśād, asti pāṣaṇḍānām api Tamasaḥ sutā Śraddh" êti. ten' âiṣā Tāmasī Śraddhā bhaviṣyati.

3.44 sakhi, ka eṣa? taruṇatara|tāla|taru|pallavo lambamāna|kaṣāya|piśaṅga|cīra|cīvaro sa|cūḍa|muṇḍita|muṇḍa|veṣa ita ev' âbhigacchati.

3.48 ājñāpayatu rāja|kulam.

3.50 yad ājñāpayati rājakulam.

3.52 evaṃ etat.

3.53 arere! bhikṣuka! itas tāvat! kim api pṛcchāmi.

3.55 are, muñca krodham. śāstra|gataṃ pṛcchāmi.

3.57 bhaṇa tāvat, kṣaṇa|vināśinā tvayā kasya kṛte vrataṃ dhāryate?

3.59 are! mukta|lajja! kasminn api Manv|antare ko 'pi mukto bhaviṣyati? tatas te sāṃprataṃ naṣṭasya kīdṛśam upakāraṃ kariṣyati? anyad api pṛcchāmi: kena te īdṛśo dharma sandiṣṭaḥ?

3.61 are! sarva|jño Buddha iti kathaṃ tvayā jñātam?

3.63 are! ujjhita|buddhika! yadi tasya bhāṣitena sarva|jñatvaṃ pratipadyase, tasmād aham api sarvaṃ jānāmi. tvam api pitṛ|pitāmahaiḥ sapta|puruṣair me dāsa iti!

3.65 are! vihāra|dāsī|bhujaṅga! duṣṭa|parivrājaka, dṛṣṭānto mayā darśitaḥ. tasmāt priyaṃ te visrabdhaṃ bhaṇāmi: Buddh'|ânuśāsanaṃ parihṛty' ārhat'|ânuśāsanam ev' ânusaratu bhavān. digambara|matam eva ācaratu bhavān!

3.69 graha|nakṣatra|cāra|candra|sūry'|ôparāga|duṣkara|parama|rahasyānam ādeśa|saṃvāda|darśanena nirūpitaṃ sarvajñatvaṃ bhagavato 'rhataḥ

3.74 evaṃ bhavatu.

3.79 are! ka eṣa kāpālaṃ vrataṃ dhārayati puruṣaḥ? tad enaṃ pṛcchāmi.

3.79 are, Kāpālika! nar'|âsthi|muṇḍa|dhārin! kīdṛśaṃ tava saukhyaṃ? kīdṛśas tava mokṣaḥ?

3.83 arhan! arhan! aho ghoraṃ pāpaṃ! kāpālikena ken' âpi vipralabdha ev' âiṣa, iti tarkayāmi!

3.86 are, Kāpālika! nanv ata eva bhaṇāmi: ken' âpy aindrajālikena māyāṃ darśayitvā vipralabdha iti!

3.90 mahā|bhāga! a|hiṃsā paramo dharmo! hiṃsā paramo '|dharmaḥ!

3.93 mahā|bhāgo yadi saṃhṛta|ghora|roṣ'|āveśaḥ saṃvṛttaḥ, tato 'haṃ kim api praṣṭum icchāmi.

3.95 śruto yuṣmākaṃ paramo dharmaḥ. atha kīdṛśo saukhya|mokṣa iti?

3.99 are, Kāpālika! yadi na ruṣyasi, tato bhaṇāmi. śarīrī sa|rāgī muktaś c', êti viruddham.

3.102 sakhi, paśya! Rajasaḥ sutā Śraddhā. s" âiṣā—

3.103 viphulla|nīl'|ôtpala|lola|locanā, / nar'|âsthi|mālā|kṛta|cāru|bhūṣaṇā, / nitamba|pīna|stana|bhāra|mantharā, / vibhāti pūrṇ'|êndu|mukhī vilāsinī.

3.104 eṣ" âsmi! ājñāpayatu svāmī.

3.110 are, bhikṣo! Kāpālinī|sparśanena dūṣitas tvam. tasmād dūram apasara!

3.114 aho arhanta! aho arhanta! Kāpālinyāḥ sparśa|sukham. aye, sundari! dadātu, dadātu tāvat punar aṅka|pālim!

3.114 are, mahān khalv indriya|vikāra saṃvṛtttaḥ! tasmād kim atra yuktam? bhavatu. picchikayā sthagayiṣye.

3.115 ayi! pīna|ghana|stana|śobhini! paritrasta|kuraṅga|vilola|locane! / yadi ramase, Kāpālini, tat kiṃ kariṣyati śrāvakī?

3.116 aho, Kāpālikaṃ darśanam ev' âikaṃ saukhya|mokṣa|sādhanam. bho, ācārya! ahaṃ tava dāsaḥ saṃvṛttaḥ. mām api Mahābhairav'|ânuśāsane dīkṣayata!

3.119 bhagavan, paripūritaṃ surayā bhājanam.

3.123 asmākam ārhat'|ânuśāsane sur'|āpānaṃ n' âsti.

3.126 yad bhagavān ājñāpayati!

3.129 are, bhikṣo! mā sarvaṃ piba! Kāpālinī|vadan'|ôcchiṣṭāṃ madirāṃ mam' âpi dhārayatu!

3.131 aho, surāyā madhuratvam! aho, svādaḥ! aho, gandhaḥ! aho, surabhitvam! ciraṃ khalv ārhat'|ânuśāsane patito vañcito 'smi īdṛśena surā|rasena! are bhikṣuka, ghūrṇanti me 'ṅgāni. tasmād upaviśāvaḥ.

3.134 are, bhikṣuka. eṣa Kāpāliko—'tha v" ācāryaḥ—Kāpālinyā sārdhaṃ śobhanaṃ nṛtyati. tasmād etābhyāṃ sah' āvām api nṛtyāvaḥ!

3.139 are Kāpālika!

3.139 atha vā ācārya... ācārya|rāja... kul'|ācārya...

3.142 ācāryam ev' âitat pṛcchāmi. yādṛśī tava surāyā āharaṇa|śaktiḥ, kiṃ tādṛśī strī|puruṣeṣv apy asti?

3.145 bho, etan mayā gaṇitena jñātam: yat sarve vayaṃ mahā|rāja|Mahāmohasya kiṃkarā iti.

3.147 tasmād rāja|kāryaṃ mantryatām.

3.149 Sattvasya sutā Śraddhā mahā|rājasy' ājñay" āharaṇīy" êti

3.153 sakhi, evaṃ kurvaḥ.

3.155 n' âsti jale, n' âsti vane, n' âsti giri|bileṣu, n' âsti pātāle, / sā Viṣṇubhakti|sahitā nivasati hṛdaye mah"|ātmanām.

3.156 sakhi, diṣṭyā vardhase. śrutaṃ Viṣṇubhaktyā devyāḥ pārśva|vartinī Śraddh" êti.

3.160 n' âsti jale, n' âsti vane, n' âsti giri|bileṣu, n' âsti pātāle, / sa Viṣṇubhakti|sahito vartate hṛdaye mah"|ātmanām.

4.2 śrutaṃ mayā Muditā|sakāśād, yan Mahābhairavī|karṣaṇa|saṃbhramato bhagavatyā Viṣṇubhaktyā paritrātā priya|sakhī Śraddh" êti. tasmād utkaṇṭhitena hṛdayena priya|sakhīṃ prekṣiṣye.

4.6 aye! eṣā me priya|sakhī bhaya|sambhrānta|hṛdayā, kalita|kampataralair aṅgaiḥ kiṃ api mantrayantī saṃmukh'|āgatām api māṃ na lakṣayati! ālapiṣye tāvat.

4.6 priya|sakhi, Śraddhe! kasmāt tvam uttāpita|hṛdayā mām api n' ālokayasi?

4.10 sakhi, tathā Viṣṇubhakti|nirbhartsita|prabhāvayā Mahābhairavyāḥ karṣaṇa|sambhramato 'dy' âpi vepante te 'ṅgāni?

4.12 aho! hat'|āśā ghora|darśanā! atha tay" āgatayā kiṃ kṛtam?

4.15 hā dhik! hā dhik!

4.17 tatas tataḥ?

4.20 diṣṭyā mṛg" îva śārdūla|mukhāt prabhraṣṭā Śraddhā kṣemeṇa sañjīvitā priya|sakhī. tatas tataḥ?

4.22 vayam api catasro bhaginyo Viṣṇubhakter ājñayā Viveka|siddhi|kāraṇaṃ mah"|ātmanāṃ hṛdaye vartāmahe.

4.26 tasmād gacchatu priya|sakhī! aham api tan|niyogam anutiṣṭhāmi.

4.37 yad deva ājñāpayati.

4.46 ita ita etu mahā|bhāgaḥ!

4.46 eṣa mahā|rājas tiṣṭhati. tad upasarpatu bhavān.

4.65 yad deva ājñāpayati.

4.70 eṣa devaḥ. upasarpatu priya|sakhī.

4.85 yad deva ājnāpayati.

4.96 eṣa svāmī. tad upasarpatu mahā|bhāgaḥ!

# NOTES

**Bold** *references are to the English text;* ***bold italic*** *references are to the Sanskrit text. An asterisk (*) in the body of the text marks the word or passage being annotated.*

## Abbreviations

Full publication details are found in the Bibliography (p. lxii).

| | |
|---|---|
| B | Brockhaus (1845) |
| K (Kolkata) | Bhaṭṭācārya (1874) |
| NS (Nirṇaya Sāgara) | Paṇśīkar (1898) |
| Tr (Trivandrum) | Sāmbaśiva Śāstrī (1936) |

## Notes

1.1 The **triple world** embraces the entire scope of mundane experience: the heavens, earth, and either the intervening atmospheric realm, or the subterranean world. Seeing a **serpent** in the place of a **garland**, or a rope, serves in Indian philosophy as a stock example of perceptual illusion.

1.3 The verse as a whole refers to the concentration of the vital energies in the central, **inner channel** of the subtle body, and their movement to the summit of that channel at the fontanel, the **divine aperture** (*brahmarandhra*). The three eyes of Shiva are here treated as homologous with the three major energy-channels, so that the third eye is the symbolic "**ruse**" disclosing the esoteric knowledge of this practice and its attainment. Shiva as the lord of yoga is of course the **crescent-moon-crowned Restrainer**.

1.5 The **Man-Lion**, Nara·sinha, was the fourth avatar of Vishnu, who adopted this form in order to slay Hiránya·káshipu, a demon who had appropriated to himself the sacrifices reserved for the gods.

1.5 The third of Vishnu's avatars, Maha·varáha, the **Great Boar**, held the earth afloat when it was submerged in the primordial cosmic deluge. A popular figure in medieval India, he was frequently associated with the role of the king in upholding the order of the world. Evidence of the Chandélla devotion to him may be seen in the late tenth or early eleventh century Varáha temple at Khajuraho, with its magnificent statue of the cosmic boar in the central shrine.

1.5 In this passage, and elsewhere throughout the play, reference to the ears (*karṇa*) seems sometimes intended to allude to Lakshmi·karna, the Chedi king whose defeat is here celebrated. Thus, the **rhythmic beat of the ears** of the world-bearing **elephants** supplies the breeze that ignites the martial ardor of Gopála.

1.7 On the **sentiment of peace** (*śāntarasa*), refer to the introduction. It is here that Krishna·mishra is taking a clear stand on the controversy surrounding its inclusion among the aesthetic emotions.

1.15 The *Viṣṇupurāṇa* relates that when the gods had been conquered by the titans in battle, Vishnu commanded them to churn the sea of milk using the **Mándara mountain** as the churning-staff, so as to obtain the elixir of immortality.

1.15 Madhu·máthana (⌜*Mahumahaṇa*⌟ in Prakrit), the **slayer of Madhu**, is an epithet of Vishnu, due to his killing of the demon Madhu, who was intent on destroying the creator Brahma.

1.16 As detailed in the introduction, the Chandéllas traced their origin to the moon-god, and therefore stemmed from the **lunar line**. Their rivals, of the Kala·churi dynasty, ruled the region of **Chedi**, around the upper valley of the Nármada river to the south of their own domains.

1.18 **Lord Naráyana**: a common epithet of the god Vishnu.

1.18 Párashu·rama, or **Axman Rama**, the sixth Vishnu avatar, is also known as Jamadágnya, after his father Jamad·agni. His legend takes varied forms in the epics and *purāṇa*s but always alludes to tensions between brahmins and kshatriyas, and the former's resentment towards the latter. To avenge the brahmins, Párashu·rama twenty-one times slaughters all the kshatriyas that he can find, leaving the earth free of them in the end.

1.20 **Jamad·agni's son**: see note to 1.18.

1.38 **Indra became Ahálya's lover**: The "Ramáyana" recounts that Ahálya, wife of the sage Gáutama, was seduced by the god Indra, himself disguised as a sage. **Brahma came to his own daughter**: Sarásvati, Brahma's wife, having been created by her consort is considered also to have been his daughter, for which reason some legends treat their marriage as incestuous. **Moon-god played with the wife of Guru**: The planet Mercury (Budha) was the son of the union of the Moon-god (Soma, Indu) with Tara, though she was the wife of Jupiter (Brihas·pati, or Guru), for which reason her jealous husband reduced her to ashes.

1.39 The eight limbs of the Yoga system of Patañjali are self-restraint (*yama*), regulation (*niyama*), posture (*āsana*), breath-control (*prāṇāyāma*), withdrawal (*pratyāhāra*), meditation (*dhāraṇā*), concentration (*dhyāna*) and absorption (*samādhi*). As they are spoken of as characters here, I have adopted as designations, the **Restrainer** and the **Regulator**.

1.48 On the evolutionary pattern of the cosmos (*pravṛtti*), and the devolution (*nivṛtti*) through which it is dissolved, refer to the introduction.

1.51 **Kuru and Pándava**: the warring clans of the "Maha·bhárata," the Káuravas and Pándavas, were descended from the brothers Kuru (also known as Dhrita·rashtra) and Pandu.

1.58 **Black night** (*kāla|rātri*) besides referring to moonless dark nights, is also a term for the end of the eon, personified as the terrible goddess Durga.

1.63 Because *māyā*, the creative, cosmic **Illusion**, is never ontologically identified with the supreme self, or *ātman*, who is called here the **Man**, she is said to bear her progeny without having consummated her marital relation. In the Sankhya philosophy, the relationship between prime nature (*prakṛti*) and the Soul, or Person (*puruṣa*), is similarly conceived as precluding any genuine union of the two, but the present work, following the teachings of Adváita Vedánta, considers Illusion, unlike nature according to Sankhya, ultimately to be without any ontological status at all.

1.82 The character Intuition (*Viveka*) is frequently referred to simply as the **King**.

1.87 The **Lord Supreme** (*param'|êśvara*) is none other than the *ātman-brahman* that Adváita Vedánta considers to be the universal self, or soul.

1.90 Here, as well as in 1.91–92, there is a mild double-entendre: the **person** (*puruṣa*), or **man** (*puṃs*), may be taken as either a male human being, subject to the wiles of women, or the self, or soul, seduced by cosmic illusion.

1.98 The body, with its nine orifices, is called the **nine-gated citadel**. Once again, a similarity between the Sankhya philosophy and Adváita Vedánta is in evidence, given the role of **Thought** (*manas*) in the emergence of corporeal existence (see note to 1.63 above). However, as is stressed in 1.99 [28], here it is a question of there being, in reality, one universal self underlying all individual persons, while for Sankhya each individual's soul is identified as a single, discrete *puruṣa*.

1.101 **Mind** (*citta*) appears here to be no different than Thought. The precise evolutionary development described here thus differs slightly from that taught in Sankhya, where intelligence (*buddhi*) arises from nature, and in turn produces egoism (*ahaṃkāra*), which then gives rise to thought (*manas*).

1.109 **wakefulness, dream, sleep, and transic repose**: the four principal states of consciousness described in many passages in the Upanishads, in particular, the *Māṇḍūkyopaniṣad* with the accompanying *Gauḍapādakārikā* (DVIVEDI 1894).

1.112 The emergence of the multiplicity of beings from the original unity of Brahman, the **supreme Man**, is here analogized to the sin of brahminicide.

1.115 **Illusion's Game**: The several editions of the *Prabodhacandrodaya* are not at all consistent in the titles of the acts, or even in using such titles at all. In this instance, and in others where possible, I follow Tr. In the *Ṭīkā* by Bhaṭṭottarācārya-Maheśvara, published in B and K, the first act is entitled *Saṃsārāvatāraḥ*, "Entry into *Sansára*."

2.2 **Shrines** (*tīrtha*), originally referred to points of passage on river embankments and fords, which often had religious associations; the term was generalized to include most holy sites and places of pilgrimage. Sometimes also translated here as "holyplace."

2.2 The **four stations** (*āśrama*) **of** orthodox Brahmanical **life**: celibate discipleship, householdry, dwelling in a forest hermitage, complete renunciation.

2.5 **Laughing at his own jokes**: lit. "laughing with wit" (*prajñay" ôpahasan*).

2.6 The region of **Radha** was in the southern part of what is today West Bengal. During the period in which our play was composed, the Sena dynasty of Bengal appears to have been the dominant power in the region.

2.9 **Guru's thought**: the system of the Mimánsaka teacher Prabhākara, ca. early eighth century, on whom see Jha (1978 [1911]). **Kumárila**: the great Mimánsaka philosopher of the seventh century, who was noted for his critiques of Buddhist thought and for his efforts to reconcile the Mimánsaka and Vedánta systems, as will be seen in act 6. For a recent investigation of aspects of his philosophy, see Taber (2005). **Shálika** is without doubt Shálika·natha·mishra, the author of several commentaries on Prabha·kara's system during the tenth century. **Vachas·pati·mishra**, also active during the tenth century, is famed for having commented on all six of the major Brahmanical philosophical systems, though in the present context he is certainly mentioned as the author of the *Tattvabindu* on Mimánsa. **Great Sea** (*mahodadhi*) and **Great Vow** (*mahāvrata*) have puzzled many of the *Prabodhacandrodaya*'s commentators, though the *Candrikā* may well be correct in its assertion that these are the proper names of a disciple of Shálika·natha·mishra and his rival who represented the opposing school of Kumárila. No works attributed to them are in any case known to exist.

2.11 The text here seems to anticipate criticisms of Adváita Vedánta, later to be well known from the work of the *viśiṣṭādvaita* thinker Ramánuja, to the effect that the Adváita of Shánkara was in fact a form of "concealed Buddhism" (*prachannabauddha*).

2.12 **Aksha·pada's system**: the sage Aksha·pada, also called Kanáda, is traditionally considered the founder of the Vaishéshika philosophical system and the author of its fundamental text, the *Vaiśeṣikasūtra*. Like the Nyaya school, which emphasized logic and the theory of knowledge, and with which Vaishéshika is often paired as Nyāya-Vaiśeṣika, it appears to have been closely affiliated with Shivaism, including the distinct **Páshupata** system, which became particularly prominent during the late first millennium CE.

2.14 **Dualist and nondualist paths**: this somewhat crass joke is not found in the Trivandrum text and, though included in other editions, may well be an interpolation.

2.17 Hypocrite in fact utters the mantra-syllable *huṃ*, used here as an imprecation.

2.20 **Turkestan**: The Chandéllas had already come into conflict with Turkic raiders of northern India before our play was written. Kirti·varman himself was attacked, unsuccessfully it appears, by Mahmud, the governor of the Punjab during the reign of Sultan Ibrahim of Ghazni (1059–99). See, for instance, DIKSHIT (1977: 108).

2.24 **Gauda** refers to Bengal in general, the region in which **Radha** was found.

2.38 **Lotus-born god**: The creator Brahma, born from a lotus sprung from the navel of Vishnu. **Cowstuff**: *gomaya*, or cowdung, is in many contexts a purifying substance.

2.42 **Age of Snake-eyes**: The Third Age in the cosmic cycle, the penultimate period of decline, is the Dvápara·yuga, the "age of twos," corresponding to the roll of two in the game of dice. It is followed by the Kali·yuga, the "age of craps," the roll of one using the oblong four-sided dice that were current in ancient India. Of course, my translation is rather loose: "snake-eyes" in gamers' parlance properly refers to double ones using two six-sided dice and not to the throw of two in the ancient Indian game.

2.50 The variant readings of this verse present special problems. Where the Trivandrum edition, which we follow here, reads "**to remedy the annihilation of his clan**" (*kulocchedavidhiṃ cikitsur*), other editions have "desiring the means to terminate his clan" (*kulocchedavidhiṃ cikīrṣur*). In the first, Hypocrite is speaking of Magnus Nescience's arrival in Varánasi in order to save his faction; while the second alternative must refer to Intuition's installation in the city. However, it seems to be the former alternative that construes most clearly with the dialogue that follows, in which Egoismo expresses doubts as to whether the city can be saved by their faction.

2.52 **Conqueror of the City**: Shiva, the tutelary deity of Varánasi.

2.53 **Cultists**: The term *tairthika*, referring originally to those who perform devotions at the sacred sites by the rivers, or *tīrtha* (see note to 2.2 above), was extended in meaning to denote adherents of religious traditions and schools of thought of which one does not approve. As employed in the present work, its connotations accord roughly with those of "cultist" in current usage.

2.54 For *kīrtiḥ*, "**fame**," NS reads *tīrthaṃ*. Adopting this reading, the line means, "has learning, asceticism, and has [made] pilgrimage,"

2.65 **Nihilists**: *nāstika*, lit. "nay-sayers." While the precise denotation shifts according to context—in some instances it refers just to traditions that deny the possibility of liberation, in others to those that deny the principle of *karman*—Krishna·mishra consistently uses it to qualify those who refuse the authority of the Veda.

2.68 **Materialism** (*lokāyata*): though not quite accurate, this has become the established translation convention. *Lokāyata* perhaps more accurately means the "worldliness," which accords well with the alternative designation, Charváka, "hedonism." Note that the character Hedonist here speaks Sanskrit, probably reflecting the fact that this tradition was an offshoot of Brahmanism, and not a heresy originating outside of the Brahmanical fold. The sole surviving philosophical text of the school, the *Tattvopaplavasiṃha* of Jaya·rashi Bhatta, was clearly the work of a Brahmanical author.

2.68 The **Vachas·pati** mentioned here is Brihas·pati, the eponymous founder of the Charváka philosophy, and not Vachas·pati·mishra, the famous polymath mentioned in 2.9 [3] above.

2.70 **Poli Sci**: *daṇḍanītividyā*, literally the sciences of justice and governance.

2.73 This verse is absent from the Trivandrum edition and is not glossed in any of the published commentaries. It may well be an interpolation.

2.76 **Fasting** (*ṣaṣṭhakālāśana*): eating once every sixth meal, i.e., once in three days.

2.85 **Eight-limbed salute of the Age of Craps**: the Age of Craps, or Kali·yuga, is the fourth in the sequence of eons, and characterized by degeneration in all respects. It is named for the worst throw in the game of dice, and so is equivalent to "craps" in American gamblers' jargon. The phrase "eight-limbed salute" refers to a bow in which one is fully prostrate as a sign of respect, here turned to humorous derision by taking the simple act of planting one's bottom on a cushion as a "salute."

2.91 **Great folk** (*mahājana*): as used here, this term, which may also refer to "great men" or to roughly what we call the "public at large," designates particularly that community which is charged with adherence to and the transmission of the Vedic traditions.

2.92 **Three Vedas**: "Rigveda," "Samaveda" and "Yajurveda." The "Atharvaveda," often counted as the fourth Veda, was slow to be included in the Vedic canon, and well into the medieval period one therefore sees reference to three and not four Vedas. As the convention had long since become associated symbolically with various other triplets—the three main divinities, three points of the trident, three eyes, etc.—it continued to be employed even after the status of the "Atharvaveda" had come to be generally accepted.

2.94 **Kuru·kshetra** is the region around Delhi and the site of the war narrated in the "Maha·bhárata."

2.107 **Ultimate Person** (*Uttamapuruṣa*): referring here to Jagan·natha, the chief divinity of the famous temple in Puri, Orissa. In grammatical usage the expression is equivalent to "first person," though it is not clear that a pun about egotism is thereby intended.

2.112 **Lex** (*dharma*): see introduction.

2.114 **The Creator was preoccupied**: the Creator of course is Brahma, whose bliss it was to create; Shiva is the **god who wrecked Daksha's sacrifice** and is passionately in love with the **pale goddess** (Gauri), or Párvati; **Daitya's foe** is Vishnu, depicted as recumbently posed, after love with his wife **Lakshmi**, on the great serpent Shesha who lies in the cosmic sea.

2.126 **Madness-juice**: the secretion that appears on the temples of male elephants in musth, indicative of their sexual energy and aggressivity.

2.128 **The gods' lord terminated Vritra**: Indra, according to the Vedic myth, was the slayer of the demon Vritra, the son of Tvashtri, who is the architect of the gods and sometimes called the Hindu Vulcan. **The crescent-crested god cut off Brahma's head**: the Purāṇas tell us that Brahma originally had five heads, not four. When he and Vishnu entered into a dispute as to which of them was preeminent, the Vedas, to the astonishment of both, declared Shiva to be foremost. The fifth head of Brahma then denounced Shiva in a rage, whereupon the latter became manifest as the terrible god Bháirava, who promptly removed the creator's offending head. **Káushika slaughtered Vasíshtha's sons**: Káushika is the clan-name of the sage Vishva·mitra, who was Vasíshtha's implacable rival. (The latter was responsible for arranging the Veda during the third world-age.) In the course of their contest, Vasíshtha continued to advance spiritually, despite his enemy's efforts to provoke him to renounce the path of ascetic self-perfection, so that Káushika went so far as to slaughter Vasíshtha's hundred sons, but even this did not phase him.

2.135 The interpretation of this verse is in some respects problematic. *tanoṣy aṅgāni tuṅgāni cet* literally means, "if you make [their] limbs prominent." The clearest of the commentarial explanations is that given in the *Prakāśa* (published in both B and NS), where we read: *puṣṭāni cet karoṣi tat tadā brahmāṇḍalakṣair api prāptaiḥ śamakathā kutaḥ?* "If you make them fat, then where, on obtaining even a hundred-thousand galaxies, might there be mention of tranquility?" The image is one of insatiable craving that continues to swell even after one has devoured the whole world.

2.166 **Himálaya's daughter**: Párvati, the wife of Shiva.

2.172 **Sculpted image** (*śālabhañjī*): the term originally referred to "games in which girls used to gather different flowers from the branches of trees ... These games were depicted in sculpture ... and slowly any sculptural figure came to be styled *śālabhanjikā* irrespective of the presence or absence of the *śāla* tree and the sex of the figure sculptured." (Sivaramamurti, p. 1.)

2.176 **False is the law ... false the fruit of heaven**: I have adopted here the reading of NS against Tr, for the former seems to me to be the more amusing of the two. In Tr we read: "false is the law, false is what's said in the treatises, and an obstacle to happiness" (⌜*micchā dhammo, sokkhaviggharāïṃ micchā satthappalavidāïṃ*⌟).

2.182 **Where Magnus Nescience is Chief**: The title of the act is found in the *Ṭīkā* by Bhaṭṭottarācārya-Maheśvara, published in B and K.

3.9 The **four stages** (*āśrama*) refer to note to 2.2 above.

3.10 **True Faith** (*sāttvikī śraddhā*) is that form of Faith that partakes of the principle of spiritual purity (*sattva*) among the three qualities (*guṇa*) articulated in Sankhya theory: purity (*sattva*), passion/energy (*rajas*), and dullness/obscurity (*tamas*). The forms of Faith involving the last two will be introduced below.

3.12 **Jánaka's daughter**: Sita, the faithful wife of Rama, was kidnapped by the ten-faced ogre Rávana, thereby setting in motion the central events of the *Ramáyana*. **Her Excellence Three**: the Three Vedas were stolen from Brahma, who had been inattentive to them, by the titans Madhu and Káitabha. Vishnu, in the form of the horse-headed divinity Haya·griva, avenged the gods and recovered the sacred texts. **Madálasa**, the daughter of the king of *gandharva*s, was abducted by **Patála·ketu**, a chief among the *daitya*s, who, like the titans, vied with the gods. Taken with her beauty, he magically created a dark haze, under the cover of which he carried her off to his palace. She was later rescued by and then married to the prince Kuvalayáshva.

3.23 **Nudist cult**: *digambara*, the "sky-clad" order of the Jains. Krishna·mishra, however, seems not to be speaking here of a particular order, but rather expresses derision of Jainism in general, for which reason "nudist cult" seems closer to the pejorative sense in which he intends the designation.

3.26 **The saints** (*arhat*) are the Jinas, those who have attained perfect liberation in the Jain religion.

3.26 The **city of nine gates** is a euphemism for the human body, with its two eyes, two ears, two nostrils, mouth, anus and urethra.

3.26 The **supreme Victor** is here the Jina, the omniscient teacher of Jainism.

3.27 The **soiled individual mass** (*malamayapudgalapiṇḍa*) is in Jainism the material component of a person's existence, the body.

3.29 **If the Sages play with your mate**: this appears to be simply a calumny hurled at the Jains by their detractors. As will be seen throughout the remainder of this act, sexual impropriety is attributed to all the non-Brahmanical traditions.

3.35 Given the rigorous insistence of Jainism on the principle of **harmlessness**, or non-violence (*ahiṃsā*), it is depicted here as the virtue that has privileged access to reports emanating from that tradition.

3.35 **Darkness:** *tamas*, the principle or quality (*guṇa*) of obscurity and dullness as explained in the Sankhya philosophy.

3.41 According to the theory developed in the *Yogācāra* school of Buddhist philosophy, **latent dispositions** (*vāsanā*) established in the substratum of **consciousness** by one's actions (*karman*) are the basis for ongoing rebirth and all the experiences of the world that accompany this process. All acts and processes are transient, and external appearances are consciousness' projection. Progression on the path of Buddhist practice uproots these dispositions, as one advances to the transformation of consciousness that is identified as awakening.

3.53 **Ascetic** (*kṣapaṇaka*) is used here to refer to the Jain.

3.57 **You dissolve in each instant**: the general Buddhist teaching of impermanence was developed in later Buddhist philosophy into a doctrine of the momentariness of all aspects of the phenomenal world. Many of the non-Buddhist schools objected that, if this were so there could be no personal identity over time, and hence no basis for the moral order of *karman*, or for the path to liberation. Despite the rejection of the doctrine of universal momentariness, however, Krishna·mishra expresses concurrence with the more general Buddhist notion of the impermanence of conditioned things, as will be seen in 5.71–74 [15] below.

3.58 **Something of the nature of consciousness**: consciousness, conceived as dynamic and changing, but nevertheless individual, was generally regarded by Buddhists as the basis for personal identity. This response did not convince those who believed that only the strict, one-to-one identity of an enduring self (*ātman*) could be good enough to serve our moral and religious reasoning.

3.60 **Omniscient lord Buddha**: the Jains may have been the first to characterize their teacher as "omniscient" (*sarvajña*), though the Buddhists began to speak of the Buddha in this fashion early on as well. However, their understandings of just what constituted "omniscience," and those of other Indian religious traditions, differed in several respects and were subject to considerable debate, as is parodied here.

3.69 **The omniscience of the Blessed Lord**: cosmology and the related astral sciences were something of a speciality of the Jains, who accordingly attributed the basis for their theories about these matters to the omniscience of the Jina. Due to the divergence of Jain views in these areas from those prevalent in other schools, their cosmological traditions were criticized, particularly by Brahmanical thinkers.

3.71 Jainism conceives the **vital soul** (*jīva*), as a substance of determinate magnitude, almost a ghostly simulacrum of one's body. Its ability to form connections with objects beyond the bounds of one's body is therefore regarded by the Buddhist disputant as incoherent.

3.75 **Shaivite philosopher** (*somasiddhānta*): Here *soma*, primarily meaning the moon, as well as the sacred *soma*-plant of the Veda, was given a mystical interpretation so as to refer to Shiva as *sa-umā*, he who is "with the goddess Uma (i.e. Párvati)." Though the term seems to have designated a particular Shaivite school, the details remain obscure, and in the present case it is used just as a label for the Kapálika, or Skullman.

3.78 **No divide**: the Kapálika teaching here is presented, like the Adváita Vedánta that Krishna·mishra favors, as a type of monism. For Adváita, ultimately there is only Brahman, while for the Kapálika only Shiva. So it is not in this case the general philosophical standpoint that is criticized, but rather the extreme transgressiveness of the Kapálika. As will be seen later in the play (5.32), the worship of Shiva per se was regarded as conformable to Brahmanical orthodoxy. And in 3.84 below, the Skullman himself aligns his doctrine with the Vedánta.

3.81 **Great Meat** is sometimes encountered in tantric contexts as a euphemism for the sacrifice of human flesh. There is no straightforward translation of *pāraṇā*, the **feast fulfilling our ritual vow**, which may refer to the feast concluding a fast, or sacraments consumed in the fulfillment of a ritual, as is the case here. The **Great Terror** is Maha·bháirava, a wrathful form of Shiva.

3.84 **Párvati's Master** is of course Shiva.

3.84 The **fourteen worlds** are listed in Gode & Karve (1957: 1202).

3.88 **My Lord's Lady**: referring here to Párvati, Shiva's consort.

3.97 The **glad goddess**, Mridáni, is Shiva's consort Párvati.

3.102 **Daughter of Desire**: this is the form of Faith who incarnates the quality of *rajas*, "energy, passion" according to the Sankhya philosophy.

3.116 **Mahābhailava:** The Prakrit text exceptionally uses the Sanskrit diphthong *ai* here, as similarly at 4.2.

3.121 **To release the beast from its snare**: When Shiva is spoken of as the "lord of beasts" (Pashu·pati), the "beast" is said to refer to the bound souls of creatures, while the "snare" (*pāśa*) describes the conditions that bind them to the mundane round.

3.125 **"A woman's mouth is always clean"**: Compare *Mānavadharmaśāstra*, v.130: "The mouth of a woman is always pure, likewise a bird when he causes a fruit to fall; a calf is pure on the flowing of the milk, and a dog when he catches a deer." (BÜHLER 1886: 192).

3.138 **Eight major powers**: usually listed as the ability to become atomically small (*aṇiman*), to be weightless (*laghiman*), to practice teletransportation (*prāpti*), to fulfill one's wishes (*prākāmya*), to be immensely large (*mahiman*), to exercise lordship (*īśatva*), to coerce (*vaśitva*), and to be immensely heavy (*gariman*).

3.141 **Betel-leaf**: to pass to another a betel-leaf that one has already chewed is perceived as a consummately disgusting gesture. This gross gag must have had an eleventh-century audience in stitches, and would probably seem just as funny today.

3.146 **Both**: presumably Skullman and Skullgirl, but possibly Skullman and the Buddhist monk.

3.163 The **Great Terroress** is Maha·bháiravi, the wrathful consort of Shiva as Maha·bháirava. Note that the Prakrit text in 4.2 below spells Maha·bháiravi retaining the Sanskrit diphthong *ai*.

3.166 **Charlatans' Charades**: Title as given in the *Ṭīkā* by Bhaṭṭottarācārya-Maheśvara, published in B and K.

4.5 This may be one of the few instances of bitextuality (*śleṣa*) in our text. The phrase may be read either as *nāra/kapāla*, "human skull" or as *nāraka/pāla*, "guardian of hell," though it is the first reading that is surely primary. The second would suggest that the Great Terroress's earrings resemble those worn by a guardian of hell, i.e., that she was done up like the devil.

4.8 **Black Night**: see note to 1.58. Here, it is clearly Maha·bháiravi who is so designated.

4.23 The four altruistic attitudes of **benevolent love, mercy** (or compassion), **rejoicing in the good of others, and equanimity** were first clearly thematized, it appears, in early Buddhism, where they are called the "four immeasurables" (*catvāry a/pramāṇāni*), and their emphasis represents one of several points of convergence between Buddhism and Adváita Vedánta.

4.25 **Shrine of the Wheel** (*Cakratīrtha*): the precise identity of this place of pilgrimage is at present unknown, and the term may well have been used at one time or another to designate any number of different sites.

4.25 **Hermeneutics**: the Mimánsa philosophy. Whereas this is treated here as being within the scope of the discursive intellect, personified as Lady Intelligence, the teaching of Úpanishad must be directly realized by Intuition.

4.35 The source of the verse quoted here has not been precisely identified, though it very closely resembles, and so may be a paraphrase of, a verse by the eighth- or ninth-century playwright Murāri: "Rama Beyond Price" 1.4 (Törzsök 2006).

4.36 **Veda-lady**: here and at 4.64 we find several variants in the designation of the female gate-keeper, including *vedavatī*, *vegavatī*, and *vetravatī*. The last, found only in K, was adopted nevertheless by Pédraglio (1974), no doubt because the meaning "staff-bearer" suggests the gate-keeper's function. However, given the peculiar position of the Vedic tradition in Krishna·mishra's allegory, not as the ultimate teaching but as an organizing principle for those teachings considered acceptable (5.39), it may be that the first alternative is to be preferred, and so has been adopted here.

4.40 Despite the evident misogyny in this passage (as at several other points throughout the play), it is important to recall, as the commentators in fact insist, that "man" and "woman" are not quite intended here in their everyday sense. For "man" is the unchanging inner self, while "woman" designates the body, whether male or female, and all else that belongs to the realm of Illusion.

4.45 **Incorporeal Man** of course refers to the absolute *ātman*. "Woman," used here as the cipher for the material world that is ultimately illusion, being insentient is said to know **nothing at all.**

4.53 **Five arrows and flower bow**: the standard attributes of Kama.

4.57 **Calming words of sage Vyasa**: an expression almost equivalent to the "Hindu canon," as Vyasa is taken to have been the arranger of the Veda, and the author of the "Maha·bhárata" and the *Vedāntasūtra*, together with other major works. That he is thus explicitly considered to have composed the key text of Vedánta philosophy perhaps held special significance for Krishna·mishra.

4.61 **The master of the Gandíva bow**: Árjuna, the famous hero of the "Maha·bhárata," to whom the "Bhágavad·gita" is revealed. The **Sindhu-king** is Jayad·ratha, who violated Dráupadi, the common wife of Árjuna and his brothers.

4.76 **Durga** is here designated by her epithet Katyáyani. Her killing of Máhisha, the buffalo-demon, is a well-known mythological image, and widely portrayed in painting and sculpture.

4.102 **Ten Chariot's son**: Rama, the son of Dasha·ratha. The **demons' lord** is his arch-rival Rávana, king of Lanka.

4.119 **Vows of the Páshupatas**: the Shaivite Páshupata ascetics covered their bodies with dust, for which reason the dust-laden breeze is frequently described as an ascetic in Sanskrit poetry.

4.122 **Scientia**: Though the term used here is *vidyā*, the name of Wisdom Moon's sister, the commentaries specify that in this instance *vidyā* refers rather to the liberating knowledge of Brahman itself. Nevertheless, as will be seen in 6.148, Scientia, by eliminating

Nescience and preparing the way for her brother's birth, may well be considered as "drawing the mind to the point of freedom," for which reason I believe that Krishna·mishra did not intend to give *vidyā* an alternative sense here.

4.123 The shrine of the **Primordial Késhava** marks one of the most sacred centers of Varánasi, where the Váruna River merges with the Ganges. Refer to Eck (1982).

4.128 **Your tusk-tips**: referring to Vishnu as the Great Boar (see note to 1.5 above).

4.128 **Your steps have traversed**: addressing Vishnu as the Dwarf incarnation (Vámana), who humbled the demon Bali by striding over the universe in three steps. This is, again, one of the avatars who had particularly strong associations with kingship in medieval India.

4.129 **Go·várdhana mountain**: a celebrated hill in the region of Máthura, that was lifted aloft by Krishna for a period of a week in order to shelter the cowherds from the violent storms sent down by Indra.

4.129 **Wives of the gods' rivals**: the vermilion in the hair of the *asura*'s wives is visible because they are bending in submission.

4.129 **You submerged the three realms**: referring to the Man-Lion (see note to 1.5above).

4.129 **Káitabha**: see note to 3.12.

4.129 **Beloved of the crescent-moon-crowned**: Varánasi is the sacred city of Shiva, but both he and Vishnu cooperated in the creation of its sacred geography. In the present context, therefore, this epithet of the latter recalls the ancient accord of the two divinities.

4.129 **Mount Mándara**: see note to 1.15.

4.129 **Vaikúntha**: the form of Vishnu associated with his presence in the Vaikúntha paradise. As noted in the introduction, this may have been a form of the deity particularly honored by the Chandéllas.

4.129 I am grateful to DÁNIEL BALOGH for suggesting that this passage displays a clear pattern of prosody meriting treatment as verse. Its four lines are each characterized by a staccato opening of six short syllables, followed by a variable number of three syllable feet—usually antibacchius but also amphimacer in the last line—and closing with an additional final syllable (counted as heavy regardless of actual prosodic weight). It thus resembles verses of the class known as *daṇḍaka*, though it does not correspond precisely with any of the *daṇḍaka* patterns whose definitions we have been able to locate. (See, for instance, GODE & KARVE (1957), Appendix A, pp. 26–27.)

4.131 **Intuition's Endeavor**: as in Tr. The same title is given in the *Ṭīkā* by Bhaṭṭottarācārya-Maheśvara, in B and K.

5.8 **Saltreetown**: *Śālagrāma*, though used to name a place here, no doubt also refers to the polished, black river-stones that are honored as representations of Vishnu. The *Nārada Pañcarātra* is quoted as saying: "Hari [= Vishnu] is to be always worshipped in images; but when these are wanting, then alone other objects are to be used for this purpose. Of these objects, again, *śālagrāmas* are the best, for a *śālagrāma* stone is the celestial form of Vaikúntha." (BANERJEA 1956: 394.)

5.8 **Shrine of the Wheel** (*Cakratīrtha*): the precise identity of this place of pilgrimage is at present unknown, and the term may well have been used at one time or another to designate any number of different sites. See also the note to 4.25.

5.8 **Helmsman** (*karṇadhara*): lit. the "rudder-holder." This is clearly a pun, also meaning the "controller of Karna."

5.26 **Philosophy of Logic**: the Nyaya philosophy, who is dispatched evidently in an effort to "reason" with Nescience.

5.29 **Heretical doctrines, accompanied by their sophistries**: the distinction here between *āgama* and *tarkaśāstra* corresponds roughly to that between doctrine and philosophy, though, in the present case, the latter is evidently disparaged, hence "sophistries."

5.30 **Their addenda**: the text in fact mentions both the *upaveda* and the *vedāṅga*. The former are the subsidiary sciences of medicine, archery (or the martial arts more generally), music, and architecture; while the latter are phonetics, prosody, grammar, etymology, astronomy, and ritual.

5.32 **The teachings of Vishnu, Shiva, the Solar Divinity**: the three prominent theistic currents of the medieval period are thus ranked among the Vedic traditions. It is here that the work makes clear that the condemnation of the transgressive Kapálika in act three is by no means a blanket condemnation of Shaivism.

5.35 **Lady Hermeneutics** ...: Mimánsa here reflects the Dharma (**Law**), and is accompanied by the Sankhya (**Number**), Nyaya (**Logic**), Vaishéshika (**Atomism**), and grammatical sciences (**Linguistics**, lit. the "Great Commentary" [on Pánini's grammar], *Mahābhāṣya*).

5.39 **Nihilistic factions**: see note to 2.65 above.

5.39 **Their doctrines' analyses of reality** (*āgamānāṃ tu tattvaṃ vicārayatām*): i.e. the scriptural and philosophical dimensions of the traditions concerned.

5.40 **aural revelations** (*śruti*): the Vedic texts that are presumed to be without human author but received through the audition of the ancient sages.

5.43 **Herons**: as herons do not in fact consume carrion, the reference to them here is not quite appropriate. At least one of the commentaries (the *Nāṭakābharaṇa*) seems to have been aware of this difficulty, and accordingly glossed "heron" here as *gṛdhra*, "vulture." I think it more plausible, however, that the author was referring to the crane or stork, heron-like birds that do sometimes feed on carrion.

5.44 **The materialist system**: the mauling of the Lokáyata by all parties fairly well reflects their treatment in the philosophical polemics of medieval India.

5.44 **The Buddhists installed themselves ...**: In the list of locations and peoples given here, I have generally preferred the readings of NS to those of Tr. The members of the first group, from **Sind** to **Orissa**, are mostly well known. In the second group, **Panchála** is the Gangetic Doab, **Malva** is Malwa, to the west of modern Madhya Pradesh, **Abhíra** is situated in southeastern Gujarat, and **Anárta** in the region of modern Kathiawar. It is remarkable that the story seems to leave most of Northern India in the hands of the defeated party. As the author clearly regards the Dravidian south to be beyond the pale (6.80 [12]), one wonders just what was gained by the momentous victory of Intuition and his party, besides, not insignificantly, the Chandélla realms and Varánasi.

5.46 **Self-Intoxication** (*mada*): though the term covers a broad range of meanings, including drunkenness and madness, the contrast with altruism seems to warrant this interpretation here.

5.48 **Deviations from yoga**: the commentators list lust, anger, greed, etc., in fact just the factors that had been supposedly "killed in battle." This may not be so inconsistent as it appears: so long as nescience is present, even in a dormant state, all of these affects have the potential at least to be reborn. Nevertheless, the phrase *yogopasarga*, when it occurs in *Yogasūtra*, 3.37, is treated by the commentaries on that text as referring to the various accomplishments that arise in connection with advancement in the practice of yoga, that become dangerous temptations for the adept: "One who longs for the final goal of life, the absolute assuagement of the three-fold anguish, how could he have any affection for those perfections which go counter to [the attainment] of that [goal]?" (Vachas·pati·mishra in Woods (1914: 266).)

5.53 The **Inner Man** is the *ātman*, while the **mischief-maker** is *manas*, or thought.

5.55 **Vyasa's Speech-goddess**: the form of the goddess Sarásvati who is regarded as the muse of sage Vyasa (4.57 [13]).

5.72 **Fifth state**: the four stations of Brahmanical life (see note to 2.2 above) are followed by death, here counted as the fifth. The body is **five-natured** in that it is composed of the five elements (see note to 1.1).

5.102 The **secret** that is disclosed here appears to be primarily the contemplation of Brahman, which remains hidden until one is suitably initiated by one's guru. The course of initiation, as understood in the Adváita Vedánta tradition, is in fact the subject of Act Six, in particular 6.135–145 [28].

5.126 **Field-commander**: the soul as witness of the phenomenal world in which it is enmeshed is referred to literally as the "knower of the field" (*kṣetrajña*). "Field-commander," though perhaps a free rendering, seemed a better translation choice and offered the possibility of a small tribute to Leonard Cohen.

5.128 **Water-offering**: the offering for the Manes and departed relations.

5.131 **The Dawn of Dispassion**: as in Tr. The title in the *Ṭīkā* by Bhaṭṭottarācārya-Maheśvara, in B and K, is nearly synonymous: *Vairāgy'|ôtpattiḥ*

6.11 **To be executed or imprisoned**: here the reading of K, *vadhye nigrāhye*, seems clearer than the *vadhyasya nigrāhyasya* of the other editions consulted.

6.13 This enigmatic phrase recalls the author's strict adherence to Adváita Vedánta, according to which the absolute *ātman-brahman*, as a perfect unity, is at once both the **self-luminous** subject and the **sovereign** domain of awakened gnosis.

6.18 **Willfulness**: although *saṃkalpa* is broadly equivalent to "intention, volition," in the present context it seems a more distinctly negative affect.

6.23 Refer to note to 5.48 above.

6.24 In Vyasa's commentary on *Yogasūtra*, 3.51 the **Honeyed One** (*madhumatī*) names a particular state of attainment that arises in the course of the advancement of contemplative practice: "The purity of the sattva in that Brahman ... who has directly experienced the Honeyed Stage is observed by those-in-high-places, the gods ... [who] invite him. 'Sir, will you sit here? Will you rest here? This pleasure might prove attractive. This maiden might prove attractive...' Thus addressed let him ponder the defects of pleasure.' (Woods 1914: 285–86.) Although honey frequently serves as a metaphor for the sweetness of spiritual accomplishment, it is Vyasa's description of this state that corresponds most closely to Krishna·mishra's elaboration of it.

6.27 Knowledge of the cosmos, and above all the Mount Meru world system, is discussed in the commentaries on *Yogasūtra*, 3.26: "As a result of constraint upon the sun [there arises the intuitive] knowledge of the cosmic-spaces (*bhuvana*)." (Woods 1914: 254.) "Constraint" is Woods' translation of *saṃyama*, which might be better expressed in this context as "intense concentration."

6.36 Following here the reading of B. Other versions, including Tr, give the hypermetrical *y" âsau.*

6.55 As the *Kaṭha Upaniṣad*, 1.2.23, tells us, "This self cannot be attained by instruction, nor by intellectual power, nor even through much hearing." (Radhakrishnan 1953: 619.) Accordingly, Úpanishad's capacity to instruct remains mysterious to Úpanishad herself.

6.62 **Mándara mountain**: refer to 1.15 and 4.127 above.

6.67 The reference is to a tale recounted in the *Mānavadharmaśāstra*, II.151–3: "Young Kavi, the son of Aṅgiras, taught his (relatives who were old enough to be) fathers, and, as he excelled them in (sacred) knowledge, he called them 'Little sons.' They, moved with resentment, asked the gods concerning the matter and the gods, having assembled, answered, 'The child has addressed you properly. For (a man) destitute of (sacred) knowledge is indeed a child, and he who teaches him the Veda is his father....'" (BÜHLER 1886: 58)

6.80 **The prattle of Dravidian girls**: roughly equivalent to "Greek to me" among English idioms.

6.84 The **Ritual Section** (*karmakāṇḍa*) is those portions of the Vedic corpus, excluding the Upanishads, that are concerned primarily with the sacrificial rites. Their interpretation is the special concern of the Mimánsaka philosophy.

6.93 The text here alludes to *Īśa Upaniṣad* 2: "Always performing works here one should wish to live a hundred years." (RADHAKRISHNAN 1956: 569.)

6.94 The conditioned activities of the **agent** (*kartṛ*) and **enjoyer** (*bhoktṛ*), though attributed to the self by the Mimánsakas, are considered to be illusory in Adváita Vedánta.

6.96 The idiom adopted here once again resembles that of Sankhya, wherein the active principle of nature (*prakṛti*) arranges itself as the manifest world in evolutionary progression before the sight of the passive individual soul, or *puruṣa*, which is in no respect an agent.

6.98 The **seven spheres** are the seven superior realms of which the lowest is the earth.

6.104 Refer to note to 6.84 above.

6.105 **Extension** (*atideśika*) is the general principle, applicable in any science, whereby a rule formulated in one context may be stipulated as extending to certain additional cases. In the Mīmāṃsa system in particular, the principle is set forth in Śabara's comments on *Mīmāṃsāsūtra* 7.1.12. (GODE & KARVE 1957: 42.)

6.109 The late seventh-century Mimánsaka philosopher Kumárila Bhatta is noted for his trenchant criticisms of Buddhist thought (on which refer in particular to ARNOLD (2005) and TABER (2005)). In Adváita legend, Kumárila, engaging in self-immolation as an act of expiation, was met by Shánkara, setting the stage for the latter's debate with and eventual conversion of Kumárila's leading disciple Mándana·mishra.

6.112 The source of this citation is *Muṇḍaka Upaniṣad* 3.1.1, paraphrasing "Rig Veda" 1.164.20.

6.118 In this verse, those **whose supreme idea is two or three distinctions** refers to the Vaishéshika school of atomistic philosophy, those who **elaborate the rules** are the Nyaya logicians, and those who **divide person from primal nature** the proponents of Sankhya. In the last mentioned, the **great one** (*mahat*) is an alternative designation for intellect (*buddhi*), nature's first evolute, which in turn produces **egoism**. Refer to note to 1.101 above. Clear summary accounts of these systems may be found in HAMILTON (2001), ch. 5 and 7.

6.119 For many forms of Indian theism, such as those associated with the philosophical schools just mentioned, a supreme and eternal god, usually called the **Lord** (*īśvara*), is affirmed, but not one that creates the universe ex nihilo. The Lord serves, rather as does the Platonic Demiurge, to give form to the chaotic matter that exists independently of him. In the present passage, the theists understand the teaching of Úpanishad, that the universe arises from and subsides in the supreme Brahman itself, to imply the mutability, and hence the impermanence, of the Lord. The final objection to Úpanishad, referring to **prime matter** (*pradhāna*), adopts the perspective of Sankhya, which, in its theory of matter, disagreed with the atomism of the Nyaya and Vaishéshika schools.

6.120 There are some difficulties in the interpretation of this passage, and the commentators are not quite in accord about it. It seems clearest to take it as maintaining that the argument that applies to middle-sized objects such as pots—that they are causal results and thus not absolute realities—applies in turn to the atoms or prime matter of which those objects are thought to be composed. The attempt to find an ultimate material cause, therefore, issues in a reductio ad absurdum and so must be rejected.

6.121 The first lines of the verse recall *Gauḍapādakārikā*, II.31: "As dream and illusion or a castle-in-the-air, so, say the wise, the Vedāntas declare this cosmos to be" (DVIVEDI, p. 50), which is in turn reminiscent of the verses concluding the Buddhist *Vajracchedikā Prajñāpāramitā*: *tārakā timiraṃ dīpo māyāvaśyāya budbudam, svapnaṃ ca vidyudabhraṃ ca evaṃ draṣṭavya saṃskṛtam*. The examples of perceptual illusion favored in the last lines of our text—**like silver in a shell, or a snake in a garland**—are very much favored in the writings of Shánkara.

6.127 The **Dándaka forest** included the vast tracts of wilderness in Maharashtra and the Deccan, and was the setting for much of the action of the "Ramáyana."

6.127 **Slayer of Madhu**: as an epithet of Vishnu, Madhu·súdana, used here, is synonymous with Madhu·máthana (see note to 1.15).

6.130 Úpanishad is describing here, from her perspective, the same events recounted at 4.126, where Nescience's allies were described as taking flight from Varánasi, and then amplified in the discourse of Faith concerning the progress of the battle (5.26).

6.134 The source of the verse quoted is "Bhágavad·gita," 16.19.

6.136 **Smiling**: other versions of the text read here *sakopam*, "angrily," though "indignantly" is perhaps what is really meant. But, in the context, Úpanishad might be better taken, as Tr suggests, to be smiling, though with a measure of mockery no doubt.

6.146 This verse concerns several of the so-called "great utterances" (*mahāvākya*) in which the highest teaching of the Upanishads is thought to be found. Three of them are discussed briefly here: **I am this** (*eṣo 'smi*), **"not"** (*n' êti*), and the famous **thou art that** (*tat tvam asi*). In citing them in this order, Krishna·mishra is following the traditional pattern of Advάita Vedánta instruction as explained by Shánkara in his *Upadeśasāhasrī*. There, the movement from the initial affirmation of self to its negation is described in verses I.18.20–25: "Just as the pain of a son is superimposed upon himself by a father, though himself suffering no pain, so [pain] is superimposed by the bearer of the 'I'-notion (= the intellect) upon its Ātman which is ever free from pain. This superimposition is negated, as if it were a thing acquired, by the words, 'Not thus! Not so!' ... [which] negates all things, including the notion of agency which is superimposed upon the Ātman." (MAYEDA 1979: 174.) The entire chapter from which these words are drawn is in fact concerned to unpack the significance of "thou are that," which Śaṅkara summarizes in saying (I.18.220): "In oneself should one see Ātman, the inner Ātman which is denoted by [the word] 'Thou.' Thence one sees all to be Ātman—that is, the One Apart which is meant by the sentence ['Thou art That']." (MAYEDA 1979: 195.)

6.148 In the present case, the double meaning of the English **conception** nicely captures the sense of *saṃkalpa*. The divinities are of course exempt from all carnality, so their birth is a matter of pure conception alone.

6.162 NS here reads *svāyaṃbhuvo muniḥ*, the "self-emergent sage." The reading of B and Tr, *sāyaṃ gṛhe muniḥ*, though more difficult, is more evocative and seems to suit the context particularly well.

6.169 **Mura's foe** (*Murāri*) is Krishna, who vanquished the demon Mura.

6.169 Verses 33 and 34 appear to belong uniquely to the Keralan recension of the *Prabodhacandrodaya* edited in Tr; they are to be found in none of the other editions consulted and are no doubt interpolations.

6.174 **Living Liberation**: as in Tr. The same title is used in the *Ṭīkā* by Bhaṭṭottarācārya-Maheśvara, in B and K.

# METERS USED

The following meters are used in this text:

*āryā* Act 1 [11], [16], Act 2 [39], Act 3 [5], [6], [24], [25], Act 5 [24]

*drutavilambita* Act 6 [4]

*gīti* Act 5 [1]

*hariṇī* Act 1 [25], [26], Act 3 [14], Act 4 [13], Act 5 [17], [23]

*irregular* Act 4 [32]

*mālinī* Act 2 [10], Act 4 [12], Act 5 [10]

*mandākrāntā* Act 1 [2], Act 2 [36], Act 5 [18], Act 6 [9], [23], [24], [36]

*praharṣiṇī* Act 1 [17], Act 4 [29]

*pṛthvī* Act 2 [11], Act 5 [12]

*puṣpitāgrā* Act 1 [13], [21], Act 2 [13], [35], Act 6 [6]

*śālinī* Act 3 [26]

*śārdūlavikrīḍita* Act 1 [1], [5], [12], [19], [29]-[31], Act 2 [1], [3], [5], [7], [9], [17], [18], [28], [30]–[32], [34], Act 3 [1], [3], [4], [9], [13], [16], [18], [22], Act 4 [1], [6], [9]–[11], [14], [19], [22], [24], [30], Act 5 [5], [7], [9], [14], [16], [29], [31], [32], Act 6 [3], [5], [8], [14], [19], [21], [22], [28]–[30]

*śikhariṇī* Act 1 [14], [20], Act 3 [15], [21], Act 4 [20], [21], [23], [28], Act 5 [2], [28], [30]

*śloka* Act 1 [6], [9], [15], [22], [28], Act 2 [2], [4], [8], [14], [19]–[21], [26], [27], [37], [38], Act 3 [2], [7], [10], [20], Act 4 [2], [8], [31], Act 5 [3], [4], [8], [11], [15], [19], [20], [25], [26], Act 6 [2], [11], [25], [27], [35]

*sragdharā* Act 1 [4], [7], Act 2 [15], [33], Act 4 [26], Act 5 [33], Act 6 [33], [34]

*unknown* Act 3 [19]

*upajāti* Act 1 [8], Act 2 [12], [16], Act 3 [23], Act 4 [7], [15], [17], Act 5 [6], [22], Act 6 [10], [17], [18], [20]

*upendravajrā* Act 2 [25], Act 3 [17], Act 6 [16], [26]

*vaṃśamālā* Act 3 [12], Act 6 [15]

*vaṃśastha* Act 1 [24]

*vasantatilakā* Act 1 [3], [10], [18], [23], [27], Act 2 [6], [22]–[24], [29], Act 3 [8], [11], Act 4 [3]–[5], [16], [18], [25], [27], Act 5 [13], [21], [27], Act 6 [1], [12], [13], [31], [32]

*viyoginī* Act 6 [7]

## THE CLAY SANSKRIT LIBRARY

The volumes in the series are listed here in order of publication.
Titles marked with an asterisk* are also available in the
Digital Clay Sanskrit Library (eCSL).
For further information visit www.claysanskritlibrary.org

1. The Emperor of the Sorcerers (*Bṛhatkathāślokasaṃgraha*) (vol. 1 of 2) by *Budhasvāmin.* SIR JAMES MALLINSON
2. Heavenly Exploits (*Divyāvadāna*). JOEL TATELMAN
3. Maha·bhárata III: The Forest (*Vanaparvan*) (vol. 4 of 4)* WILLIAM J. JOHNSON
4. Much Ado about Religion (*Āgamaḍambara*) by *Bhaṭṭa Jayanta.* CSABA DEZSŐ
5. The Birth of Kumára (*Kumārasaṃbhava*) by *Kālidāsa.* DAVID SMITH
6. Ramáyana I: Boyhood (*Bālakāṇḍa*) by *Vālmīki.* ROBERT P. GOLDMAN
7. The Epitome of Queen Lilávati (*Līlāvatīsāra*) (vol. 1 of 2) by *Jinaratna.* R.C.C. FYNES
8. Ramáyana II: Ayódhya (*Ayodhyākāṇḍa*) by *Vālmīki.* SHELDON I. POLLOCK
9. Love Lyrics (*Amaruśataka, Śatakatraya & Caurapañcāśikā*) by *Amaru, Bhartṛhari & Bilhaṇa.* GREG BAILEY & RICHARD GOMBRICH
10. What Ten Young Men Did (*Daśakumāracarita*) by *Daṇḍin.* ISABELLE ONIANS
11. Three Satires (*Kaliviḍambana, Kalāvilāsa & Bhallaṭaśataka*) by *Nīlakaṇṭha, Kṣemendra & Bhallaṭa.* SOMADEVA VASUDEVA
12. Ramáyana IV: Kishkíndha (*Kiṣkindhākāṇḍa*) by *Vālmīki.* ROSALIND LEFEBER
13. The Emperor of the Sorcerers (*Bṛhatkathāślokasaṃgraha*) (vol. 2 of 2) by *Budhasvāmin.* SIR JAMES MALLINSON
14. Maha·bhárata IX: Shalya (*Śalyaparvan*) (vol. 1 of 2)* JUSTIN MEILAND

15. Rákshasa's Ring (*Mudrārākṣasa*)*
by *Viśākhadatta*. MICHAEL COULSON
16. Messenger Poems (*Meghadūta, Pavanadūta & Haṃsadūta*)
by *Kālidāsa, Dhoyī & Rūpa Gosvāmin*. SIR JAMES MALLINSON
17. Ramáyana III: The Forest (*Araṇyakāṇḍa*)
by *Vālmīki*. SHELDON I. POLLOCK
18. The Epitome of Queen Lilávati (*Līlāvatīsāra*) (vol. 2 of 2)
by *Jinaratna*. R.C.C. FYNES
19. Five Discourses on Worldly Wisdom (*Pañcatantra*)*
by *Viṣṇuśarman*. PATRICK OLIVELLE
20. Ramáyana V: Súndara (*Sundarakāṇḍa*) by *Vālmīki*.
ROBERT P. GOLDMAN & SALLY J. SUTHERLAND GOLDMAN
21. Maha·bhárata II: The Great Hall (*Sabhāparvan*)
PAUL WILMOT
22. The Recognition of Shakúntala (*Abhijñānaśākuntala*) (Kashmir Recension) by *Kālidāsa*. SOMADEVA VASUDEVA
23. Maha·bhárata VII: Drona (*Droṇaparvan*) (vol. 1 of 4)*
VAUGHAN PILIKIAN
24. Rama Beyond Price (*Anargharāghava*)
by *Murāri*. JUDIT TÖRZSÖK
25. Maha·bhárata IV: Viráta (*Virāṭaparvan*)
KATHLEEN GARBUTT
26. Maha·bhárata VIII: Karna (*Karṇaparvan*) (vol. 1 of 2)
ADAM BOWLES
27. "The Lady of the Jewel Necklace" & "The Lady who Shows her Love" (*Ratnāvalī & Priyadarśikā*) by *Harṣa*.*
WENDY DONIGER
28. The Ocean of the Rivers of Story (*Kathāsaritsāgara*) (vol. 1 of 7)
by *Somadeva*. SIR JAMES MALLINSON
29. Handsome Nanda (*Saundarananda*)*
by *Aśvaghoṣa*. LINDA COVILL
30. Maha·bhárata IX: Shalya (*Śalyaparvan*) (vol. 2 of 2)*
JUSTIN MEILAND
31. Rama's Last Act (*Uttararāmacarita*) by *Bhavabhūti*.
SHELDON POLLOCK. Foreword by GIRISH KARNAD

32. "Friendly Advice" (*Hitopadeśa*) by *Nārāyaṇa* &
"King Víkrama's Adventures" (*Vikramacarita*). Judit Törzsök
33. Life of the Buddha (*Buddhacarita*)
by *Aśvaghoṣa*. Patrick Olivelle
34. Maha·bhárata V: Preparations for War (*Udyogaparvan*) (vol. 1 of 2)
Kathleen Garbutt. Foreword by Gurcharan Das
35. Maha·bhárata VIII: Karna (*Karṇaparvan*) (vol. 2 of 2)
Adam Bowles
36. Maha·bhárata V: Preparations for War (*Udyogaparvan*) (vol. 2 of 2)
Kathleen Garbutt
37. Maha·bhárata VI: Bhishma (*Bhīṣmaparvan*) (vol. 1 of 2)*
Including the "Bhagavad Gita" in Context
Alex Cherniak. Foreword by Ranajit Guha
38. The Ocean of the Rivers of Story (*Kathāsaritsāgara*) (vol. 2 of 7)
by *Somadeva*. Sir James Mallinson
39. "How the Nagas were Pleased" (*Nāgānanda*) by *Harṣa* &
"The Shattered Thighs" (*Ūrubhaṅga*) by *Bhāsa*.*
Andrew Skilton
40. Gita·govínda: Love Songs of Radha and Krishna (*Gītagovinda*)*
by *Jayadeva*. Lee Siegel. Foreword by Sudipta Kaviraj
41. "Bouquet of Rasa" & "River of Rasa" (*Rasamañjarī & Rasataraṅgiṇī*) by *Bhānudatta*. Sheldon Pollock
42. Garland of the Buddha's Past Lives (*Jātakamālā*) (vol. 1 of 2)*
by *Āryaśūra*. Justin Meiland
43. Maha·bhárata XII: Peace (*Śāntiparvan*) (vol. 3 of 5)*
"The Book of Liberation" (*Mokṣadharma*). Alexander Wynne
44. The Little Clay Cart (*Mṛcchakaṭikā*) by *Śūdraka*.
Diwakar Acharya. Foreword by Partha Chatterjee
45. Bhatti's Poem: The Death of Rávana (*Bhaṭṭikāvya*)*
by *Bhaṭṭi*. Oliver Fallon

46. "Self-Surrender," "Peace," "Compassion," and "The Mission of the Goose": Poems and Prayers from South India (*Ātmārpaṇastuti, Śāntivilāsa, Dayāśataka & Haṃsasaṃdeśa*) by *Appayya Dīkṣita, Nīlakaṇṭha Dīkṣita & Vedānta Deśika.* YIGAL BRONNER & DAVID SHULMAN
Foreword by GIEVE PATEL

47. Maha·bhárata VI: Bhishma (*Bhīṣmaparvan*) (vol. 2 of 2)* ALEX CHERNIAK

48. How Úrvashi Was Won (*Vikramorvaśīya*) by *Kālidāsa* VELCHERU NARAYANA RAO & DAVID SHULMAN

49. The Quartet of Causeries (*Caturbhāṇī*) by *Śūdraka, Śyāmilaka, Vararuci & Īśvaradatta.* CSABA DEZSŐ & SOMADEVA VASUDEVA

50. Garland of the Buddha's Past Lives (*Jātakamālā*) (vol. 2 of 2)* by *Āryaśūra.* JUSTIN MEILAND

51. Princess Kadámbari (*Kādambarī*) (vol. 1 of 3) by *Bāṇa.* DAVID SMITH

52. The Rise of Wisdom Moon (*Prabodhacandrodaya*)* by *Kṛṣṇamiśra.* MATTHEW T. KAPSTEIN
Foreword by J.N. MOHANTY

53. Maha·bhárata VII: Drona (*Droṇaparvan*) (vol. 2 of 4)* VAUGHAN PILIKIAN

54. Maha·bhárata X & XI: Dead of Night & The Women (*Sauptikaparvan & Strīparvan*).* KATE CROSBY

55. Seven Hundred Elegant Verses (*Āryāsaptaśatī*)* by *Govardhana.* FRIEDHELM HARDY

56. Málavika and Agni·mitra (*Mālavikāgnimitram*) by *Kālidāsa.* DÁNIEL BALOGH & ESZTER SOMOGYI